D1140453

STAYING POWER

WITHDRAWN

WITHDRAWN

WITHDRAWN

WITHDRAWN

STAYING POWER

PETER WALKER
AN AUTOBIOGRAPHY

920.
X14405

ST PAUL'S SCHOOL LIBRARY

BLOOMSBURY

To Tessa, in gratitude

First published in Great Britain 1991
Bloomsbury Publishing Limited, 2 Soho Square, London W1V 5DE

Copyright © 1991 by Peter Walker

The moral right of the author has been asserted

Cartoons by Peter Brookes, Cummings and Garland

A CIP catalogue record for this book
is available from the British Library

ISBN 0-7475-1034-2

Typeset by Rowland Phototypesetting Limited,
Bury St Edmunds, Suffolk
Printed in Great Britain by
Clays Limited, St Ives plc

CONTENTS

FOREWORD

I think political commentators owe me a small debt, as I owe them many.

Over the years there seems to have been an unhealthy preoccupation with my future. In the early 1970s and 1980s, they flatteringly speculated that I could become the next leader of the Conservative Party. At other times, they were just as fervent in speculating that Margaret Thatcher was about to sack me!

The continuing presence of a committed 'wet' in the heart of a dry Thatcher Cabinet clearly has a fascination. I hope this book sheds a ray of light on how and why it came about.

The clash of approaches between myself and Margaret Thatcher is undeniable. The sudden espousal of *laissez-faire* economics and monetarism was anathema to me, being completely contrary to the traditional Disraelian Toryism on which I had been brought up. I have tried to explain in the following pages that I did not see myself as the rebel I was portrayed as during all those years, but as a keeper of the Tory flame.

It is not always easy to argue the Middle Way of Macmillan or Tories like myself. The search for the right blend of compassion and efficiency to provide a decent life for everyone can be represented as, well, wet. It lacks the drama and glamour of conviction politics. But I have not wavered in my passionate belief that there is this middle course between the deadening hand of state control and allowing market forces total freedom. The middle course as I see it recognizes the benefits which can flow from government and industry working together and seeks to fulfil society's obligation towards those least able to succeed by themselves.

I was delighted, however, to be able to play a prominent part in the privatization programmes and the spread of ownership to ordinary people. I hope I was able to make a positive contribution to a range of issues at home and abroad and certainly was able to influence many decisions from within the Cabinet.

The book, I trust, will speak for itself.

That I have enjoyed more than thirty years in Parliament and so many in office is due to remarkable good fortune. I have been lucky to have the benefit of good helath, dedicated parents, a marvellous wife and family and the chance, at an early age, of a degree of financial independence which has allowed me to devote so much of my life to politics.

I am grateful to the school teachers who inspired me; elder statesmen who encouraged me as a young politician; businessmen who gave time advising me on the creation of my own business; steadfast friends like Charlie Morrison, Ian Gilmour, Alick Buchanan-Smith and four outstanding Parliamentary Private Secretaries, Tony Berry, who sadly lost his life in the Brighton bomb attack, Michael McNair-Wilson, who was struck by illness but with great determination recovered to lead a full life, Stephen Dorrell, now a minister with a big political future ahead of him, and Colin Shepherd who guided me so skilfully in my days as Welsh Secretary.

Politicians are handicapped without good secretaries. I have been particularly lucky in having Sue Cornford as mine throughout much of my time in Parliament, working long hours, showing great patience and becoming a firm friend of the family.

In writing the book, I am grateful for the great help I have received from John Lewis. I came to know John in my early days in Parliament when he was political correspondent of the *Birmingham Post*. I have benefited from his wisdom and writing throughout most of my political life and am now grateful for his research and pulling together of the book, not to mention the repeated removal of my split infinitives.

I also owe debts of gratitude to Ian Gilmour and Jack Warden, whose memory is legend among political correspondents, for reading a draft of the book and making helpful suggestions; and to the staff in the Commons reference library who fielded enquiries with their customary courtesy and skill.

1

YOUNG PATRIOT

The wheel has turned full circle.

Throughout the Thatcher years, I thought of myself as being still in the mainstream of Conservatism. 'Rab' Butler was the key figure in preparing policy when I joined the Conservative Party in 1945 and he was a liberal Tory. Anthony Eden was in the same liberal Tory, property-owning tradition. Harold Macmillan, with his big election success in 1959, was an obvious liberal Tory. Alec Douglas-Home was in much the same mould. Ted Heath's views, except, initially, on Europe, were close to mine. I had a run from 1945 to 1974 when I was, all the time, at one with the Tory leadership.

Then suddenly, to my dismay, there was a radical change with the arrival of 'Thatcherism' and obeisance to a single sacred measure of money supply.

I thought we had learned the lesson of our 1945 defeat when the nation was still shocked by the slump of the 1930s and we were blamed. We realized then we must have economic policies which would unite the country and stop future mass unemployment. As a young man, I watched 'Rab' Butler, Iain Macleod and Harold Macmillan prepare those policies. It was these policies which returned us to power and they were executed with enthusiasm by Churchill, Macmillan, Alec Douglas-Home and Ted Heath. The issue which caused the Ted Heath Cabinet the greatest distress was the rise in unemployment to more than one million.

It was easy to see why Thatcherism did emerge. In its periods of office, Labour not only increased unemployment, but also followed policies which plunged us into debt, as it hankered after old, discredited, Socialist solutions.

Margaret and others were caught on the rebound and over-reacted. Throughout the first part of the century we opposed *laissez-faire* Liberalism and favoured protectionism and government intervention for social reasons. Under the new Prime Minister we had a party quoting Adam Smith from the last century and Milton Friedman from this. Fortunately, a good deal was rhetoric and we did not adhere to strict *laissez-faire* policies or the results could have been worse, but then neither did we pursue with sufficient vigour the One Nation approach to which I was committed.

It is a happy coincidence that at the moment I am leaving the Commons after thirty years as an MP, the wheel has completed its turn and the party shows every sign of returning to this traditional 'One Nation' brand of Toryism.

I watched John Major come to the Commons as an eager young backbencher, enthusiastic for the traditional policies advocated by the Conservative Party. I saw him as a skilful Cabinet Minister, a man of immense ability, quality and character.

I have been involved with five remarkable Conservative leaders. Harold Macmillan brought a sense of unity to the country, recognized the winds of change in Africa, sensed that Britain's future was with Europe. Alec Douglas-Home possessed a rare combination of integrity, dignity and desire for his nation to succeed. I wish he had been given more time in office. It was typical of him that he served happily as Foreign Secretary under his Conservative successor. Ted Heath negotiated our entry into Europe, saw the emerging problems of the Third World and tackled with passion the problems of rising unemployment in the best Keynesian manner. Margaret Thatcher's energy and determination in pursuing the policies in which she believed made her one of the leading figures of the world. History may well judge that if the Soviet Union and South Africa emerge as prosperous democracies she, of all Western politicians, will have played the leading role.

Is it possible John Major has the best qualities of all these Prime Ministers? I believe he possesses the thoughtfulness of Harold Macmillan, with a similar desire to unite our country. He possesses the dignity and integrity of Alec Douglas-Home. He shares the visions of Ted Heath on Europe and his distaste of unemployment. I think that in a different way he will show the same enthusiasm and determination displayed by Margaret Thatcher. If we finish the century with such a Prime Minister, we will be blessed.

Within a short period John Major had stopped the widespread political damage being done to the Conservative Party by the poll tax. In a matter of weeks he had made clear a positive attitude to Europe and become one of the most respected and admired leaders in the European Community, a Prime Minister who will now have great influence on the way that Europe develops.

I spoke to him not long after he had become leader and said I wanted to be as helpful as possible to his government, but hesitated in case by reputation as a leading 'wet' I did him more damage than help with the party's small right wing.

I should never have expressed such doubts to John Major. He said, 'Peter. You know me well enough. I am my own man. I will pursue and advocate policies I believe are right. A Prime Minister cannot be effective if all he is doing is looking over his shoulder at each faction in his party and reacting to them.' He would welcome my support.

The policies he follows will be those he considers right for the nation. The baptism of criticism will benefit him. It has made everyone in the party realize their electoral fortunes depend on his success.

No doubt he will attract critics from the right, but they are small in number. It was never true that 330 of the 370 Conservative MPs were Thatcherites. They were loyal to the party leader, wanted the party to win and were willing to believe the monetary policy would help. They were essentially neutral, the same people who supported Ted or Alec Douglas-Home.

I remember, in 1982, a group of the more liberally minded Tory MPs going through the list of Conservatives for hard-line monetarists. We finished up with sixteen. Some of the sixteen will be vocal and complain that we are departing from the policies of the previous leader. John Major will come out with his own manifesto and his own policies.

My forty-six years in the Conservative Party have been more exhilarating than I could have hoped in my wildest dreams. My journey through those years, intriguingly, has marked similarities with that of Margaret Thatcher.

We both grew up during the war in an atmosphere of fierce patriotism, an emotion we have retained throughout our lives. Like other working-class couples, my parents, Sydney and Rose, linked this patriotism with a belief in unremitting endeavour, 'getting on', their children working hard at school and everywhere else. We were, however, only too well aware of the need to understand the harsh blows life can deliver. My father was hit by the slump from 1929 to 1931 and for eighteen months found it impossible to get a job. My mother told me how he cycled from factory to factory every day in the best Norman Tebbit tradition. She talked of the agony he felt because he was unable to provide for his wife and their first child. I arrived in 1932, after he had got back to work.

If anyone seeks the cause of my hatred of unemployment, they need look no further. My father became a shop steward with the strong belief that workers should have power to negotiate. After his own experience, he was passionate about stopping mass redundancies. A sympathy for those thrown out of work and an appreciation of what it can mean to families may have helped me in handling the two miners' disputes in which I later became embroiled.

If my father's loss of his job gives the impression of a childhood of gloom, however, it is misleading. It was just the reverse. I remember it as being warm and cheerful.

It is fascinating to look back at life in the typical three-bedroomed semi-detached house we occupied, as a low-income family, in Harrow in the 1930s and compare it with half a century later.

The house, which was built in the late 1920s, was considered a good three-bedroom semi. Every bedroom had a fireplace for a coal fire in the winter. Cooking was done in the oven or over the fire in the kitchen where there was a coal grate, blackened every day by the proud housewife. Baker and milkman called each day with their horse-drawn vehicles. Small suburban gardens were the source of intense pride, families making sure they planted the right plants at the right time of the year.

In the family structure, grandparents were particularly important. One grandfather seems to have been a great character, six foot three inches tall with a mop of curly hair, an entrepreneurial builder who died in his 80s. My grandmother, I remember, was proud and lived in a rather grander semi-detached in Wembley. She always entertained us at Christmas and was a great cook.

Parents hoped their offspring would pass the eleven-plus and go to a grammar school. The standard of teaching at my primary school was of the highest order. I can still remember every teacher. The headmistress was strict, but an enthusiast in creating team spirit. The percentage of Welldon Park pupils who went on to grammar school was extremely high and the school was rightly proud of its record.

My brother, Sydney, went to the local grammar school at Harrow and I went to Latymer Upper School in Hammersmith, considered then, as now, to be one of the best day schools in London.

It was a typical working-cum-lower-middle class upbringing. We rejoiced in the great institution of the Saturday morning cinema for which most children payed their tuppence for a diet of cartoon, comedy and then cowboy film. The bad men always got shot.

At a tender age we went to Sunday School and when older to the full church service. We both belonged to the cubs and the great event was the annual camp. The cub leader, Miss Wildman, also took us both for piano lessons. I am afraid she succeeded with neither. She failed with my brother because he could play everything by ear anyway. I was just hopeless.

I was seven when war was declared. The family was thrown into turmoil by a dilemma of whether to evacuate us two boys. Canada and South Africa were offering safe havens for London children. After a great deal of agonizing, my parents decided that Sydney and I should go to Canada, but a week before we were due to leave they changed their minds and said they could not bear to let us go. The ship we were to have sailed on was torpedoed in the Atlantic.

For a youngster, war was exciting. A major event was the building of an Anderson shelter in our garden. My brother and I slept on two top bunks, our parents beneath, and it became a second home. We did our homework in the shelter, used a radio there and for at least two years, from the beginning of 1940, we slept every night in the shelter. The road where we lived was in the line of bombing raids, close to Northolt Airfield where Spitfire squadrons were based.

One of my tasks each week was to collect scrap metal and scrap paper which were turned into munitions. Another was to deliver the weekly rota for the two hours of fire-watching each night. The fire wardens, who included both my parents, were trained to use a stirrup pump and to throw sandbags on incendiary bombs; they were also given steel helmets. During the worst raids, it was a hazardous job with shrapnel falling from the shells of our own anti-aircraft guns. We were lucky that a bomb which did land in our front garden did not explode. If it had our house would have been flattened.

The open-air type of life seemed to suit us. It was probably responsible for our good health. None of us suffered from colds or 'flu.

At primary school the air-raids meant that lessons stopped, we went into a brick shelter and were read to or shown film slides.

Even travelling to Latymer each morning could be an adventure.

The tube train windows were covered with a protective netting to stop glass flying during air-raids. To discourage people from pulling off the netting, posters warned: 'Forgive me the correction, but this netting is here for your protection.' On one occasion, I remember, someone had written underneath: 'Forgive me for the alteration, I cannot see the bloody station.'

Like other families, we kept our own chickens as part of the war effort, but they all died of natural causes. They became so much part of the family that none of us could bring ourselves to kill them.

Street life was important. We played in the street. There were far fewer cars and fewer dangers. Roller skating, cycling, gang play and conker fights all took place there. There was no fear of burglary or mugging. Doors were left unlocked. Young children were able to go about where they liked, without fear, and from the age of eight I was allowed to go to professional soccer matches and became a supporter of Fulham. Children from different backgrounds mixed fairly freely. Those from families who considered themselves middle class and dressed and spoke 'better' did not take part in the rougher kind of game. I remember Kenneth Adams was sent to a private school and was looked upon as being different.

The entrepreneurial spirit was alive in the street. The Rose family, with five children, were tough business people. They bred pet rabbits which they sold to the other children at a healthy profit. I joined in all the games and organizations. Football and cricket were played in the nearby recreation ground, particularly at school holidays.

I had my first business experience as well, as an assistant to the milkman during the school holidays. I liked it. I was fond of his horse and while I started early in the morning I finished about lunch-time and was given the princely pay of threepence a week for my Monday to Friday shift. At that time there were few restraints on the employment of children. This was just as well as I also did two newspaper rounds, getting up rather earlier than my friends, and receiving for it the enormous figure of fourteen shillings a week.

Holidays were a rarity. I can remember going on holiday with my parents only twice, one week at Bognor Regis and another week at Sandown in the Isle of Wight after the war. They simply did not have the money to spare and during the war there was too much uncertainty.

In the early years of her marriage, my mother did not go to work because she felt it was her duty to look after the children, but the war changed her attitude. She decided she had an even greater duty to help the war effort, first by making blackout blinds at a local factory in a school and later making jettison fuel tanks for RAF bombers. Making the tanks meant that she could not leave the factory until the job was complete and she had to stay at work during the height of the air-raids.

Latymer also cut across the class structure. Sons of factory workers and bankers, solicitors, accountants and architects mixed easily. Never, as far as I know, was there any sense of class distinction. If you were marked out, it was because you were good at sport or on the academic side. One of my greatest pals was Graham Glenister, the son of a senior partner in a sizeable firm of solicitors. They lived in a large house in Stamford Brook which I used to visit, particularly during the holidays. I recall going one Christmas when the Glenisters had been given an entire leg of pork. At a time when food rationing limited you to eightpence worth of meat a week this was luxury.

My first glimpse into stockbroking came through the father of another friend, John Cornell. John's father would really be shocked at the transformation in the Stock Exchange, which now works totally on electronic machinery and screens. I remember being at their house when John's father came in looking angry and asking for a large whisky. He said that when he had rushed to the jobber for a new issue of shares, he had been told by some wretched young stock-broker, 'Do you realize there is a queue here, sir?' He had replied, 'There has never been a queue the whole of the time I have been on the Stock Exchange. I have sometimes lost my shirt and tie trying to get the stock I wanted. As far as I am concerned, the first man to the jobber gets the stocks.'

My school friends went into a variety of different jobs. One with the rather unfortunate name of Dicky Drain and probably the best brain at Latymer has become a highly respected academic at York University. Peter Cook ended up by being a distinguished doctor.

What we did not consider as a family was that either Sydney or I should go to university. No member of my family had been to university. We did not know anyone who had and I had no great desire to go since I knew nothing about them. Doubtless if I had stayed at Latymer, I would have been told of the importance, but leaving at sixteen, before the sixth form, university did not come into the reckoning. Leo Amery was later to warn me I must compensate, which is what I did.

2

LIGHTING THE FLAME

I was steeped in national politics. Churchill was a hero and the other members of the War Cabinet were well known to me. Both my parents were active in politics, but party politics came as a surprise. When the 1945 General Election was declared I had no idea what it was about.

The 1940 General Election, of course, was cancelled and I had been three when the previous one took place, only seven when the coalition was formed.

I do remember Mrs Attlee coming to my Welldon Park primary school. She was fund-raising, as I recall it, for lifeboat men and I was running the bookstall. She bought a book by Walter de la Mare and asked me if I read much. I said I did and she said I had a good stall. She was just the wife of a distinguished politician. To me Mr Attlee and Mr Churchill were members of one government. I had not thought of them as opponents.

To understand what was happening, I turned first to my parents and asked them about the differences between the parties. My father said Labour believed in nationalization and the Conservatives in free enterprise. I recall he gave a curious example of razor-blades manufacturers. He said I could buy EverReady or Gillette blades. Competition meant there was a choice, with each company trying to produce better and cheaper blades. Without the competition there would have been inefficiency and no choice. My mother said the Socialists were weak at defending the country. When, before the war, Churchill was warning of the menace of Hitler, they had wanted to disarm.

I was soon given a taste of what party politics was about. My

8

parents formed, with two or three others, a Conservative Party branch in the Roxeth ward of Harrow West, a less affluent area of three-bedroom semi-detached houses in which factory and lower-paid office workers lived.

They asked me to deliver leaflets. I did so without commitment because I wanted to decide for myself which party to support. There were four candidates for the constituency, Conservative, Labour, Liberal and Commonwealth, a left-wing party led by Richard Ackland. I went along to hear them all. The main argument of the Conservatives was that we must keep Churchill as our leader. After all, the war with Japan was still raging.

Other issues revolved round the economy, nationalization and unemployment. Labour blamed unemployment on the Conservatives and the Tories responded by blaming the 1929 Labour Government.

To hasten my education in party politics, I went to the public library, which was held in the evenings in my old Welldon Park primary school and run by the deputy headmaster, Mr Goodhead. I asked him to recommend me two books about each of the main parties. I forget what they all were, but one was George Bernard Shaw's *Intelligent Women's Guide to Socialism, Capitalism, Sovietism and Fascism*. I came to the conclusion I was a Conservative.

Now at secondary school, Latymer Upper, I followed up my momentous decision by forming the Walker Anti-Labour League. One of the boys who helped was appropriately called Butler. We produced leaflets in longhand, with carbon copies, and put them in the desks of masters we knew were keen Socialists.

When Churchill was defeated, I was shocked. To a thirteen-year-old it seemed unbelievable that this great man, whom the whole nation had cheered to the echo on VE Day, was being kicked out. On VE Day, I had been with thousands of others in Parliament Square, standing by the Treasury wall, to cheer him as he drove through. How could they reject him? It was my first experience of the brutality of politics.

The excitement of the election was over, but at thirteen my involvement in politics was only beginning. The Conservative agent for Harrow West was Arthur Kelting. Like many others commissioned during the war, he returned to become a Conservative agent, a job with a middle-class salary and social status. He went on to become a considerable figure in the property world and deputy chairman of Hammersons. Arthur Kelting called on my mother to ask if I could join a Young Conservative branch he was setting up.

My mother protested that I was only thirteen, two years below the minimum. Arthur said it did not matter, as no one asked about age. One Friday evening I went along to the Conservative headquarters in Lowland Road with ten others. Arthur Kelting asked who wanted to become chairman. None of the others wanted the job and, much to my surprise, I was elected. The organization grew quickly and we had to divide it into two groups, one for those under twenty-one and another for those over twenty-one and under thirty. I stayed chairman of the under twenty-ones.

Politics was a family affair. My parents were on the Roxeth branch committee and I remember going to my first dinner at a local pub called the Tithe Farm wearing my father's old dinner jacket.

About this time I had my first fateful meeting with Leo Amery, the former Conservative minister. If later I was to be regarded as being a comparatively well-read candidate, digesting the heavy newspapers each day and gobbling up the political biographies and history, Leo Amery was largely responsible. I spoke at a Conservative Conference in Central Hall, Westminster in 1946 and made a very silly speech. Wearing a school blazer and at the age of fourteen, I started: 'Ladies and Gentlemen. I am a young Conservative.' The spectacle of this young boy in a school blazer brought down the house. Leo came up to me afterwards and said, 'That was a very fine speech, young man.'

He invited me to have tea at his great house in Eaton Square. This marvellous man took me upstairs to his library and talked to me about politics. It happened on five or more occasions.

He gave me two pieces of advice around which I have built my life. If I refer to them again in the book it is without apology. They have been central. He stressed the importance of being widely read and of being financially independent. When I told him I wanted to be an MP, I remember him asking: 'You do realize that you will have to wait until you are twenty-one?'

He gave me a number of reasons for being financially independent. He said one day I might be a junior minister with a wife and children. If I disagreed with the government on an important issue, I might want to resign. But if I did so without a stable financial background, I could lower the standard of living of my new family. I would face a nasty dilemma. He knew that on many occasions ministers compromised. They decided the issue was not so important after all and that they would soldier on to avoid their wives and children suffering.

He added another reason. In my lifetime, improved communications would mean that the world would shrink and become a small place in which events in one part would affect all the others. Every politician would have to have an understanding of international affairs. Either I could see the world at my own expense and see what I wanted or I could see it at someone else's expense and see what they wanted to show me.

Leo Amery gave me yet another sound tip. He said it was extraordinary that human beings spent so little time thinking. He believed he had benefited greatly from trying to put aside at least an hour each day to think alone. It made his life much more interesting and fuller and I should try it. Inspired by this great man, a pre-war Cabinet Minister, I decided to follow the recipe and it has helped to put events into perspective.

I felt rather like Dick Whittington as I stored the advice to be acted upon later.

That chance meeting with Leo Amery was critical to my future, but others were influential too. The deputy head of my primary school, Mr Goodhead, who advised me on books to read, was one. Another was the maths master at Latymer, Mr Stollery. He had more influence than he could have guessed. When he wanted to set a mathematics problem, he opened this pink newspaper I had never seen and gave examples. 'Here is a British war loan, three per cent stock, standing at 106,' he would say. 'What is the yield for a person with so much stock?' The paper from which he was framing his questions was the *Financial Times*.

The first time he gave an example I bought an *FT* at the station and took it home and told my father about it. With what I have always thought was great percipience, my father, a capstan operator, told me that if I wanted the newspaper he would give me tenpence a week to buy it each day. It earned me a reputation. I know Nigel Spearing, the Labour MP who was then a prefect at Latymer, has told others he remembers seeing this twelve-year-old boy studying the *Financial Times* on the tube between Harrow and Hammersmith. As likely as not, I would have had a comic in the other pocket.

There was no monopoly of ideas. If Mr Stollery encouraged me in capitalist ways, another teacher at Latymer, Wilf Sharp, an English teacher, a Socialist and an admirer of George Bernard Shaw, widened my horizons in other directions. He was good at drama, possessed a grand sense of humour and we had good-tempered and refreshing political dialogues in class. I learned from him that it is possible to have differences, but still argue them with humour and tolerance.

A third teacher, 'Milky' Parrish (Parrish was the name of a famous baby food at the time), taught me to think deeply for the first time about my Christianity. My brother and I always went to church and to Sunday School, but 'Milky' provided another dimension. He formed a somewhat pretentiously named Philosophy Club at which he would give terrific lessons on how to think and the spiritual values of man. His strong Christian views gave force to his belief in the self-determination of the individual. I have combined his advice with what I got from Leo Amery. I do pray and my hour's meditation does fit into a Christian view of life.

The friendship I formed with Leo Amery was similar to ones he had enjoyed when he was younger. In his youth he had worked closely with and been influenced by Lord Milner and been active in a group which recognized Joseph Chamberlain as its leader.

I quickly became an admirer of Chamberlain. He was an outsider in politics, a businessman among landowners and lawyers, and a provincial among Londoners. This enabled him to see the implications of political doctrines at the grass roots, rather than relying on the textbook of political economy. Chamberlain abandoned doctrines when they became irrelevant to industrial experience. He realized that Britain's industrial dominance was gone. The problem for the future was how to promote the greatest happiness for the masses and how to increase their enjoyment of life. He supported tariff reform to ensure a market for British industry. He actually proposed to finance old-age pensions out of the proceeds of protective duties.

Chamberlain, like Disraeli, opposed Marxist materialism through a set of imaginative and constructive new policies. He wanted to transform the Conservative Party from a party of sound administration and cautious ameliorative reform into one with a positive and dynamic creed. This creed would avoid the dangers of class conflict inherent in the Conservatism of the market economy.

Leo Amery encouraged me to read widely, but particularly Edmund Burke. He warned me that there were two things I would miss by not going to university. One was the art of reading, the other the art of conversation. At university I would have been surrounded by people of high ability and good conversationalists.

'You must try to read as much as your contemporaries and seek the company of conversationalists,' he said.

I read, read and read. I was devouring four or five books a week. I later applied the same approach to business. In my insurance broker's business, I insisted that even junior executives read the *Financial Times* and magazines like the *Banker*. I would deliberately ask them about a particular article and if they had not read it, I was critical. I am glad to say that all my children devour books.

My reading confirmed my growing belief in practical Toryism. Burke attacked the arrogance of what he called 'private stock of reason' and of the intellectual who believed that he could reform society without taking notice of the collective feelings of his compatriots. What he was attacking was very much like the ideology of Marxism or the believer in extreme *laissez-faire* of today. Institutions which worked well in one society might not work in another.

Burke attacked the French Revolution because the French had not adopted the empirical methods of the American colonists and ignored the need for practical reforms. He was not hostile to reform, but realized it must be absorbed into a national tradition. He did not believe there were any general laws of politics. Governments wrestled with the practical problem of how to rule equitably in the historic circumstances facing a country. His theory of balance, his awareness of the connections between tradition and reform and his distrust of ideology make him a founding father of Conservative thinking.

Years later I was often to be accused of being a 'rebel'. I never saw myself like that. Throughout my career, I have wanted to stick to the traditional, practical Toryism of Burke and others.

My two years' National Service, mostly spent in the army's Education Corps, confirmed me in the type of Toryism I wanted. It brought home to me that as a nation, we were wasting ability. Society placed more importance on an individual's background than his skills or intelligence.

In typical services fashion I was confused initially with another Walker and was lucky enough to spend six weeks in the company of Covent Garden porters. I learned to appreciate their wit, keen minds – and total lack of education. They were highly intelligent, but suffered from a low standard of literacy. In the Education Corps,

I discovered that many people could be encouraged to study for the first time in their lives.

Social division and discrimination were offensive to me and when I came out of the army I was relieved to find this attitude shared by the Conservative leadership of the time. Rab Butler, for example, produced workers' and industrial charters and a positive industrial policy focused on giving workers a more fulfilling part in employment.

No wonder that I later had some differences with Margaret Thatcher over the direction of policy.

Years later Jack Kennedy struck the same chord. I looked upon him as both a realist and an optimist who did not regard problems as an excuse for inaction. The Kennedys, Bobby and Jack, endeavoured to turn the anger and protest marches of the time into constructive reform. Both found it offensive that there were still ghettos of chronic social and economic deprivation. The problems of inner cities had to be tackled because they were a threat both to national interest and to national morality. Like Macmillan, the Kennedys concluded that the ideologues of left and right set higher store by the symmetry of their theories than by the solution of real problems. They thought that government should combine private initiative and public responsibility, working together for the common good.

Sharing and holding to these convictions of the 1960s, I later questioned the new Conservative leadership's heavy emphasis on the philosophical importance of the free market, apparently defining freedom as absence of control.

I set out my thinking in the Iain Macleod Memorial Lecture of 1978. I warned that in far too many areas of our life there were still two nations. In the inner cities, for example, we often had poverty and unemployment contrasting starkly with the prosperity of many of the suburbs. We had two nations in housing and the 'them' and 'us' attitudes in the workplace. The problem was compounded by racial tensions. Blacks and Asians were concentrated in the deprived inner city areas, with poor housing, high unemployment, lower education standards.

I said that progressive Tories had now to reformulate their philosophy, forty years after Macmillan's 'Middle Way'. It was no longer enough for governments to provide a minimum of welfare and a framework of law and order and leave individuals to get on with it. Real freedom would come only when people could take advantage of what Iain Macleod had described as the 'pursuit of excellence'.

The *laissez-faire* free market forces advocated by the Liberals in the nineteenth century and a number of modern economists on the right had little in common with real freedom. *Laissez-faire* only encouraged a disastrous battle on the shopfloor. The market economy, provided it worked properly, gave consumers a wide choice, but people were more than consumers. They were workers, managers, householders and students. Freedom for them included freedom from humiliation and the restraints of poverty, from unfair discrimination, from arduous toil and from the debilitating effects of slum housing. 'It means a society thriving on diversity, but undivided by class, race, regional disparities or generation gaps,' I said.

I had attempted to set out what had been the Tory tradition throughout my political life. I was therefore saddened at the hostility that this speech provoked.

3

GETTING ELECTED

At the age of sixteen I sought new pastures in more senses than one. My father took a new job as an engineer with British Acoustics in Gloucester, partly because he liked the idea of moving to 'attractive countryside'. This was understandable. Like many others at that time, the HMV factory at which he worked in Hayes were dark, dirty and noisy. The job was oily and the washing facilities inadequate, so that many of the engineers suffered from dermatitis. On top of that, he had a long cycle ride each day between Harrow and Hayes.

I left school after matriculating about the same time and was given the choice of staying with an aunt in London and going into the sixth form of Latymer, or going with my parents. I chose to go to Gloucester, but did not want to begin again at a new school.

Work sounded exciting and I already had an idea of what I wanted to do. Mr Ross, who served on the local Conservative committee in Harrow and possessed the only car in the road, was in insurance. He had told me it was interesting and offered a good career. The labour exchange in Gloucester had a vacancy for an office boy at the General Accident Insurance Company in Brunswick Road, Gloucester. With the advice of Leo Amery ringing in my ears – 'Make certain of your financial independence' – I took it and began a business career I describe more fully in a later chapter.

The move did not stop, or even seriously disrupt, political activity. We all quickly became involved in the Gloucester party. I immediately joined the Gloucester Young Conservatives and by a series of accidents quickly became chairman of a lively branch with a regular attendance of two to three hundred.

My mother became chairwoman of the Conservative women's branch. Our candidate was Tony Kershaw, who nearly won the seat and later became the MP for Stroud and a Foreign Office minister.

The big bonus was that I now had the chance to see my cricketing heroes, Worcestershire. I was always keen on cricket. Throughout the war I saw marvellous matches at Lords when the army, navy and RAF played each other and the British Empire eleven appeared. Many of the famous players were on display. I went to Lords with a friend called Bobby King. Bobby was passionate about cricket and we both collected Wisdens. For no explicable reason, I decided my favourite county was Worcestershire and I learned a great deal about the pre-war history of the county.

I suppose the names of great players like the Nawab of Pataudi, who had played for Worcestershire, caught my imagination. Living in Gloucester, I was able, for the first time, to see my heroes in the flesh. I used to catch the early morning bus from Gloucester to Worcester with my haversack, lemonade bottle and sandwiches and return on the last bus back. Now, when I go to the lovely county ground and see little boys with haversacks, I think, 'That was me.'

It turned out to be rather more than a boyhood passion. The longstanding allegiance to Worcestershire cricket can have done me no harm when a few years later I went before a Worcester selection committee and was able to say proudly that I was a life-time supporter of the county cricket club.

Then came a change in our family financial circumstances.

My grandmother died, leaving two big houses in Hampstead to my father. They would be worth £400,000 to £500,000 today. He sold them each for £2,000, but that was a great deal of money.

The money was a merciful release for my father. It gave him the happy prospect of doing something different. He had for many years endured a job he did not like. The fault was his father's. No doubt with the best intentions, my grandfather had told all his six or seven sons they must be apprenticed in a skill. One became a cabinet maker. My father, without consultation and to his dismay, was apprenticed to an engineering firm. The important munitions work he did during the war meant that he did not have to go into the army, but he hated the job.

The new-found capital was his opportunity to get out of engineering and he bought a little grocer's shop at 31 London Road, Brentford, for £3,000. When he purchased it, the turnover was £150 a week, with fifteen pounds as profit. A few years later he had built up the turnover to £1,200 a week.

Back in London, I joined the Brentford and Chiswick Young Conservatives, served my two years' National Service, and returned to become chairman of the local Young Conservatives. It was not a question of outstanding ability being recognized wherever I went! Once you were known to have been chairman of one branch you were a hot candidate for any vacancy in another.

I became chairman of Home Counties North area where my treasurer was a civilian pilot called Norman Tebbit. There was one uproarious annual general meeting. We came to the treasurer's report and someone said the left-hand side of the balance sheet did not add up. Four hundred people started doing the sum and agreed that it was not correct.

I looked at Norman and he looked slightly embarrassed. Then someone else got up and said, 'I have added up the right-hand side of the balance sheet and that does not add up either.' I had to say I was terribly sorry and that we would have to look into it.

Poor Norman and the area agent came in to see me with all their papers. I always remember because the final balance was drawn up on a Co-op tea-bag. What had happened was that Norman had been literally flying off everywhere and at the last moment had rushed to get all the figures together and made a mess of it.

Years later, when I was in the House of Commons, my good friend Norman came to ask me to propose him for the candidates' list. This I was delighted to do and advised him how to become better known and more likely to be adopted as a candidate.

In those days, the Young Conservatives was an active organization. As area chairman of Home Counties North, I would be speaking virtually every night of the week at a branch meeting. We covered the whole of Essex and Middlesex, so I had to catch a train to part of Essex or a tube to somewhere else. The meetings themselves were, on average, between sixty and eighty strong. If you were invited to speak at the bigger branches, like Bromley or Beckenham, you faced audiences of 700 or 800 young people.

I did become well known and I made some successful speeches at party conferences. One outcome of all this frantic activity was that in 1955 I was asked to do one of the radio party political broadcasts at a time when radio was important. Harold Wilson, Richard Crossman and Hugh Gaitskell were among the Labour team speaking on radio. It was a departure for a party to choose an unknown figure to do a political broadcast, but an unknown twenty-three-year-old created considerable interest, and it was certainly a good idea to have a young person appealing to the young voters.

Weekend schools organized by the party were packed and we usually took over several hotels. At this point, I started meeting the leaders of the party. It was as chairman of an area weekend school that I first met Iain Macleod.

I was impressed by him from the beginning. When Harold Macmillan took over as leader, Iain, then Minister of Labour, came down to a weekend school and I remember asking him about the difference between Anthony Eden and Macmillan. He said it was summed up beautifully for him when the government faced a major Ford strike at Dagenham. The phone rang and his private office said the Prime Minister wanted to speak to him. He thought, 'Oh God, he is going to be just like Anthony. Whenever anything like this happens, he will be phoning me every five minutes to ask what is going on and what I am doing about it, making suggestions.'

He wearily picked up the phone: 'Good morning, Prime Minister.' Harold said, 'Dorothy tells me there is a terribly good film on at the Odeon Leicester Square and we wondered if you and Eve would like to join us.'

As I came on to the national YC scene, William van Straubenzee, later an MP and minister, was national chairman. My immediate predecessor was Fergus Montgomery, who is still an MP. I was lucky that my chairmanship, between 1958–60, was the peak of YC membership.

Before then, however, I was to fight two elections. I was twenty-three when I first fought Dartford in 1955. Margaret Thatcher had fought it in 1950 and 1951 and met Denis there, but was now the prospective Parliamentary candidate for the more promising Finchley. She was extremely helpful about taking over the candidature of the constituency. She lived in a flat in Chelsea and I had dinner with her and Denis. I thought her able, lively and enthusiastic and I liked them both very much. She won her seat in 1959: I had to wait another two years.

We were always friendly and I was later to prompt Ted Heath to bring her into the Shadow Cabinet. Even in those days, I thought it was important to have at least one woman in the Shadow Cabinet and Cabinet and Miss Mervyn Pike had been in before. He agreed, and Margaret took over my job in the Shadow Cabinet as Shadow Minister of Transport while I moved to Housing and Local Government.

My first encounters with Ted Heath portended a quarrelsome relationship instead of the harmonious one which actually developed. It really did start badly. He came down to speak for me in the 1955 campaign when he was Chief Whip. I was twenty-two when I was adopted and he was the MP for the neighbouring constituency, so, in retrospect, it was understandable he should try to reassure my constituency party. I did not see it like that at the time.

He told my party that they had a very young candidate, me, 'and I know there are some of you who are saying he is too young.' He added: 'I don't think he is too young. He is very energetic, very able and very bright. Be assured when he gets in the House of Commons, as I am sure he will, I shall, as Chief Whip, have no difficulty in guiding him.' I was furious.

Matters went from bad to worse. The next serious encounter was when I was national chairman of the YCs. Ted was the vice-president of the YCs, with Sir Anthony Eden as president. Since Sir Anthony had stepped down, Ted was acting president.

The cause of our clash was a conference on 'Entry into the Common Market' he had called in his Bexley constituency and at which he asked me to speak. The next day newspapers carried a story that he had been attacked for his views on Europe by some of his own constituents at the conference. He wrongly jumped to the conclusion that I had leaked the story to the *Daily Express*.

He asked me to meet him in the House of Commons and I went along in blissful ignorance, thinking he wanted to discuss YC affairs. Instead he came down to the Harcourt Dining Room, where I was waiting, and told me he was not going to tolerate any more of 'this'. I asked him what 'this' was. He said, 'You come to a private meeting and then go and tell the press what happened. I know, I know, you gave it to them.'

I said, 'I don't know what you are talking about. I have not seen the *Express* and have not talked to anyone about the meeting.'

Ted said, 'I don't believe you.'

By now I was angry. I retorted, 'If you don't believe me, and you are the vice-president of the YCs while I am the chairman, we have an intolerable position. I will not continue as national chairman to have someone like you telling me I am a liar.'

He looked rather startled and said, 'Are you sure you did not give the information?' When I said 'Yes', he relented. 'I must have got it wrong. Come and have a drink.'

However, no sooner was I elected in the 1962 by-election than we were in immediate conflict over the European Community.

My adoption for the Dartford seat in 1955 was, to put it at its mildest, unusual. I think I must be the only politician to be adopted for two seats on the same night. I went to Lincoln and was placed on a short list of two and then later in the same week went to Dartford and was selected. On arriving home that night I found a telegram waiting. It was from the Lincoln party: the other person on the short list had been taken ill and they had unanimously decided to adopt me as their candidate that night.

I decided to stick to Dartford. It was nearer, though Lincoln had a smaller Labour majority.

Peter Emery had been on the short list for Dartford, so I phoned him the next day and asked him if he would be interested in Lincoln. He said he would and I phoned the local party and recommended him. Peter went off to Lincoln and they adopted him.

I later had good reason to be glad of my choice. In the 1955 election, Lincoln was the only seat which showed a swing to Labour. I hasten to say this was no reflection on Peter. Two days before polling day Geoffrey de Freitas, the Labour candidate, was walking across the bridge in Lincoln itself when a child fell into the river. He courageously jumped in to rescue the child and the story and his photograph were duly spread over the front pages of the local papers. You cannot fight that kind of luck.

I was shockingly precocious. I shudder to think how at the age of twenty-two, as candidate for Dartford I had the answer to every political problem. Others shuddered as well. There is one example I remember with particular embarrassment. The proprietor of the Gravesend and Dartford *Reporter* kindly invited me to lunch at a Gravesend restaurant and in return this awful twenty-two-year-old explained to him the solution to every problem which existed. At the end of the lunch, the proprietor said, 'Well, young man, my newspaper is independent. But fortunately for you it is a great deal more independent of the Socialists than it is of the Tories.'

Dartford was a marvellous training ground for the politics of town and country. The constituency had tough cement workers and dockers at Greenhythe and Swanscombe. It was a real community and I was lucky to have a very good agent, Charles Knight. Landed with such a youngster, he taught me a great deal about where I was going wrong. We had good results, bringing the majority down to 4,000 in 1955 and then to 1,200 in 1959. I worked the constituency hard, going down two or three times a week and canvassing between elections.

I am afraid I must have been a pain in the neck to the likeable Labour MP, Sydney Irving. I constantly challenged him to debate. As the sitting member, he quite rightly refused to give me the publicity or the chance to meet him on equal terms. But this was no perfunctory challenge. We gave no quarter. We even went to the extent of organizing a Conservative ball to celebrate his hundredth unanswered challenge to a debate.

We put up posters asking when he would meet the challenge. Left-wingers came to our aid. They ought to have known better, but in the end Sydney's executive committee, which included some nasty left-wingers, insisted that he should meet the challenge. The great day was fixed and it was a perfectly civilized debate. At the end, Sydney, with his usual courtesy, thanked the chairman for such a good meeting. I seconded and said I agreed that it was such a good meeting and such a good example of how democracy should work that we should repeat it every three months. Sydney turned ashen. We continued to ask, 'Why will the Labour candidate not debate again?' Despite this, he and I became personal friends when we were in the Commons together.

We had many well-attended election meetings, complete with hecklers. There was good humour as well. I used to give one committed Socialist heckler a lift from one Tory election meeting to the next. We would arrive and he would go to the back of the hall and I would go to the front. He would heckle and I would respond and they were lively exchanges. Then we would leave for the next meeting.

In 1959 Harold Macmillan came to Dartford just before polling day and we had a great surge of enthusiasm and a massive turnout. I had a feeling we could just pull it off, but failed by those 1,200 votes. We were naughty and forced a recount, which we should not have done with that size of majority. We were prompted because in another constituency the election officers had had a recount and discovered that a thousand votes had been put in the wrong pile.

As always my mother and father helped in my campaigning. Both were party workers and in my first campaign they addressed thousands of letters I had topped and tailed.

The constituency boundaries were redrawn later and Dartford became more Tory. I have always said that Dartford had both Margaret Thatcher and Peter Walker, but it was not until the local party got rid of both of them that the Tories were able to win the seat.

Between the elections we had Suez. The invasion presented no great personal crisis for me as it did for many others. This was partly my upbringing. The whole of my childhood had been spent with Britain at war. Here was another dictator who, ignoring all the rights we had in the canal, had decided to seize the Canal Company. I accepted that the canal was a vital lifeline to trade and communication. Trade with the Commonwealth was already a preoccupation of mine. I must also confess an emotional bond with Anthony Eden.

About this time we had a Conservative Party conference at which an emergency resolution supporting Suez was passed. Mr Lewis, who was chairman of the Welsh Conservative Party and later became a minister and Lord Brecon, proposed the motion and I seconded. I made a vigorous speech out of patriotic instinct and a vitriolic attack on Hugh Gaitskell which I now regret. I think Gaitskell was an honourable, decent and civilized man, but at the time I felt he was being unbelievably unpatriotic.

I was at the Young Conservatives meeting in the Festival Hall for Eden's last speech two days before he resigned. He received an enormous ovation when he arrived and left. He argued that the nationalization of the Canal Company was the act of an aggressor and a disaster not only in economic terms, but also in undermining the rule of law.

Even today I hesitate to change my view of the Suez operation. I cannot help feeling that what went wrong was the military execution of the operation and the American withdrawal of its support. I am influenced in this by my later experience as Parliamentary Private Secretary to Selwyn Lloyd. Selwyn told me that when Foster Dulles, the US Secretary of State, was seriously ill in hospital in America a few years later he asked Selwyn to visit him. Selwyn went quietly, and heard the American say how much he regretted withdrawing American backing for the Suez venture. He hoped Selwyn would appreciate this regret from a dying man.

After losing Dartford narrowly on my second attempt, my next chance came at a by-election in Harrow West.

In one of the frequent twists of political fate, the constituency in which I was born and did much of my early political work became the only one to turn me down as a candidate. It happened in 1960 and I blame my mother!

Much earlier she had won the chairwomanship of the women's branch and, in the process, defeated a woman from the most Tory part of Harrow West, Pinner. The woman deeply objected to my mother getting the post.

Revenge can be sweet. Years later, as I went into the Harrow West selection meeting, she appeared and said in a loud voice, 'How lovely to see you, Peter. The last time I saw you you were wearing short trousers.' You could feel the whole meeting saying, 'Yes, he is very young, isn't he?'

I think it is always true that the local boy is taken for granted, but on this occasion I had also to contend with what I can now acknowledge as a remarkable put-down by a woman who had by then become chairwoman of the women's branch. It was too much.

My next chance, at a by-election in Worcester a year later, was fortunately entirely different. The local party had applications from three or four hundred candidates and interviewed a hundred of them, including Francis Pym and William Rees-Mogg, later editor of *The Times*, now chairman of the Broadcasting Standards Council and a newspaper columnist. They narrowed the field to twenty and then a final five. No one remembered me in short trousers. As far as I was aware, nobody knew me at all.

I could claim my knowledge of the county cricket ground and my support for Worcestershire, but that was all. The chairman of the selection committee was Joe Gimpon, chairman of Royal Worcester Porcelain. As a young accountant he had been asked to liquidate the company and had said, 'I am not going to liquidate it: I am going to buy it.' The divisional chairman was Lady Sandys, a marvellous lady. Richard, her son, became a Government Whip in the Lords and a fine friend as president of the Worcester Conservative Association.

I made an early mistake by wearing my 'City' attire of a black jacket and pinstripe trousers to my first selection meeting. As a result, I discovered I did have friends or a friend at court. The agent whom I did not know knew me. He had apparently seen me in action and thought I was the best ever national chairman of the Young Conservatives. He phoned to tell me of my gaffe: 'I should not be doing this. You did very well, but for goodness' sake don't come

24

again in a black jacket and pinstripes. They have never seen them before and wondered what you were wearing. They are not like that.' For my next interview, I went in a tweed suit.

When it got down to the last five, the short list included the then Mayor of Droitwich, Roy Fabricius, who became a good friend. The other local man was a former Mayor of Worcester, Basil Edwards, who had started off as the adopted candidate for Worcester in 1945. He had fallen victim to an extraordinary set of circumstances. After he had been chosen, the Ward family intervened to say that there were two Conservative associations in Worcester and theirs had chosen Geordie Ward, so the Conservatives had two contenders for the single seat. It resulted in Basil receiving a call from the Prime Minister. Winston Churchill phoned to tell him, 'If we have two Conservative candidates, we are bound to be defeated. Obviously, I don't have the time to sort out who is the right one and in the interests of our country, Mr Edwards, I must ask you to stand down.'

Basil reluctantly stood down and Geordie got elected by four votes.

When the 1961 by-election was called Basil was immediately and properly put on the short list. These local candidates were strong, worthy, patriotic people who became my friends, but they had limited knowledge of national policy. As a former chairman of the Young Conservatives, speaking almost every night, and having fought two by-elections, I was able to make the best speech at the selection conference and obtained eighty-five per cent of the votes.

I fought a vigorous non-stop contest in my own style, consciously ignoring the advice of my predecessor. This did not stop Geordie, an old-style politician, giving it.

He told me that I must arrive at the committee rooms at eleven o'clock each morning, allocate a room to myself, marked 'Silent, Man at Work', read the newspapers, then go round to the Union Club for lunch. Everyone had lunch there and I would find out what was going on. 'Don't have the club claret. It is all right, but have some of their half bottles. They are very good and very reasonable.'

After lunch I was advised to slip into one of the club armchairs and have a nap, getting the steward to wake me about three o'clock, before going out for a hard hour's canvassing and then back to my hotel to bed. The hotel was to rouse me at 6.30 p.m. with a light meal before I went to my evening meeting. I was to tell my supporters that I had to get back early to prepare my speech for the next day. 'I tell you, Peter, the important thing in Worcester is that when you arrive at the eve-of-poll meeting, the people of Worcester like you to look fresh and not tired and exhausted.'

Needless to say, I worked from early morning to late at night.

At the end, I had half Geordie's majority, but there was an explanation for this. The by-election was held when the Liberals were riding particularly high. The true position was revealed in the next election in 1964. Worcester was virtually the only seat in the country where there was a swing to the Conservatives, not against the by-election, but against the 1959 general election. It was the second best result in the country. Majorities in all the neighbouring constituencies, including that of Sir Gerald Nabarro, tumbled. If you take the second 1964 election and apply to it the national swing, I should have lost by 2,000. In fact, I won by 3,500.

Sir Gerald's generosity briefly threatened the 1961 by-election campaign. He wrote: 'I am thrilled you have been adopted as my neighbour. I am prepared to make seventeen speeches on your behalf.' The last thing I wanted was Gerald speaking every night during the campaign. I wrote back and said the offer was terribly kind, but if he spoke once it would be enough.

We finished the by-election on an uproarious note. The day after I won I gave a lunch at the Raven Hotel at Droitwich for the agents who had run the campaign and I had some fun at the expense of the area agent, Jack Galloway. He had had to look after the Small Heath by-election at the same time as Worcester and I had teased him that he spent more time at Small Heath. Unkindly, I spotted an old rusty sword in a Worcester antique shop and bought it for five pounds. At the end of the lunch I gave the workers mementoes and Jack six bottles of whisky, but then arranged for the head waiter to bring the rusty old sword on a cushion bearing the label 'To Jack Galloway, for winning the battle in Small Heath'.

At the time it seemed hilarious. There were roars of laughter. There was a great cine film of Jack Galloway leaving the Raven at about three o'clock that afternoon with three bottles of whisky under each arm, struggling to carry the sword as well.

I continued to work Worcester hard after the election. I spent every weekend from Friday evening to Sunday evening going round. Between the surgeries for constituents, I would knock on doors. I was fortunate in having enormous press coverage and was able to build up a strong personal following. My predecessor was a nice man, but had not been a terribly active constituency MP.

As I became established, I began to feel a strong affinity with the West Midlands as a whole. Much later I was to draw up a manifesto for the Midlands, but the early ties were strengthened by my association with the *Birmingham Post*. When I first became an MP, the *Post* asked me to do a regular fortnightly column with Brian Walden, then Labour MP for a Birmingham seat, doing the alternate week. The difficulty from the paper's point of view was that Brian and I agreed on almost everything, defeating the idea of having two opposing attitudes. Although this arrangement continued for several years, the editor, David Hopkinson, did not really get the clash of party opinions he wanted.

Something else drew me to the West Midlands, a region with a high number of marginal seats and of critical importance if any party is to win power. This was Joe Chamberlain, a Birmingham man and very much, as I have already said, my sort of Tory. The Chamberlain tradition lived on in my early days as an MP. Tory leaders like Sir Frank Griffin were very much in the Chamberlain mould, committed to making Birmingham hum industrially and in other ways.

I was especially fortunate to have Worcester as my seat. If you wanted to produce a microcosm of England, Worcester is it. You have a cathedral city, the old and the modern, industry and agriculture and village cricket; the village pubs are for the locals. If, with hindsight, I could choose any constituency to represent, Worcester would be it. From a narrow party organizational point of view, it is important that the population is relatively stable. The Worcester electorate was remarkably stable. In my surgeries, I have now seen 30,000 people. If I have been able to do anything for them, they will have told not only their neighbours, but also all their relatives. This just does not happen in suburban Birmingham or London.

You can more easily form social links as well. I organized dominoes and darts teams which went round the villages. I do not play billiards or snooker, but was still president of the local league. Visiting the local pubs was a good way of getting to know people in a totally relaxed atmosphere. You would go to a village pub in, say, Ombersley or Hartlebury, and have a night in which you played darts and crib, and the local people came to know you as an individual and not just a public figure.

I led a cricket team which played two or three local villages each year. This turned out to be a mixed blessing. It was fine when I was in my late twenties and early thirties, but as I got older I began to suspect they put on village fast bowlers at both ends in the hope of forcing a quick by-election. It was rather frightening and I was grateful when the villages disappeared from my constituency in a boundary commission reorganization and I was no longer at risk.

I carefully did not offer a similar challenge to the new village which came into the constituency.

4

KICKING OVER THE TRACES

I arrived in the Commons in a dream. The extent of my ambition was to become an MP: I had thought no further. Like Stanley Baldwin when he first entered Parliament, I spent hours in the chamber itself.

Luck gave me a head start. I got immediate credit for my maiden speech, which was not nearly as impressive as it apparently sounded. I normally speak without notes, but on this occasion was terrified at the prospect of my maiden speech and wrote copious ones. When I got up to speak my hand was trembling so badly, I could not read them and immediately put them down. Commentators like Tom Lindsay in the *Daily Telegraph* referred to 'this remarkable maiden speech without notes'. If only they had known.

I remember I received kind notes from Maurice Edelman, the Labour MP for Coventry North whom I had never met, and Sir Edward Boyle, who was speaking from the government front bench.

Edward became a firm friend, if sometimes a little removed from ordinary life. We have one lovely story about his vagueness. Just after our daughter Shara was born, Tessa and I were walking in St James's Park with our son Jonathan, who was about two years old and toddling. Edward saw us, congratulated us on the new baby, then, looking towards Jonathan, declared, 'Isn't he big?' He was a lovely man and a friend, but lived in a rarefied atmosphere. The worst thing he did was to help to destroy the grammar schools. I argued that as our educational spokesman he was wrong to put so much emphasis on comprehensives. He would reply, 'Peter, I went to a comprehensive school, Eton, not based on ability and talent. Eton has done well and I want everyone to have their Eton.'

Once in the Commons, I was immediately plunged into the anti-EEC entry campaign. The early influence of Leo Amery, this time as the imperialist, was at work again.

In 1949 the party had brought out a document called *The Imperial Charter* which argued the importance of Commonwealth trade. I was persuaded to believe in this fantastic imperial connection and that it could be revitalized. I reasoned that the Community was a French and German creation based on protectionist, inward-looking policies.

It was proposing external tariffs against the rest of the world. And it was totally white while I believed that Africa and Asia were the emergent powers. I was against racial prejudice and convinced it was necessary to have a more outward-looking Europe, one with good relations with Africa and Asia. I could not see the 'Six' doing that.

I argued that there was an alternative. The Community's single biggest customer was Britain. The Community's biggest group of customers was the European Free Trade Association, in which Britain was dominant. I urged the government to invite all Commonwealth countries to reach an economic agreement with EFTA. Some might not wish to do so, but they should at least be given the chance. The Commonwealth often had the raw materials, Britain had the manufacturing capacity. We would then have a big block able to tell the Six: 'If you put up tariffs against us, we will retaliate and put up tariffs against you and cut off raw material supplies.' We would add more in sorrow than in anger that we did not want this to happen. We wanted maximum trade, but if forced would adopt this tit-for-tat policy. I thought that by adopting that approach we could make Europe far more outward-looking, which seemed preferable to Britain becoming simply the seventh member of the Community.

Nobody seriously challenged my view and I became more and more confident that I was right. What is more, I did not believe we were telling the Commonwealth the whole truth about what the external tariff barrier would mean for them. I entered the House of Commons on 15 March and by 1 June was committed to touring the Commonwealth to tell them what they faced.

I had no idea that a young MP threatening to tour the Commonwealth could cause concern in the Cabinet. I was a nonentity without political clout. But I have discovered since that the Cabinet did discuss my visit and decided that I could stir up public opinion and endanger the negotiations. As I was a six-months-old MP they could scarcely send a Cabinet Minister to follow me and repair the damage. That would be acknowledging the importance of my tour. Instead they would send the chairman of the backbench Foreign Affairs Committee, Sir Tufton Beamish.

I had no formal organization for my visits, but people from the Commonwealth wrote to me and I wrote back to say that I would be coming out to Australia or wherever on certain dates and would be grateful if they could organize meetings.

In India, I met Moraji Desai, leader of the Janata Party, who later became his country's Prime Minister. He gave me his reflections not only on the EEC, but also on world politics, meditation and thought. I met groups of Indian Parliamentarians, went to the Indian Parliament and addressed the Chamber of Commerce in Delhi.

I flew to Australia and spoke to the most fabulous meetings. The Australians were extremely worried about Britain joining the European Community.

The peak of my political career came at Adelaide. Six hundred people took part in a rousing meeting at the end of which the chairman declared he would now ask Don Bradman to propose a vote of thanks. Don Bradman thanking me, the Worcestershire supporter! I met him three times in the space of about forty-eight hours and could not believe my good fortune.

When I discovered Sir Tufton was to follow a couple of weeks later to say how wrong I was, I behaved outrageously. I warned my audiences in Australia and other countries that I was to be pursued by this man, Sir Tufton Beamish. I deliberately stretched out the name . . . Sir . . . Tufton . . . Beamish. Audiences giggled at the name for a start. I described him scornfully as a distinguished Parliamentarian, but then went on to urge them to ask him a series of questions.

'I want you to say: "But Sir Tufton, what about this?" and "Sir Tufton, what about the effect on that?"'

I left all these people with their eyes gleaming. Poor Sir Tufton was met by the most hostile audiences imaginable and, in Auckland, had to be rescued by the police.

For the first time, I discovered I had powerful allies in my defence of the Commonwealth. Shortly after announcing the tour, I received a remarkable telegram from the south of France saying: 'Deeply admire your courageous tour of the Empire. Please be my guest in Fredericton, Canada. Let me know the date of your arrival and departure and the names of any distinguished Canadians you would like me to invite during your stay.'

The author of the invitation was Lord Beaverbrook. I arrived in Fredericton to discover half the airport was named after him and I stayed at the Beaverbrook Hotel, passing the Beaverbrook Gymnasium and the Beaverbrook Theatre. At the university in New Brunswick, there was the Max Aitken Library and the Lady Beaverbrook House. Everything was owned by the family.

He occupied one floor of the hotel where I stayed as his guest. Although he was over eighty, I discovered how he still sought to control his newspapers when I was sitting in my bedroom and heard him dictating to a tape recorder in the adjoining room.

Each day he had copies of the *Evening Standard* and the *Evening News*, the *Daily Mail* and the *Daily Express* flown out. Each day he commented. I heard him dictating: 'Mr So and So. The printing on Page 1 is terrible. There is something wrong with our paper or our printing, please get it right. I see in today's *Express* we have another photograph of Sir Roy Welensky. I know we support him, but this is the eleventh successive day we have had his photograph and our readers will be bored. Don't use it for the next six days.' His final comment: 'I see the *Daily Mail* has an advertisement for Home Electrics which is four column inches bigger than the one in the *Daily Express*. Mr So and So, we don't accept advertisements which are smaller than those of the *Daily Mail*.'

On the second day I was there, he asked me if I would like to meet some of the university's professors for lunch. He then summoned his male secretary to tell him: 'Get me six professors for lunch.'

There were less congenial sequels to my early relationship with Lord Beaverbrook. The first was the South Dorset by-election in 1962, in which Angus Maude was standing. Lord Hinchinbrook, who gave up his title, stood as an anti-Market candidate against him. I thought that was wrong. We all had our own views on the issue, but had been given total freedom. There was no vendetta or even a squeeze and I believed that in these circumstances it was wrong to stand against an official Conservative candidate when only the Labour Party could benefit.

I was asked to go down and speak for Angus, and said I would.

I told my audience that I was against the negotiations, but I had had freedom to express my views at party conferences, in the Commons and elsewhere. In a democratic party, there were differences, but we must remember there were also a whole range of policies on which we were united against the Socialists. My good friend and chum, Hinch, was wrong.

The Beaver ordered a hatchet job to be done on Walker. There were three *Express* reporters at the meeting, including the late lamented George Gale. The next day I had the front page, the editorial and a feature article attacking this wicked man who had given up the cause to support the official Tory candidate.

The second sequel involved another by-election two years later and was even more awkward. Sir Alec Douglas-Home had summoned me to No. 10 to tell me the Devizes by-election was critical. If we could hold this by-election, we could well win the coming general election. If we lost it badly, we could lose the general election. He would like me to go down and run the campaign. Any Cabinet Ministers I wanted to speak would come and Central Office would be told I was in complete command.

Of course, I accepted and realized immediately that I must have the support of the Tory press, the *Daily* and *Sunday Express* in particular. I phoned Lord Beaverbrook at his Leatherhead home on a Sunday and asked to speak to him. There was a long pause before I was told he would speak to me and then another before he came on the phone. I explained that there was a crucial by-election. The Prime Minister had asked me to run the campaign and I wanted the backing of his newspapers. He asked me who the candidate was. It was Charlie Morrison, the son of John Morrison, the famous chairman of the Conservative backbench 1922 Committee. What were his views on Europe? I said I did not know, but he was of good farming stock and of a distinguished family and I would guess was enthusiastic about the Empire and British agriculture. There was another silence and then: 'I will support.' Nothing else. He had put down the phone. However disenchanted he was with me personally, Beaver knew where his priorities lay. No candidate has ever had the support that Charlie had from *Express* newspapers in that successful campaign.

I did also lunch with Lord Beaverbrook at his flat next to the Ritz. He adopted the disconcerting practice of having a blank note pad at the side of his plate. If you said anything interesting, funny or witty, he wrote it down. If you got to the sweet course and there was no entry, you knew he was unbelievably bored.

During this phase the *Daily Mirror* and others described me as an 'angry Tory', but I did not see it like that. The main difference I had with the leadership was over Europe and I did not think of myself as a rebel. I felt, perhaps naively, I was arguing a cogent case and that was what being an MP was all about.

Some derive enjoyment from being labelled a rebel. I did not. I look back with some surprise to find that I was. I certainly was not the conventional rebel. The first profile of me was by Anthony Howard in the *New Statesman*, accompanied by a Vicky cartoon. I must be one of the last of a generation of politicians to be the subject of a Vicky cartoon. Anthony argued that I was opposed to going into the Common Market for reasons quite different from the right-wingers in the party. I was objecting because I felt it would be bad for Africa and Asia, while right-wingers were mainly concerned about kith and kin arguments. I was constantly being grouped with thirty-odd rebels who had completely different motives.

He was right. I was arguing a left-wing case against the Community. I felt there was a coherent alternative.

Derek Walker-Smith, Sir Derek, Conservative MP for Hertfordshire East, became a close associate in the fight and we wrote a leaflet *Call to the Commonwealth*. I could not help thinking that here was a senior ex-minister leading the fight with a young MP of only a few months' duration.

The Commonwealth commitment went hand in hand with an abhorrence of racial discrimination and immigration controls. Like others I came later to realize that the sheer numbers of immigrants, particularly from Asia, meant there had to be some control, but I detested the concept. What we were describing as 'immigrants' were citizens of the Empire. I was left with the nagging certainty that many of those who were pressing for controls were racist.

While I may have been regarded as liberal on immigration, I caused some raised eyebrows on law and order. I can see now that there was an apparent or real contradiction in my attitude to capital and corporal punishment. I was against hanging, but in favour of birching. I think I must have retained from school days a belief that a quick caning was a perfectly good punishment. There was a direct relationship between crime and effect and I took the view there was no permanent damage. I am horrified at the idea of birching now, but at that age I saw it as a punishment to be administered if people repeated crimes of violence.

Hanging was something else. My distaste started at school when I was asked to do an exercise saying what was wrong with the following sentence: 'The judge said, "I sentence you to death. Perhaps that will teach you a lesson."' I found it a conclusive argument. The whole idea was repugnant.

In these early days in the Commons, much of my time was taken with national issues, but they sometimes had a particular constituency application. Agriculture fell into this category. Leo Amery was responsible for my early interest in the subject, which tied in with my anti-EEC stance. He wrote a book called *The Balanced Economy* in which he argued strongly that for the sake of the balance of payments, security in time of war and social reasons, it was lunacy to destroy our agriculture as we had nearly done in the late 1920s and early 1930s.

So much for theory. I knew nothing of the detail of agriculture. Burned into my memory was my experience when I first became candidate for Dartford and was summoned to meet the NFU. I remember my first question was: 'What will you do about the flax marketing scheme?' I was forced to say that I was terribly sorry, I did not even know there was a flax marketing scheme. To which my questioner replied, 'That's the bloody trouble. There isn't one.'

You do not enjoy that kind of luck too often. I vowed I would not be at risk on agriculture again. This was particularly important in heavily agricultural Worcestershire.

Soon after I was chosen for Worcester, I went to the NFU and said that I did not know the detail of their problems, but if I was lucky enough to become an MP I wanted to be the best briefed on agriculture in the Commons. I did not want to meet them when the farm prices were fixed and interest rates were high and everyone was complaining. It would be far better to set up a committee of the brightest people in the different spheres of agriculture, some on the dairy, arable, corn and cereal side, some from the fruit side. This would meet every three months, not to have a long argument with me or the government, but to brief me. Any points farmers wanted put forward or argued in Parliament I would listen to and, if I agreed, I would raise them in the Commons.

The effort turned out to be a good investment for me as well as the farmers in a way I could not have guessed at the time. When I became Minister of Agriculture many years later, I really did know a great deal about agriculture.

5

MARKED OUT

Selwyn Lloyd was responsible for shooting me on to the front bench.

It happened in a most unpromising way. Like many others, I was disturbed by Harold Macmillan's 'night of the long knives' when he sacked so many members of his Cabinet, among them Selwyn. I thought that, as Chancellor, Selwyn had taken a series of unpopular, but basically correct measures to stop inflation rising. They included hire purchase controls. He was terrified at where inflation might lead and sent a warning minute to Cabinet saying that if things went on like this inflation would reach four per cent . . . .

He was dismissed ruthlessly. Then some months later when all the economic indicators were improving, this ridiculous young MP, me, made a weekend speech saying that he hoped, as the economic trend continued to improve, the party would express its gratitude to Selwyn Lloyd, who had taken all the measures necessary to bring about the improvement.

I did not mean it to be critical of Reggie Maudling, whom I liked, but I thought Selwyn had taken all the punishment and was now being vindicated. The following week I received a note from him saying that he had never seen a more stupid way of destroying a political career at birth than my silly speech. But he was nevertheless grateful. I was more than generous, if also foolish.

He suggested we should have lunch and we formed a friendship which was to stick. When Alec became leader and brought him back into the Cabinet, he asked me to become his Parliamentary Private Secretary.

The job was excellent training. Here was a man who had been Secretary of State for Defence, Foreign Secretary, Chancellor and now Leader of the House. As Leader, he did all the negotiations with the Opposition. If there was a dispute between two Cabinet Ministers, the Prime Minister Alec asked him to arbitrate.

He told me to sit at a particular desk for all meetings. If they were sensitive, I was to work at my desk, but continue to listen. He showed me all the Cabinet papers. He was out to teach this young boy all he knew about politics and he did teach me a terrific amount. I sat in on meetings between him and Harold Wilson and again when he had in several Cabinet colleagues to thrash out a particularly difficult problem.

My 'filing' became the subject of hilarity. Since there were no cupboards in the room, we kept the drink in a filing cabinet. If, at about six o'clock, Selwyn was having a meeting and he thought he should offer everyone a drink, he would suddenly shout out, 'Walker. Do the filing.' All those present would look sympathetically as the young MP responded to the barked order by rushing across to the filing cabinet – only to see him, much to their relief, produce the gin and whisky.

In a small way, I was able to help Selwyn in his new job. The Opposition was delighted with the choice because they considered he was not particularly articulate from the dispatch box. As his PPS, I helped him with his first big speech as Leader. Conscious that there was a problem, I borrowed from the Commons library all the speeches he had made in the previous fifteen years, read them all and found what I thought was the reason he was not an effective speaker. The short explanation was that whenever he made a point, he wanted to explain the thinking behind it. There could be ten sentences explaining why something was being done. Someone would interrupt in the middle of an explanation and he would be knocked off his track.

Diffidently, I told him what I thought I had found wrong with his speeches and that in a Parliamentary speech, lasting perhaps thirty minutes, you simply had to make point after point after point. He mumbled and agreed. I am glad to say that first speech was punchy, with no explanations, and was declared a terrific success. Even the jokes came off. Just how much he enjoyed himself was brought home to me as we walked to his room after the speech and during the vote at the end of the debate. The man who never relished big speeches asked, 'When is my next speech?'

Obviously, it was Selwyn who recommended me to Alec for

promotion to the front bench after our narrow 1964 General Election defeat. Typically, he made a joke of it. He came back from lunch one day and said, 'Alec wants to see you at three o'clock. He is horrified at the speech you made at the weekend.'

I said, 'What speech?'

He said he did not know what I had said, but he had never known Alec more annoyed about any speech. I protested that it was a speech on housing attacking the Labour Party. 'I can only tell you Alec is furious.'

I went along to Sir Alec's office with a press hand-out of what I had said and ready to demand to know what my leader was talking about.

I knocked on the door and at his invitation sat down, looking daggers. He said, 'Peter, I would like you to join the front bench. I want you to join Ted's team on economic affairs.' I gulped and realized that I was the victim of yet another of Selwyn's practical jokes.

As I walked out of his room, I remembered my differences with Ted Heath over Europe and the scene when I was candidate for Dartford. What was life going to be like as number two to Ted?

Selwyn was a lonely man because his marriage had broken up early. His daughter, whom he adored, was going into the theatre and she was with repertory companies away from home. He went home to an empty flat and later when Tessa and I were married he came and stayed with us frequently.

Later still I advised him against becoming Speaker of the Commons when it was offered. He quite rightly ignored my advice. What I had not taken into my calculations was that, as Speaker, you can never be lonely. You are always having people to dinner; you are surrounded by people. And he was an excellent Speaker.

He taught me some things without saying a word. Though he had been so ruthlessly sacked by Harold Macmillan, he would never utter a word of any description against him, even to someone as close as his PPS. At all the functions we attended when both Selwyn and Harold was present, it was always Harold who was deeply embarrassed. Selwyn was relaxed and charming, but you could sense Harold's unease about sacking a man for doing the right things. It was a lesson to me that Selwyn gained strength from doing that. If he had started attacking Harold, it would have been discounted as the reflex hostility towards someone who had dismissed you.

I hope I would have done it naturally in any event, but when Margaret Thatcher sacked me from the Shadow Cabinet years later, I was particularly careful not to utter a single word of acrimony against her. Not only was Selwyn right in human terms, he was right tactically. To have attacked Harold would have let Harold off the hook.

The same year I became Selwyn's PPS, we suffered the Profumo scandal. I knew Jack Profumo and when the allegations were made and he denied them, I believed him totally. Walking out of the Commons on the Friday he made his denial, I saw George Wigg and Barbara Castle, two of the Labour MPs who had been after Jack, muttering together in what I thought was a vicious way. I thought, 'Thank God, he is free of them.' But he was not. He had lied.

I liked him as a person and was upset when the full story emerged.

The day after his resignation, Central Office phoned me to say that Jack was due to speak to the annual women's rally in his constituency the following day and would I go in his place. I could not think of a more difficult engagement, but said I would. Every television camera and every newspaper was present and I was in a dilemma about what to say to convey my sympathy and start reuniting the party. Though it must have been far from his mind, the Bishop of Southwark provided my salvation. That morning he had delivered a blistering attack on Jack and so I began with a blistering attack on the bishop. I genuinely thought it was unforgivable that a Christian bishop, with hostile political views, should make a vicious assault in this way.

I was able to win the cheers of the women of Stratford-upon-Avon and say comforting things about Jack. Jack and I have remained close friends ever since and I was delighted when he was honoured by the Queen for his fabulous work at Toynbee Hall in the East End. For years when I was writing for newspapers, I told them to send the fees to Toynbee Hall.

We did have another point of contact. There is a club called The Other Club, started by Winston Churchill. Important politicians of all parties, including former Prime Ministers, are members and there has never been a leak, despite the fact that the politicians are from different parties. Jack was a member of the club and when the scandal broke he resigned. About a year later the members unanimously asked him to come back and he has been a regular attender ever since. He is an honourable member and a decent man.

I was by now getting my domestic arrangements worked out. Life was often fun. After managing his by-election campaign, I became close to Charlie Morrison. I would sometimes drive down to Devizes to spend the week-end with him and his wife, Sara.

Ian Gilmour became a friend of us both and we decided to share an office, with a secretary each and a research assistant between us. Sara and Charlie also wanted accommodation when they were in London and though Ian had a house at Isleworth he wanted somewhere to stay when there were late-night sittings. As a bachelor I needed accommodation close to the Commons. We found a big flat in Gayfere Street. We each had a bedroom, and shared a drawing room; there was also a big room in which our three secretaries worked and another room in which our research assistant delved. We got on well together. I went into the Shadow Cabinet in 1965 and Charlie was appointed under me as Shadow Minister for Sport. Ian had been editor of the *Spectator*. We all had 'wet' tendencies and became known as the 'Gayfere Street set'.

Tessa became Ian's secretary. I thought she was lovely, lively, attractive and had a marvellous personality. What is more she shared the views of Charlie, Ian and myself about politics. Unknown to the others I began to take her out and we quickly fell in love. Our liaison was not as secret as we thought. The illusion of secrecy was smashed one day when Tessa walked into the Commons to be told by a policeman: 'He has just gone out, madam.'

Pleased as I was with my first front bench appointment, I was nervous about joining Ted Heath's team because of our earlier differences. Fortunately, we were thrown together quickly by the 1965 Finance Bill. It was the most controversial Socialist bill you could devise, introducing the capital gains and corporation taxes and taxes on overseas earnings.

Ted divided our attack on the bill into three parts, each with its own leader. I was the leader on capital gains, Tony Barber on the corporation tax and Edward Boyle on the overseas financial provisions. We met each morning and I quickly built up a rapport with Ted.

We launched probably the most ruthless amending campaign against a Finance Bill this century, and it was successful. The skill with which it was conducted was almost certainly responsible for Ted's beating Reggie Maudling for the leadership. Ted's team was seen to have performed well. On at least one night we defeated the government.

It was ironical that ten years later, in 1975, Margaret Thatcher made a deep and probably decisive impression by the way she conducted our case against the Finance Bill, having been put in charge of the operation by Ted. In the space of ten years two people were elected to the leadership of the Conservative Party because of the way they had handled the fight against the Finance Bill.

The campaign against the 1965 Finance Bill gave me an early insight into Ted's passion for doing the right thing. One day when we were debating the bill, a Tory backbencher made what could only be described as a totally dishonest speech, using statistics in a misleading way. I was sitting next to Ted and he was fuming with rage. In the voting lobby afterwards, he went up to the MP and told him he had made an incredibly bogus speech. He said, 'This is a bad piece of legislation and should be opposed with total honesty and integrity.' Fiercely opposed to the legislation as he was, he was not going to fight dishonestly.

It was Ted who told me of Alec's resignation. He was head of the party's research department in Queen Anne's Gate, a job he had been asked to do by Alec. I went for an appointment there one afternoon and was left waiting for an hour. It became quickly clear why.

Ted arrived to tell me Alec had resigned. I immediately said, 'I hope you are going to stand.' He said he was. I wished him every success and promised my support. 'Well,' he said, 'you had better organize my campaign. The election is next Tuesday.'

I could scarcely believe it. I asked him if he was serious and should he not have someone more senior to do the job. He said, 'Yes, I am being serious. I want you to organize the campaign.'

Even then I asked, 'Do you really mean it or do you intend to run the campaign yourself and ask me to do some things for you? If you mean me to run it there may be some things I suggest you will not be terribly keen about.'

He said, 'If you are running it, I will listen to your suggestions. If they are silly, I will reject them. Otherwise I will support.'

I told him bluntly there were one or two people who would want to campaign vigorously for him, but would lose him votes. He should ask them to stay out of the campaign until Tuesday. I explained that one was thought to be hostile to Alec and had soured relations. Both would create the fear that they would be appointed either Foreign Secretary or Chancellor, if he was elected, and this would put off potential supporters.

Ted agreed, and asked these two supporters to stay out of London. They were extremely disgruntled, but did as they were asked.

We ran the campaign from my flat and office in Gayfere Street. Luckily both Charlie Morrison and Ian Gilmour were in favour of Ted. Tony Barber came and helped and, very important, so did Geoffrey Lloyd. Geoffrey, the leader of the Birmingham Tories, was highly influential with the knights of the shires. We had a meeting of ten people and allocated ten MPs each to approach. We did it on the basis that if they knew them well, they should make the approach. If they did not, they would find someone who did.

We checked and double checked and if there were still doubtfuls we invited them to see Ted.

On the eve of the election we had some bad polls and Ted was depressed. I assured him, 'I can tell you you are going to win and tomorrow morning I will give you the figures.'

He said he was sure that the other side was saying the same thing, but I insisted that if anybody was found to have last-minute doubts they would be put in touch with him and that there were only four really undecided.

On the morning of the election, I phoned him the figures. The vote I gave him was the figure he got. I gave two more to Reggie Maudling than he obtained, and two less to Enoch Powell.

The flavour of these tense few days are caught in extracts from notes I made at the time.

Monday, 26 July: 'Press magnificent. *Daily Mail*, *Daily Mirror*, *Daily Sketch* all came out with editorial for Ted. *Telegraph* on the fence editorially, but (in news columns) violently pro-Reggie due to Harry Boyne [the paper's lobby correspondent] being a close chum of Reggie. Phoned Ted at 8.30. He was very delighted and buoyant at press. At 9.15 a.m. Robin Chichester-Clark phoned to say that Reggie Maudling was wandering round the House of Commons with William Clark and Michael Clark Hutchinson, meeting Scottish members as they came off the trains from Scotland and talking to lobby correspondents who were assembled there. I therefore sent Charlie Morrison over to the House and joined him myself for a few minutes later to see that lobby correspondents were contacted by our own people . . . Early editions of the *Evening Standard* ran a story by

Robert Carvel, a staunch Maudling supporter, giving the impression that Maudling was just ahead. By later editions they had had to make their story sound as though things were neck and neck . . .

'I considered that from 4 p.m. to 6 p.m. was a crucial time in the lobby as correspondents might agree among themselves that the battle was going one way or the other and it was important to fight any bandwagon effect for Maudling. Our own people had been buoyant throughout the day as a result of the morning press, while Maudling people had obviously been rather bitter and depressed. They were now beginning to feed the press with extravagant figures as to the measure of their support. I therefore phoned Ted and suggested he should walk through the lobby at about 5 p.m., looking his most buoyant and confident and when stopped by any of the lobby should express to them his confidence in the result. This he did and it proved to be a successful operation.'

Tuesday 27 July: 'The morning press was certainly bad in the sense that it gave great publicity to the *Daily Express* and National Opinion Poll saying that Maudling was more popular with the public than Heath. The figures we telephoned to newspapers the night before appeared in all the London papers, however, and must have helped steady opinion. Telephoned Ted at 8.15. His first comment was, "These polls are certainly bloody. I really don't believe anybody thinks I have less energy than Reggie." I comforted him with the view that he would certainly obtain 150 votes and this was sufficient. He told me that Peter Thorneycroft had contacted him to say he would be voting for him and that Henry Brooke was also supporting us. He asked what time I wanted him to go to the House and I suggested he went along in order to vote, spent ten minutes in the smoking room and then left the House. This he agreed to do. Keith Joseph phoned to say that Margaret Thatcher was voting with us and also Ted Gardner . . .

'Went with Charlie to vote and thereafter to the smoking room where I had a drink with Reggie. We discussed Formentor. The smoking room was crowded, with views differing. Went off with Charlie to Buck's for an early lunch. Just as we were leaving, Marcus Kimball informed us that Richard Stanley was celebrating upstairs the victory of Maudling. He was so convinced he would win on the first ballot. Returned to the House of Commons, arriving at about five minutes past two. Went up to the committee floor. Waited outside room fourteen where the result was to be declared. Corridor crowded with members . . . .

'At 2.15 p.m. the doors of the committee room were opened and MPs crowded in. I stayed at the doorway. Sir William Anstruther-Gray duly stood up and announced that votes had been cast in the following way: Edward Heath 150, Reginald Maudling 133. I did not wait for further figures, but dashed to the phones to ring Ted. Lobby correspondents followed me and I gave them the figures I knew through door of telephone booth. Ted's line was engaged. Told them to interrupt call. Eventually got through to Ted and informed him of the result with the words "You've done it", giving him the two figures I knew. He asked me to go straight across to his room. When I arrived, Tony Barber was already there. Ted, smiling, warmly shook me by the hand and said, "You've done marvellously." I expressed the view to Ted that it would be wrong for anybody to approach Reggie and that he must concede without any pressure.'

We had an awkward few hours after the result was announced. I had arranged for Ted to receive the verdict in my Commons office, in what had been the St Stephen's Club. It was obvious from a quick look at the figures that he was so far ahead of Reggie that he would win a second ballot and we assumed Reggie would want to stand down.

There was, however, the immediate problem of the media outside. It was important that Ted should not be forced to comment before Reggie had had time to think and to concede. So we quickly jumped into my car outside St Stephen's and drove to Gayfere Street.

We sat there for up to two hours, having left a message with the whip's office that if Reggie wanted to speak to Ted he was at Gayfere Street. For me it was an highly instructive two hours. We used it to have a fascinating discussion on what was wrong with the Tory Party and what he would do as leader. I reminded him that a few months before he had said, 'You and I are going to have a tough and difficult task to modernize this party.' He asked me if I thought he should keep Edward du Cann as party chairman. I said I thought it would be a mistake to change him. He was doing well enough with the party generally, but not being tough enough in making internal changes to the organization. I said it was important to bring Iain Macleod back into the centre of things. He agreed.

Then Reggie phoned through to say that he was standing down. Typically he wished Ted every success and offered any help he could give. Ted went to the Commons to meet the press and make a statement.

As I went across the Members' Lobby, coming straight towards me was Reggie Maudling. He offered his congratulations and then asked why he had lost. It was an awful moment. I liked Reggie a great deal and I just fluffed up some nonsense, saying that he had been close to winning.

One of the real reasons we won was the care we took to make sure that everyone was contacted by someone they liked. Reggie worked on a different system with a small group, including Lord Lambton and William Clark, approaching everyone. Some people liked them, others did not. It was not the same as an approach from a close personal friend. We also paid a great deal of attention to getting across Ted's appeal in the media, but for all that the polls had often been against us.

Ted's other big advantage was that he was considered to be energetic and good at the dispatch box. Reggie was considered laid back and lazy. There were no differences on policy. When I had lunch with Reggie a while later and compared notes, we found that forty-five MPs had told both sides they would be voting for their man.

The day after his election, Ted called me in and said he wanted to make me Shadow Minister of Transport, but not give me a place in the Shadow Cabinet. I looked disappointed, but he insisted he was doing it for me. If he put me straight into the Shadow Cabinet there would be a great deal of resentment and hostility towards me personally. Tory MPs would accept that I had done well and should be given a post, but not in the Shadow Cabinet.

I told him I thought he was totally wrong. I said that if I was good enough to organize his campaign for the leadership and had been successful as his number two on the Finance Bill team, the idea that at thirty-three I was not old or experienced enough to be in the Shadow Cabinet was nonsense. There was not going to be an election for another three years, so that I would probably be at least thirty-six before I could hope to be in government. To think that you debarred anyone from the Shadow Cabinet or Cabinet who was under forty was crazy. I mentioned William Pitt, but he said he knew the Parliamentary party and was doing what was in my interest.

I went back to Gayfere Street and told Ian Gilmour what had happened. That evening, before the announcement, Alec Todd, Conservative Central Office's chief press officer, came in and congratulated me. Ian said it was a good appointment; but silly not to put me in the Shadow Cabinet. Alec said, 'But you are in the Shadow Cabinet. Here is the list I have just given to the media.'

Ted had decided I should be there after all, but he had not phoned or contacted me. He just announced it. About midnight, he did phone. He simply said, 'You're in.'

I was lucky that shortly after I had become Shadow Transport Minister, Labour introduced a disastrously big Transport Bill which gave me ample targets. It should have been five bills.

Following my experience of team work on the Finance Bill committee, I set up a similar team for the Transport Bill. I put two MPs in charge of each section of the bill. It was their job to talk to the industries concerned and then to draft and put down hundreds of amendments. We broke Parliamentary history in the number of amendments we tabled.

It was also fun. Barbara Castle, who was the Transport Minister and in charge of the bill, introduced an incredibly Socialist provision for quality and quantity licensing. Every lorry was to have a licence. The road-haulage industry hated it and then the garages were drawn in. They hated it too. I said that if we had the entire road-haulage industry on our side, we must organize major rallies and marches. It was clear that if we could bring in the Motor Traders' Association and all the garages, we could make a big impact. This is what happened.

Central Office had no money, so we decided to make the whole thing self-financing. We printed thousands of leaflets with a cartoon figure called 'Bill' and the slogan 'Let's kill Transport Bill'. We persuaded the motor traders to buy them for all their garages, road haulers to buy them for their lorries and the traders to sell them at a profit to the general public. The profits were ploughed back into producing more posters.

Rallies were organized by the motor traders and road-haulers associations throughout the country. Each was attended by one of our transport team. We were getting rallies of a thousand at Bristol and a thousand at Manchester.

In London we had a spectacular procession. As the first part arrived at Downing Street, the last part had not left Hyde Park. I spoke, the Young Conservatives took part and it was the first fun campaign against a piece of legislation.

Michael Heseltine was a member of the team opposing the bill.

This was the first time he worked with me and it was his first front-bench job. I was impressed with his qualities. At the end of the campaign, we had a dinner and the team gave me a copy of the bill in perspex with a miniature silver bus on top. Jack Weatherill, who was to become Speaker, was the whip on the team.

Tragically, my number two, David Webster, MP for Weston-super-Mare, died twenty-four hours after coming back from a skiing holiday during which he contracted pneumonia. David was beginning to do well politically, but did not have a significant outside job. He stretched himself financially and died without wealth. I paid for his son to go to Harrow.

The legislation itself became bogged down in Parliament. Barbara left in a reshuffle and Dick Marsh replaced her and cancelled most of the bill. Dick Marsh was a friend. When he came to the House, I heard him make a good speech and dropped him a note to say so. Later on he sent me a note saying that we ought not to start a correspondence, but he wanted to congratulate me on a recent speech I had made. For reasons I cannot quite understand, people said we looked alike. People went up to him and said, 'Hello Peter', just as they said, 'Hello, Dick' to me.

We started with a good personal relationship which had not existed between me and Barbara. She was an excellent Parliamentarian, but we did not find each other easy to deal with. I had said from the start that whatever else happened, we must never be rude to her because she would play her woman-hurt scene. She would love us to be rough. Instead we must be courteous and it would drive her mad.

In practice, she did not speak much outside Parliament about the bill. I was told that she was chastised by the Labour whips for not getting sufficient grip of the legislation. Much of the work was left to her number two, Stephen Swingler. He died suddenly of a heart attack.

Whenever Barbara spoke, we were always charming. You could see her thinking, 'Why can I not arouse these people?' One night she could stand it no longer. Addressing a women's rally in Central Hall, Westminster, she ridiculed the idea that the Conservative Party was a party of gentlemen. She told them, 'You should come across to the Commons and see how beastly and rude they are to me night after night on the committee stage of the Transport Bill.'

I raised her comments as a point of order with the chairman of the committee on the bill. This was a criticism of his chairmanship, I suggested. Did he remember any of these things taking place? Not one of my members could remember any incidents which would justify the charge!

Barbara tried to agree a timetable with me, but I was forced to tell her it was a controversial bill and the only way we could compromise would be for huge chunks of it to be dropped.

I was to have equally unhappy dealings with her after we returned to power in 1970 and I became Secretary of State for the Environment. She wrote to me and said the M40 route planned through the Chilterns was a disgrace and that fool Fred Mulley had agreed to it. The Ramblers Association, the Council for the Preservation of Rural England and all the other organizations were against it. If I was prepared to quash it and go for the alternative, she would publicly stand up and say I was right and that all the organizations backed me. It would be marvellous for my reputation as an environmentalist and it would be reversing a decision taken by someone who had no understanding of what it was about. 'I am wondering whether, even at this late hour, I could prevail upon you to consider the proposed route down Beacon Hill for the extension of the M40,' she wrote. When I looked at the scheme, I discovered the route went within a few hundred yards from her home and she had strong personal reasons for wanting to stop the road being built. There was no mention of this in her letter. The alternative route was far worse than the one Fred Mulley had chosen. I called in the organizations and all favoured the Fred Mulley route. I confirmed it.

With the General Election getting closer, Ted reshuffled his shadow team. My new portfolio, as Shadow Minister of Housing and Local Government, was a hot potato. One of my first tasks was to take a position on the Redcliffe-Maud report which recommended fundamental changes in local government. I had no strong views. I had never been involved in local government. John Redcliffe-Maud was anxious that there should be all-party support for the proposals and I invited him to lunch.

I expressed the view that the single-tier local authorities he envisaged would be far too remote from ordinary people. I remember citing housing. Knowing my own Worcester constituency, I did not think a single county housing authority would work. Under his proposal, the city of Worcester would have no functions. He was proposing fifty-eight local authorities, leaving cities like Leicester and Coventry with no council of their own.

I said I wished to consult the party and that I would personally visit every area of the country to hear the views of Conservative councils at all levels. We fulfilled the promise. All-day conferences were organized with Tory councillors in each region on a succession of Saturdays. They were well attended. Some county councils were in favour of unitary authorities because they felt all power was going to go to them. Most of the districts were against it.

At the party conference that year, I said I thought that local government should keep two tiers. The functions which were better provided over a wider area, like education, roads and planning, should go to the counties, the others to the districts.

In the welter of later criticism of my proposals, I cannot help recalling that I got an enthusiastic standing ovation from that conference for my stand. What is more the decision was praised in every single publication with the exception of the *Economist* and the London *Evening Standard*.

At the same time as my political career was blossoming, so was my personal relationship with Tessa. Romantically, we got engaged in Paris, but not without complications. At the time, anyone going abroad was allowed to spend only fifty pounds a year currency allowance.

I spent the whole of my allowance to fly us out on an early morning plane to Paris, have an expensive lunch, propose and put on the ring on the banks of the Seine. On the way back, the plane was late and we arrived to meet rather drunken and merry photographers and pressmen in my Gayfere Street flat. They had been invited by Central Office to report the engagement and while waiting had drunk every drop of alcohol in the place.

It seemed the natural thing to do to marry at St Margaret's, Westminster, and have the reception at the House of Commons. Iain Macleod and Ted Heath were there. Sydney, my brother, was my best man and we set up house in Cowley Street where we still live.

Marrying Tessa has been my greatest joy. A man is lucky to marry someone who is beautiful and lively. He is fortunate if that someone is loving and kind and a perfect mother to five children. To marry someone who combines these gifts is truly remarkable. Tessa has a great love of reading, she is interested in politics, in education and in people and she also combines a strong sense of duty with a strong sense of humour. She has given me twenty-two years of happiness for which I can never be grateful enough.

It was not all plain sailing. As the General Election approached, Enoch Powell rocked the boat dangerously on race. The issue was constantly in the newspapers and there was undoubtedly widespread racial prejudice, probably rather more among Labour supporters than ours. It was the same pattern as in the United States, where the most vehement hatred was expressed by the poor whites.

I found all racial prejudice obscene. My strong views may have been related to my Christian commitment. As a Christian, you cannot accept that there should be different treatment of races.

I knew Enoch reasonably well. I sat next to him in the Shadow Cabinet. I admired his great intellect and that of his wife. I still think she is a wonderful person, but his Birmingham 'rivers of blood' speech was inexcusable.

There was no question of his views being stifled in Shadow Cabinet or him being outmanoeuvred. I remember the Shadow Cabinet had a meeting on the Wednesday to discuss our position for a major immigration debate on the following Monday, at which Quintin Hogg was to be our spokesman.

This was the most crucial point in the coming week's business. Quintin explained the line he was going to take. Ted asked for comments and suggestions and there were a few. And then, as he sometimes did when there was a particularly important issue, he went all the way round the table asking if there was any additional comment. Enoch, sitting next to me, said he had no comment.

Enoch then left the meeting to alert, on the following day, all newspapers and television stations to the fact that he was making an important and controversial speech on immigration on the Saturday. To those on the inside, it was a calculated act of defiance, if not betrayal.

Once the speech had been made Ted phoned all the members of the Shadow Cabinet and said that Enoch had contradicted all we had agreed and he was going to sack him. We all accepted he had no choice.

As it was we went into the election appearing to adopt more right-wing policies than we intended. The policy was fixed by a famous meeting of the Shadow Cabinet at Selsdon Park.

It started with Michael Fraser, who was then head of the party's research department, reminding Ted that he was seeing the press at twelve o'clock on the Saturday to obtain publicity in the Sunday papers. Ted asked us, 'What on earth shall I say?' Iain Macleod said it was quite easy. You went out and told the newspapers we believed in law and order and that was bound to secure a good press. Ted took the advice and all the Sundays were filled with this hard line when we had not discussed law and order at all.

The thing we did discuss which gave a right-wing tilt to our economic policy was a prices and incomes policy. I and others argued we could not rule out a prices and incomes policy since economic circumstances might force one upon us. Iain, who was by then Shadow Chancellor, did not agree.

He said that I and others were quite right in one respect. We might have to have an incomes policy, but to explain in a manifesto that you might have to do it under certain circumstances was grey. Manifestos had to be black or white. Either we said we were going to have an incomes policy and it would be superb or that we would not have one at all. We should say we were not going to have one and if a few years on we changed our minds we would have to explain there were special circumstances. As far as the manifesto was concerned, it should not be blurred. No 'ifs' or 'buts'. Everybody said he was right and so it got into the manifesto.

I admired Iain Macleod for his powers of oratory, his sense of humour and his interest in the young. By chance, Eve, his wife, was born in Hanbury in my Worcester constituency, where her father had been vicar, so there was an additional link. As Minister of Health he emerged as a powerful figure, one of the few to damage the reputation of Aneurin Bevan, and I had high hopes that he would one day lead the Conservative Party. When he resigned following the election of Alec Douglas-Home as leader, I felt he was mistaken and was sad at the loss. Ian Gilmour and myself were perhaps his closest friends during that period. We would meet at least once a week to discuss ideas and the speeches Iain should make. We wanted him back into the centre of British politics and were delighted when Ted Heath became leader and he came back as Shadow Chancellor.

In constant pain from his back and neck, a gambler who played for high stakes, he possessed an immense love of life, a passion about social problems and the wish to see the Tories as a great reforming party.

I am afraid Iain was not, however, as at ease on economics as he was in other areas. He did not understand the subject. When he became Shadow Chancellor and I was Shadow Transport Minister, he asked me if I would brief him on economic and financial affairs. Apart from anything else, I had been Ted's number two on the Finance Bill. I found that he was not familiar with what was happening and for eight Sundays I went to see him at his Potter's Bar home to give him day-long briefings. We did a different subject each time.

On his appointment as Chancellor, I was still nervous. I knew he could be a terrific success, but I also knew he could slip because he had little feel for the issues. Though he had an excellent brain, he was unhappy in the use of phrases about the economy. The tragedy is that he died so quickly when he had so much to offer across a range of policies.

I did have readjustments of my own to make. I remained against EEC entry for a long time, well into the '60s, but was constantly being brought up against counter-arguments. Ted, with whom I was working closely, argued that while I may have had a case in the past it had now gone. He pointed to the change in the pattern of trade, and added that countries like Denmark wanted to join the Community. Both Ian Gilmour and Charlie Morrison took the pro-Market view. Reluctantly, I came to accept that the position had changed and I could no longer maintain my opposition.

I became more and more convinced of the wisdom of my conversion when I became a Minister, attended EEC Councils of Ministers and began to see the value of co-ordinated European action.

I represented the UK on the regional policy council and there met Hans-Dietrich Genscher, who was the Minister for the Interior in Germany. He and I became friends and used to plan strategy together. The friendship was also a considerable personal convenience to me, since Germany had a large squadron of helicopters. Whenever I wanted to see him or move round Germany, I had one of his helicopters. I started to see Europe at work and wanted Britain to play a full part in it. Since then, I have no doubts that closer ties with the Community are essential.

6

LANDING LUFTHANSA

So much comes back to Leo Amery. As I said, he impressed on me in one of our early discussions the importance of being financially independent. I had already made a start. I was introduced to pay incentive schemes at a tender age. My weekly pocket money was adjusted if specified tasks were completed, like mowing the grass or helping to dig the chicken run. On Saturday mornings, I used to accompany Jerry the milkman for threepence. During the school holidays, I went with him for the whole week and received more.

My two newspaper rounds called for a sophisticated study of organization and methods. You had to report to the newsagents at 6 a.m. and did your round on a cycle. You quickly developed the best method of delivering the papers. You knew gardens you could cross to deliver to a neighbour and the strategic points at which to park your bike to enable you to put the maximum number of papers through the maximum number of doors in the shortest possible time. I pedalled hard and was delighted if I broke my record for a particular round.

One of the areas in which I delivered was Harrow on the Hill, including Harrow School. Many years later I was asked by the headmaster to speak to the school's sixth form and to dine with him first. When he came to the door I was able to tell him that the last time I had stood upon the same doorstep was to deliver the newspaper.

Undoubtedly my reading of the *Financial Times* at the age of thirteen gave me a head start. It must have been uncanny to see a young boy wearing school blazer and satchel riding on the tube each day between South Harrow and Hammersmith reading the pink paper.

After we moved to Gloucester, I became an office boy at the

General Accident Insurance Company on a princely eighty pounds a year. My job was to open the post, put stamps on outgoing letters, keep a record of each one, do the filing and, of course, make the tea in the morning and the coffee in the afternoon. I also had to write out motor insurance cover notes. Fortunately, it was a small office with only about ten staff and I saw every type of insurance transaction.

Through dealings with the local brokers and agents I discovered where the business was created in a city like Gloucester. The staff were eager to teach me what they knew and encouraged me to take my Chartered Institute examinations. This was the sound technical knowledge I needed.

Mr Cotterell, the manager, was impressed by his energetic sixteen-year-old and explained carefully the different types of insurance. He stressed the importance of reading the insurance press and I became an avid reader of the *Post Magazine*, the main journal of the industry.

I suppose he was coming to the end of his working life, looking forward to his pension and grumbling a great deal about head office. He would also relay to staff his latest witty exchange with his wife. 'Last night my wife tried to persuade me to spend more money and told me I should cast my bread on the water. I told her, "The trouble with you, my dear, is that the tide goes out too quickly."'

Business often came from friends and connections. Being chairman of Gloucester Young Conservatives extended my contacts. I found, for example, that I could obtain third party only insurance for a cycle for the sum of three shillings and ninepence. Many friends took out policies on their cycles. Relatives were quoted on policies for their household comprehensive, for life policy and motor insurance.

To my delight, I won the prize for selling more policies than anyone else among the inside non-selling staff of the Cheltenham branch. (Gloucester was an office of the Cheltenham branch.) This was glory. The prize was ten pounds, more than a month's salary. A Mr Barnes, the Cheltenham branch manager, came to Gloucester to present young Walker with the money. He said he was pleased that I was the first ever office boy to win the prize.

He told me that if I went on working like that, at twenty-four I could well be on a salary of £600 a year as a grade B inspector. If I kept up the momentum, I could be earning a thousand a year by the time I was in my early thirties.

STAYING POWER

In those days there was a magic about earning a thousand pounds a year. Those who earned this or more were clearly middle class and part of the establishment. It was a challenge to break the barrier. I took the first part of my Chartered Institute examinations before being called up in 1950 and continued to study while I was in the army.

The great fascination about insurance is that it does touch upon every aspect of life. Every type of firm and industry has to be insured. The breakthrough in new technology and nuclear power had enormous implications and they were international.

Towards the end of my two years' National Service I lighted on an advertisement inviting applications to become a junior American non-marine broker with one of Lloyds' brokers. I presumed that it would mean going to America and found the idea appealing, so I wrote in and got the job.

The firm was an old one called Griffiths Tate, established a hundred years earlier. The four partners ran the firm from the partners' room, sitting behind dark mahogany desks and dressed in stiff white collars. The letter of appointment read: 'Dear Walker, This is to confirm that you have been appointed a junior broker. You will be joining the American Department on 1 May. Your salary will be £300 per annum, your hours of work will be 8.45 a.m. to 5.30 p.m. Monday and Friday and 8.45 to 12 noon on Saturday. You will have two weeks holiday a year.'

Then in the all-important final paragraph, it added: 'You will wear a bowler hat to and from the office.'

I soon discovered that junior American brokers never went to America. Instead, you dealt with minor American business in the room at Lloyds. Even if it was not what I expected, it was exciting going to that room. I had read about the Lloyds market, how this great business had begun in a coffee house, and seen pictures of the room at Lloyds. Coffee houses were still important in the City. When I started at Griffiths Tate, the Captain's Room at Lloyds remained a coffee house and meeting place. The Court Tea Rooms was another. It was in a basement and run by a charming lady called Mrs Andrews. As you descended the stairs there was a large notice saying 'Gentlemen Only'. Mrs Andrews served everybody with delicious coffee and biscuits and buns.

At Christmas you had mince pies. Many youngsters who made names for themselves in the City first met in Mrs Andrews' tea rooms. I regularly met David Coleridge, who entered Lloyds at the same time as me and is now chairman of Lloyds. Another regular was David Scholey, a junior at Guinness Mahon, who is now chairman of Warburgs.

Mrs Andrews sadly disappeared after a railwayman with a haversack disturbed the gentility of her tea rooms. The story is that he sat down and asked for a cup of tea. When she said the table was reserved, he moved to another. In exasperation, she said all the tables were reserved and the poor railwayman had to leave. Even worse, two women came down for coffee. Mrs Andrews could not withstand the shocks of a changing Britain and the tea rooms closed.

My immediate superior at Griffiths Tate was John Varney, a lively and energetic broker. He trained me the hard way by giving me a pile of slips which described the various risks or alterations to risks which had to be approved by underwriters. I was told to find the underwriters and get them to agree. It seemed a tough way of starting the job. But it was the quickest way of learning your way round the room and getting to know the underwriters. I enjoyed it. It really was a great open market. The most senior people treated the most junior with courtesy and respect. As a young inexperienced broker, I could approach the chairman of Lloyds, who was an underwriter, and be treated with the same respect I would give to him.

There is a great deal of humour in the underwriting business. You learn to be a quick judge of character. Underwriters depend on the information from brokers to decide what they are going to accept and what they are going to charge. If the broker fails to tell you of a salient fact, it can be expensive. The room operates on the basis that the broker tells everything he knows about the risk. Though there were no legal sanctions, there was the strongest sanction of all. If any broker gained the reputation he could not be trusted, underwriters gave him no more business.

I studied hard to become more proficient than my rivals. I bought Chartered Institute books and read all the insurance magazines. When I had my own firm in later years I always tried to see that all those who worked for me were well informed.

My first big break came by chance when I read in the *Financial Times* that Lufthansa was going to start a new airline and purchase their first four aircraft. I wondered if there was any possibility of quoting on the insurance of these aircraft and took the initiative by contacting the German Embassy in London and asking them who would be responsible for placing insurance. They made inquiries and told me the man I wanted was a Herr von Zitzavitz, with an address and telephone number in Cologne. I phoned him at what I considered to be immense cost. Fortunately he could speak English. If he had not been able to do so, the venture would have come to a sudden death. He said he was placing the insurances the following week and had had quotations, but if my firm wanted to quote he would be willing to examine it. Perhaps I could discuss it with him on Monday morning at 11 a.m.

Excited by this opportunity and believing it would impress the directors, I entered the partners' room and told them of the progress I had made. It would be a substantial bit of business. The directors looked shocked that a twenty-year-old had come up with such a suggestion and the senior partner, Mr Parmeter, looked at me and said, 'Do you realize that the second class fare to Cologne and back could well cost thirty pounds?'

I turned in some anger and said, 'Well, sir, I will pay the fare and if we succeed in getting the business, I want half the brokerage.'

The partners smiled and the deal was struck. My difficulty was in raising the fare. My parents helped, though they did question whether I was being wise.

To overcome my limited knowledge of aviation insurance I bought the Chartered Insurance Institute correspondence course on aviation insurance and read the entire book on the boat train to the Hook of Holland. Herr von Zitzavitz said the best quotation he had obtained was three and a half per cent and he thought he would be placing the order at that rate. I told him I was certain I could place it at three and a quarter per cent. He said that if I succeeded I could have the order. I told him I would phone the next day and rushed back to London to seek out the leading aviation insurance underwriter.

The man I wanted was a Mr Lamplough of the British Aviation Insurance Company, who said he thought three and a half per cent was the right rate. I argued that we should try to get this business in what could become one of the world's great airlines. He finally agreed he would lead at three and a quarter. Once this was done, with the help of two colleagues in my firm, I was able to place the rest and phone Herr von Zitzavitz with a firm quote. He was as good as his word and placed the order.

This was a great shock to the partners. They were thrilled and excited, and staggered when they remembered they had agreed to give away half the brokerage because of their meanness about paying my fare. It was even more of a shock to one of the Lloyds' main aviation brokers, Willis Faber. They believed they had obtained the order at three and a half per cent. Quick discussions took place because Griffiths Tate had no aviation department, while Faber did. They said they would like to manage the whole business using their aviation department. It would enable it to be serviced properly without Griffiths Tate having to recruit new, skilled personnel. I said I had no wish to interfere provided I had half the brokerage.

It was not quite the end of the story. A few years later Willis Faber purchased Griffiths Tate and suggested the agreement should come to an end. I warned them that I would strongly oppose any breaking of the agreement and Willis Faber had, reluctantly, to agree. In the end, they paid a capital sum so they could have all the future brokerage.

The handling of the Lufthansa account gave me confidence. About this time, I bumped into an old Latymer friend, David Moate, on Hammersmith Station and we arranged to meet again. He suggested we should set up an insurance company of our own. We would try to interest some of the clients of his father, an accountant. Griffiths Tate said they were happy for me to do this provided any business in Lloyds was done through Griffiths Tate.

David and I started Walker Moate and Company. It was a partnership with no capital and one small room at the top of the Wool Exchange which we rented for thirty shillings a week. The furniture was borrowed. We had a fifty-pound loan from my parents. We both stayed in our full-time jobs, so we had our salaries but when the Lufthansa brokerage fell to me, I decided I would take the risk and leave Griffiths Tate to build up my own business. It was an incredible decision to take, starting my own insurance brokers in the City at the age of twenty. We had limited knowledge and no important connections and it was exceedingly hard work for several years. We went to motor dealers and tried to place their more difficult motor insurance for them.

We had a lucky break with a police sergeant. After insuring his car with us he became the organizer of the Metropolitan Police Motor Club. Could we arrange special terms for his members? I negotiated with my former employers, the General and Accident Insurance Company, and worked out a special scheme for the club.

This was the start of a range of special insurance for policemen:

special household comprehensive policy, a life policy called the Policeman's Perfect Protection policy, personal accident cover. The good thing about trying to sell insurance to policemen was that the police stations were open twenty-four hours a day. After doing my nightly Young Conservative meeting somewhere in the Greater London area, I would go off to the local police stations to build up that side of the business.

Gradually we developed more substantial business and life assurance and we placed mortgages and small pension schemes. Next we were able to take on staff. Infected by our enthusiasm, Teddy Clouston, who was with one of the life offices, announced he would like to join us since he felt we had a great future. He would create a life and pension department for our tiny firm.

I pointed out the risk. The salary would be limited, though we would offer him brokerage on the business he won. Teddy said he wanted to take the risk, joined and later, as it became larger, was made chief executive. He developed great skills in life assurance and became an expert on how to organize the life cover connected with provision for death duties. This brought us wealthy connections as we advertised in *Investors' Chronicle* and the *Financial Times*.

From the beginning, I recognized that the only really worthwhile investment in the City was in people. Whenever we had any money, I tried to take on bright people and drive the firm on further. David was a considerable entrepreneur. He had the first idea of luncheon vouchers which he launched under the name of Vantreuse Caterers. Sadly, he failed to get the support of the main eating places, like the Express Dairy, Lyons and the ABC, where large numbers of city workers ate regularly at lunchtime. Some years later his idea was taken up again. This time it was given a simpler name, Luncheon Vouchers, and restaurant chains said they would accept them.

The Moates were a talented family. David's father invented the first machine to enable you to hear a telephone from the other side of the room. Others came in later with more capital and better technology.

Another chance meeting was important. I met Edward du Cann completely by accident. I knew him as a young candidate at Conservative conferences and meetings. In the business world, he was secretary of the National Group of Unit Trusts. His salary was modest. He told me all about unit trusts and his frustration that none of them were expanding. Board of Trade restrictions on commissions were so tight that you lost money if you expanded.

He was so depressed that I suggested we had lunch and then became excited by the untapped potential he was explaining. I suggested he should start a business of his own. Having started my own, I could not see why anyone with a good idea should not do the same. He said it would need substantial capital he did not have. Though my capital was modest, I said I would put money into such a venture. I suggested we could link a unit trust with life insurance and have, for the first time, a life policy which was linked to equity values. I argued it would be attractive for a whole range of policies. I went away and with Teddy Clouston prepared just such a policy.

I also decided I would approach George Stewart, chairman of Stewart Smith and, in my view, the most enterprising of all the Lloyds brokers at that time. He had been kind and encouraging to me. He was chairman of the London and Edinburgh Insurance Company and I noticed he had launched a life fund for London and Edinburgh. Instead, I proposed, he should launch an equity-linked policy. It would be an innovation and make his company more interesting than a small participant in life insurance. He called in his actuary who said it was practical and could be attractive.

We agreed to launch a new unit trust. London and Edinburgh would give the main financial backing. We formed a company called Dillon (Edward du Cann's second Christian name) Walker. It would be the sales company and Unicorn Securities would provide the management of the trust. I tried to persuade Barclay's Bank to be the trustee. They had always been my bankers, but they thought there was no great future for unit trusts. London and Edinburgh then persuaded Lloyds Bank to become the trustees of Britain's first post-war unit trust.

Bill Fowler, who had worked at the National Group of Unit Trusts, was persuaded to join Edward du Cann. Bill was a splendid man, skilled in the administration of unit trusts and possessed total integrity. The subsequent success of unit trusts was very much due to the application of Bill Fowler.

We advertised our block offer and attracted a couple of hundred thousand pounds' investment. The City considered it a success, if on a minor scale. We continued to develop it and units sold well. The Equitas policy was launched and caused wide interest.

Life offices were not amused by having an equity-linked policy. A meeting of life insurance actuaries was convened one evening and almost unanimously condemned the policy. It gave me delight over the next decade to see the actuaries who had attacked the policies forced themselves to produce similar ones.

We then decided to launch another trust producing a higher yield than Unicorn. We called it the Falcon Trust. Attitudes to unit trusts were changing. People were now convinced they had a future. We were confident that, quite sensationally, we might be able to raise a million pounds on one block offer.

Our expectation was wildly out. We received more than seven million pounds. Not only did it break all records, it created a sensation. It was also sensational to handle. I remember using a shovel to put cheques into a bag to be taken round to a bank. Post and cheques continued to flood in, and from that moment we were a major force in unit trusts.

The final ironic twist came years later when Barclays, the bank which had originally refused to be trustees, bought Unicorn Trust and Dillon Walker.

Doing well, David Moate and I decided to go our separate ways. I was the driving force in the insurance business. David had built up other business interests, including a hire purchase business. He had also developed his father's accountancy practice.

We agreed what we thought was the right value of the businesses, Dillon Walker and the insurance business, and we divided it fifty-fifty. I took the unit trust and insurance business and had to make payments to David for his capital interest.

I was then fortunate enough to be able to purchase an old firm of Lloyds brokers, Rose Thompson Young. It had been founded in 1818 and Jimmy Young, the main proprietor, was close to retirement. The purchase made us Lloyds brokers in our own right and put us on a more substantial basis.

Rose Thompson Young was an old-fashioned firm and this created an unexpected problem. As we moved into the offices in Moorgate Hall, we found dozens of safes; there were literally safes in every room. Files were kept in safes instead of filing cabinets. To create more space, I ordered that they should be removed, not realizing the cost of taking heavy safes out of the top floor of a City building!

With Rose Thompson Young came their office in Glasgow and a young man called Ian Lang. Neither of us could have dreamed at the time that Ian would become Secretary of State for Scotland and I would be Secretary of State for Wales.

I continued the policy of trying to employ the liveliest people. Clive Sassarath, who had been with Price Forbes, was a marvellous practitioner in UK non-marine insurance. I recruited him to head the UK non-marine side of the business, which he did with great drive. I wanted to get into reinsurance, which in broking terms is one of the biggest areas of international insurance activity. I asked ten Lloyds underwriters who they thought was the brightest young man in reinsurance and to my surprise they all came up with the same name. Derek Collins was with E. W. Paine at the time. I asked him to have coffee with me. I told him I had made this survey and I wanted to create a reinsurance department. Would he leave E. W. Paine and join me? He said he had been trained by E. W. Paine, he was happy with the firm which paid him a good salary, was in a top position and had no desire to leave. I said the one thing which E. W. Paine could not offer and I could was an equity stake in the business. Mine was a smaller business and he could be chief executive of the reinsurance business. He could have a substantial equity and when the firm had progressed to a tolerable size, he could exchange the shares for those in Walker Young and become an important equity holder.

He agreed to take the risk. I told him he could fix his own salary because he would be fixing the budgets for the whole of the reinsurance section of the business. As an equity participant, he would see there were good profits and he would decide what was a reasonable salary for himself. This he did. He triumphed. He built up a substantial reinsurance business worldwide. We opened offices in Canada and Australia and did considerable business in the United States and parts of Europe. He drew round him a team of ability and talent, men who knew the detail of the business, were innovators and achieved an international reputation.

I formed another important friendship when I attended Territorial Army camps after my National Service. I met a young subaltern called Sefton Myers. He appeared to be prosperous because he had a Riley car. He offered me a lift back to London in it on one occasion and I discovered that he was with his father in the property world. He had a highly developed sense of humour and was good company; we became friends.

Sometime later he asked me to meet his father, Bernard Myers, to advise them on their future as a property company. They told me they were doing well in office and other developments, but wanted to get a stock exchange quotation. Knowing of my success in unit trusts and insurance broking, they asked me to advise them on becoming a publicly quoted company. I said they should go to the best accountants, solicitors and stockbrokers in the City. If they had the finest names in the City on the prospectus when they went public it would guarantee their success. I introduced them to Slaughter and May, who became their solicitors, to Peat Marwick, who became their accountants, and to the stockbrokers Read Hurst Brown, which had the highest reputation for dealing in property shares in the City.

I approached Read Hurst Brown and they expressed their eagerness to become brokers of the company. Bernard Myers asked me if I would become financial director.

As a friend of Sefton and an admirer of the Myers family, I was happy to do so. At that time I also had connections in the City with the major life offices which provided long-term funds for property companies. I joined the board and looked forward to it going public. Everything went well. We raised a large sum of money from the Legal and General Assurance Company at a low rate of interest, to be called upon for our development. We set up a professional team to decide whether or not to proceed with developments.

We built the first out-of-town office block in London, near Kew Bridge. It was such a sensation that the then Minister of Housing and Local Government, Henry Brooke, opened it, emphasizing to companies they could have offices outside the City of London.

We let it at eight shillings a square foot and made a considerable profit on it. Then we got on with the preparation of a prospectus and were ready for the company to go public.

A few days before the event I was telephoned by Read Hurst Brown and asked to go and see them. To their horror they had discovered that Bernard Myers had been bankrupt in the 1930s and had been found guilty of having bought black market petrol during the war. The bankruptcy had taken place in a textile firm he had been connected with at the time. He had been fully discharged from that bankruptcy and there was no reason why he should have been barred from the chairmanship of a publicly quoted company. What did stop him, of course, was the fact that he had not disclosed any of the information to any of us. I was deeply embarrassed. I had introduced somebody to top firms of accountants, brokers and solicitors, and he had failed to reveal this background. Bernard

Myers was humiliated and his son distressed, as was the whole of the family.

Bernard's explanation was that he had been discharged from the bankruptcy and there was no reason for his children to know of it. He had not believed he needed to disclose the information.

We discussed what we should do. Obviously the issue could not take place, but we would continue to act as advisers and I would continue to be a member of the board. I stayed friends with the family. Eventually there was a reverse take-over of the company and a public quotation was obtained after the Stock Exchange had been given all the facts.

The sadness was that in later years Bernard became a compulsive gambler on horses and lost a substantial proportion of his fortune. As an outside director, I had the difficult task of telling him he must leave the board of the company he had created. Sefton, who was a supporter of charity and fine causes and had many friends, tragically developed cancer in his early forties. A happy, contented family, enjoying great success, had slipped into tragedy, the son dying young and the father being forced to leave the company he had built up.

What is admirable is the character some people show when things go wrong. The younger son, Martin, who went to Latymer, came to me for advice when he was about to leave school. He admired the way I had started from nothing. He was embarrassed that his father had given him a large number of shares, so that he was rich in his own right and would have difficulty being his own person. He wanted to make his own way. I suggested he should qualify in whatever he wanted, banking, insurance, property. He should then build up whatever company he wished to establish. He went on to the technical college at Brixton, became qualified as a chartered surveyor, worked extremely hard and later joined Jones Lang Wootton. He opened their New York office and made a property fortune for himself. When his father ran into financial difficulties, Martin used all the wealth his father had given him to support both parents, living himself on the modest income of someone starting in a junior capacity in the surveying business.

By this time, the early 1960s, I knew many people in the City. There had been newspaper write-ups of the role I had played in the formation of unit trusts, the first equity-linked life policy, stories of how I had created a substantial Lloyds broking business, of my involvement in major property companies.

One thing led to another. Mr Frank Waller, chairman of the major engineering company Adwest Engineering, asked me to join his board. I did so with alacrity. It was the first time I had had the chance of seeing the problems and opportunities of a manufacturing company at board level.

When I came into the House of Commons in March 1961 I found it was possible to continue with a busy life in the City as well as being an active MP at Westminster and in Worcester.

I was an early riser and reached my City office just before 7 a.m. There I witnessed the opening of the post, a task I recommend to chief executives and chairmen. A regular examination of the incoming post gives you a good idea of what is happening in the business. I would work from 7 a.m. until the early afternoon. Commons question time begins at 2.30 p.m. If I wanted to ask a question I would be there then or, if not, between 3 p.m. and 5 p.m., depending upon the business. I would stay there until late at night.

It was as a result of a chat in the Commons with Reggie Maudling, then Chancellor, that, by a circuitous route, I first met Jim Slater. Reggie said he was interested in a profile of me that had appeared in the *London Evening News* that week. The paper had decided to do a series of young men under thirty-five who had already made a success in business. I was one of the profiles, Jim Slater was another. At a young age, he held a senior position in Leyland Motors, by far our most successful motor manufacturer.

Reggie thought it was encouraging to see bright men succeeding at an early age. I offered, if I could organize it, to arrange for him to meet the other 'profiles'. We agreed a date, I booked a room at the St Stephen's Club opposite the House of Commons and invited my fellow 'profiles' to dine with the Chancellor. All accepted, with the exception of Jim Slater. The dinner party itself was a total disaster.

To my immense disappointment, and I am sure Reggie's, the bright young tycoons produced no original ideas. They came out with all the clichés and platitudes.

But I did receive a letter from Jim Slater saying that he had been in South Africa at the time of the dinner, but if he had been present he would have liked to put the following ten ideas to the Chancellor. They were interesting ideas and we had lunch. I thought he was impressive, liked his sense of humour and we became friends.

Other 'profiles' suggested that we should form a dining club and to my embarrassment, in my absence, they called it the Walker's dining club. It met regularly for about ten years and proved to be far more lively than that first encounter with Reggie Maudling. So all was not lost in organizing that first uninspiring dinner.

Some time later I received a call from Jim Slater saying that he wanted to talk to me urgently. He told me how the future hierarchy of Leyland was about to be agreed. It was mapped out in some detail. Donald Stokes would be chief executive with Lord Black continuing as chairman. Lord Black was to retire soon afterwards and Donald Stokes would become chairman, with Jim Slater as chief executive. When Donald Stokes went, Jim Slater would become chairman. He was in a dilemma as to whether to devote his life to what he believed would be Europe's most successful car maker or should he, at this stage, start his own business?

He had, by investing, built up some capital of his own, he told me, and probably had £100,000 of his own resources he could call upon. He felt there were opportunities in investing in badly managed businesses, pulling up their management and doing well in the process.

I gave him the only advice I could. Only he could decide. Either he wanted to head an important business which would operate internationally, a business to which he had already devoted a great deal of his early life, or he wanted to have total freedom and independence to be an entrepreneur in his own right. We listed the advantages and disadvantages of both courses. I did say that if he decided to go off on his own, I would give him any help I could. I was ready to put in capital if he wanted more investment and to introduce him to the many friends I had in the City. Since he had been in manufacturing, he had few contacts in the City itself and did not know merchant and investment bankers. A few days later he phoned to say he had decided to go it alone and would appreciate my help.

It was agreed that I should put in capital and try to organize for him a syndicate of merchant bankers who might be willing to put more investment resources behind him when he wished to acquire a business. The name of the company, Slater Walker, did not mean that I had any executive role in it. From the start I made it clear that now I was in the Shadow Cabinet I intended to devote the rest of my life to politics. If we won the next General Election, I would disappear from the business scene altogether and would not be returning to it.

Jim said it would be of help if I joined the board of directors and remained active for as long as politics allowed me. It was his suggestion that, as I was one of the two investors, we should call the company Slater Walker. Later I introduced him to many of the leading banks; Lazards and the Drayton Group were among those who agreed to provide capital.

The banks and two or three institutional investors made available a quarter of a million pounds each. From the beginning Jim had not only the resources of what he and I had put in, but also a syndicate of important City banking houses to whom I had introduced him and who were happy to provide additional funds.

Jim Slater's great gift is the ability to examine propositions objectively, listen to advice and weigh their worth accurately. He never attempted to defend his original view. If a counter-argument had force and was better than his own, he recognized it.

Slater Walker was run on the basis of a Monday morning management meeting. Throughout my period with the company, my sole involvement was at that weekly meeting. I never had a secretary or desk, and I took no part in negotiations. But from ten o'clock to twelve o'clock on Mondays, I attended that meeting.

Without realizing it at the time, I see now that I did have quite an important role. As a non-executive, I questioned the executive proposals. You could almost have described me as the Leader of the Opposition. If a new idea came forward which I considered was calling upon too many resources, when we did not have the management skills or information, I would argue against it. Quite frequently such proposals were delayed or abandoned.

Jim Slater attracted around him a lively and highly motivated group of young men, but he was also in contact with other young entrepreneurs. He had close relationships with James Hanson, Geoffrey Sterling and many of the highly successful industrialists of the 1980s. All benefited from exchanging views and doing business together. Another close associate was Jimmy Goldsmith, who was a good friend during the 1980s.

Jim Slater's team did help to improve management attitudes in Britain. If he acquired a company, he took immediate and effective measures to make it profitable. One was to establish tight financial control of forecasting and budgeting. He would review the whole of the purchasing policy. Often there was an improvement in the profitability of a company purely as a result of renegotiating all the purchasing arrangements.

Complacent managements bought their raw materials and component parts from the same old firm. Buyers and sellers knew each other socially, liked each other and played a round of golf together. As a result, negotiations to get the finest price were not as tough as they should have been.

If a company had four or five million pounds of purchases, Jim was able to save half a million or even a million in costs, the whole of that sum going straight to the bottom line in profits.

He was also looking for the bright young managers who had been repressed. Young men who had been held down would be promoted to the top and give a firm added drive.

The original syndicate all did extremely well out of their investments. The Stock Exchange and the main clearing banks were enthusiastic about his achievements.

As the prospect of the 1970 General Election came closer, I had to decide how to organize the future of the businesses in which I had played an important part. My insurance-broking business, which I had built up from scratch with one room, one chair and one desk, was now one of the best firms of Lloyd brokers, expanding quickly and operating on an international scale. I thought it had one of the finest insurance teams in the management world.

By that time I had divested many of my shares, so that the key players could be shareholders, but I was still the largest shareholder. I discussed with colleagues how they would like the firm to develop. We agreed there were three choices. The first was for them to continue to expand and perhaps get a Stock Exchange quotation. I suggested if they wanted to do this, they should go on for perhaps another two or three years, enjoying their current rapid growth and then float off a proportion of their shares. The second choice was to merge with another firm of Lloyds brokers and create a bigger entity. There were at least two substantial brokers who had indicated to me that they would like to negotiate a merger. The third was to obtain a public quotation by becoming a subsidiary of Slater Walker. They would get Slater Walker shares for their shares and would always have a captive insurance business and the advantage of worldwide connections. I left it to them to decide.

Their future was involved in what happened to Walker Young

and I was going to be divorced from it. I pointed out that if they went the last route, the valuation of the firm would be lower than it should be. With me as a shareholder in both Slater Walker and Walker Young, the chairman of one and a board member of the other, there would have to be an independent valuation which would guarantee that the price was reasonable for Slater Walker shareholders. But with the growth taking place in Slater Walker they would probably be quickly compensated. At that time the prospects were extremely good. They decided on the third route.

Rothschilds were called in to provide the independent valuation. They set an exceedingly low valuation for Walker Young, to the benefit of Slater Walker shareholders, but gave my Walker Young colleagues substantial quoted shareholding and all the prospects of a fast-expanding worldwide business.

The moment the election was called I gave up business entirely, to return only when I left the Cabinet twenty years later. I had to dispose of most of my investments because of the Cabinet rules. As I quickly became Secretary of State for the Environment with responsibility for planning decisions throughout the country, I took the view it was right to get rid of all of them. This was costly, because it meant paying capital gains tax on many of my holdings, including those in Slater Walker, but it did not distress me. I knew I was financially independent and could pursue politics without worrying about the economic needs of my family.

I also decided that since Slater Walker was frequently involved in property and planning matters it would be wrong for me to have contact with former business colleagues.

I met Jim Slater on only one occasion each year, when our two families dined together at Christmas. Tessa did, however, continue to see Helen and our children sometimes saw each other.

There was only one exception in the period between our taking office in 1970 and Slater Walker getting into difficulties in 1975. That was an occasion when I was going to attend a lunch in the City and it had to be cancelled at the last moment. I said to my Permanent Secretary, Sir Antony Part, I would love to have a talk with Jim Slater on the current industrial and economic scene and asked if it would be outrageous if I lunched with him. Antony Part's view was that there was no reason I should not see him whenever I liked. I phoned Jim. He was having lunch in his own office that day with Cyril Stein of Ladbrokes and he said they would be delighted if I joined them.

Both were buoyant and doing well in the property market. I did say that if I was still part of the management committee I might be warning 'Down Jim', an expression I used when I thought the company was biting off more than it could chew. This was said as an aside, but as I left I was slightly nervous about their confidence.

It was still a great shock to me a few months after becoming a minister to open the papers to discover that Slater Walker had sold my insurance business to Jimmy Goldsmith for a multiple of the price for which they had bought it twelve months earlier. It reflected the low price we had had to accept on the Rothschild valuation. I suppose it was understandable that I was not informed. I had no connections with the business and had made it clear to Jim that I could not discuss business matters with him from the second I went into the Cabinet.

I did, however, contact some of my former colleagues: Teddy Clouston, Derek Collins, Clive Sassarath. They were all shocked and distressed that there had been virtually no consultation.

It was, alas, the break up of that excellent management team. The majority went to Wigham Poland and became the key players in a much larger firm. Derek Collins headed the reinsurance side of the bigger business, Clive led the UK non-marine side, Donald MacKie was in charge of the life and pensions side. Although Wigham Poland were much bigger, it was the Walker Young executives who took the major roles.

When, however, Jimmy Goldsmith sold Wigham Poland to Sedgwick Collins, the team did disintegrate. Clive decided that he would prefer to be part of a smaller entity and joined a small firm of Lloyds brokers, CBC, of which he is now chairman. It is a firm which has recaptured the dynamism and team spirit of Walker Young. It has as its chief executive Peter Hicks, whom I took on in the motor insurance department in the early days and who has developed a considerable reputation in Lloyds.

I was delighted that when I left the Cabinet my old friends Clive and Peter Hicks asked me to join their small but fast-expanding firm. It felt good to be back with a firm with that kind of spirit we shared in the 1960s.

Derek Collins decided to go for early retirement and a remarkable team was split up. It is spilt milk, but I think now that it was a mistake to become part of Slater Walker rather than continue as an independent Lloyds broker. There is no doubt that during the 1970s and 1980s the old firm would have been a colossal success and one of the leading firms of Lloyds brokers.

I was sad, too, in 1975 when Slater Walker's financial difficulties, together with the rise in interest rates and the fall in property values, led to the winding up of the company.

It was tragic for Jim Slater himself, a man close to his wife and children and someone who had enjoyed a big reputation, suddenly to find his house surrounded by photographers and newspaper front pages describing his downfall. Institutions which had enthusiastically backed him in the past decided to stop doing so. Knowing the family, we were all distressed. We thought particularly of the children. They were going to school when their chums were reading about their father's difficulties.

You cannot, however, keep a good man down. Jim Slater quickly paid off the debts and has become prosperous again. But he has also made it clear he is not going to be involved in any business which could expose him to the publicity the family suffered in 1975. He has continued his commercial activities on a private basis. He must also reflect that he might have done better to become chief executive of Leyland when he had the chance. He would have become chairman, and the history of the British motor industry might have been happier.

Jim Slater did have immense dynamism and a great ability to concentrate on detail and motivate all those who worked with him. He had one of the most powerful intellects I have ever met. He succumbed to the risk we all run in business, of becoming over-confident. The weather changes rapidly and smooth waters turn to threatening waves. If you have over-borrowed and interest rates go against you, you can quickly turn success into disaster.

I was lucky. I left business in 1970, after eighteen exhilarating years, a financial success. My first love was Lloyds of London. I think it is a marvellous market, even if it has had its problems. It has energy and talent. Those who prosper are those who also have integrity and respect.

All successful businesses must have the right ingredients. Executives must be able to enthuse their staff, spot and develop talent, and have a vision of what they want the business to become. It is not enough simply to react to day-to-day opportunities and problems. Then they must carry out constant and detailed analysis of what is taking place.

It is staggering that many firms, some quite large, do not have the information they should, despite a choice of computers and new technology to help them. Decision-takers are still taking their decisions without up-to-date figures and facts. I discovered at an early stage in my insurance broking firm that I could, if I wished, have on my desk every morning the basic facts about my businesses worldwide the day before.

In both service and manufacturing industry you must insist you have top quality all the time and monitor to ensure that you have it. Japanese post-war success has probably been due more to quality control than any other factor. Of the 'Western' capitalist countries, only Japan decided, as long ago as the 1950s, to make quality control a statutory requirement. It has given them a high penetration of world markets.

Above everything else, the entrepreneur must have integrity. If he is seen to act with integrity, he will win the confidence of all those with whom he is doing business, employees, customers or bankers. I have forgotten who said I should go and see my bank manager regularly even when there was no crisis, simply to give him the latest information. It is advice I have followed. Whenever I have needed a facility from the bank, I have always been confident of getting it, because I knew Barclays knew the full background.

The bridging loan which enabled me to buy Rose Thompson Young, for example, was large, but granted instantly because the bank knew how my business had been succeeding over those early years. Leo Amery would have approved.

7

IN AT THE DEEP END

My appointment first as Minister of Housing and Local Government and then, quickly, as the Secretary of State for the new and enlarged Department of the Environment, was a giant stride. Douglas Haig, the highly respected political correspondent of the *Birmingham Post* quoted another MP as describing me as a 'flashing meteor'. I certainly felt myself to be in the stratosphere.

I was being asked to take on not only a radical reform of local government, but also the setting up of a major new department to tackle the environmental and deprivation problems of the 1970s and, as it happens, the 1980s and 1990s. This was without any previous ministerial experience.

I began without even knowing where to find my office. After the heady election victory in 1970 I came up to Cowley Street with Tessa and Jonathan on the Friday, hoping that I might be in the Cabinet.

On the Saturday morning, we watched television and saw Sir Alec and Iain Macleod go to No. 10. No phone calls for me. That afternoon we were due to go to a wedding of friends of Tessa's. I could scarcely phone No. 10 and say that if the Prime Minister wanted me I would be at St Mary's Church. On the other hand, if I went to the wedding and No. 10 could not find me, that would be a disaster. We agreed that Tessa would go to the wedding and I would stay at home. Just after she left, the phone rang and I was asked to go to No. 10. Ted said he wanted me to be Minister of Housing and Local Government and later the first Environment Secretary. I drove to the church and whispered to Tessa what had happened.

Back from the wedding reception, we asked ourselves: where is the Ministry of Housing and Local Government? The telephone directory revealed it was in Whitehall, so we drove up and down Whitehall looking for my ministry. We did not find it first time. It was what is now the Treasury building. I still did not know what to do on Monday. Did I knock on the door and say: 'I am Peter Walker. I am your new minister?'

About an hour later the civil service swung into action. My Permanent Secretary, Sir Matthew Stevenson, phoned to ask if he could come round to bring me some briefing papers and arrange a car for Monday.

At thirty-eight I was a Privy Councillor, going to Buckingham Palace, being sworn in and getting my seals of office.

I did have an early brush with my civil servants. I told my private office I would like my four ministers to meet at 8.45 each morning in my office. The next morning they turned up, plus a civil servant from my private office with a notebook. He said he was to take the minutes of the meeting. I thanked him, but said I did not want minutes. He said he had been told by the Permanent Secretary that he must be there. I said he must tell the Permanent Secretary I did not want him.

The Permanent Secretary came in later and told me I was making a grave mistake and civil servants would feel they were not trusted. I said I did trust them. We would obviously go to the civil servants with ideas and if they thought these were crazy they would say so. Sir Matthew, who later became a great friend and taught me a great deal, protested it had not been done before. I explained I felt strongly. I might, for example, want to discuss civil servants. I did not want it minuted by another civil servant. Or I might want to discuss party politics. He came back a third time and said he thought he would have to have a word with the Prime Minister.

I told him there was no need to hesitate. I picked up a phone and asked to speak to No. 10. He said he did not think it was necessary. I then said, 'All right. We will have a civil servant present, but on one condition. There must always be a minister present for meetings of civil servants.' He smiled and said, 'I think you have won, Minister.' When he finally retired, Sir Matthew wrote me a note saying I was right to insist on minister-only meetings and he thought they had been a success.

These daily meetings did mean that all ministers knew what was happening throughout the whole department. Civil servants could never go to a junior minister and get him to agree to something that he thought the Secretary of State would turn down. It led to more cohesion and enthusiasm. There was another important, political advantage. PPSs could attend, so that I had, in effect, fifteen ministers and PPSs going round the Commons explaining why we had adopted this or that policy. In this way you were able to make a big impact on the Parliamentary party, where so much strength ultimately lay.

Ministers also had my programme and they were encouraged to sit in at any meetings in which they had an interest. If there was a big strategic decision on how to reorganize local government or the Housing Bill, I would call a conference of all the ministers. They were free to raise any objection they wanted. Every six months we went away for a long weekend to discuss strategy on, say, pollution or the inner cities. This was without an agenda. A great many ideas came out. The first of these brain-storming exercises took place at Paul Channon's home, but others were held in small hotels where we took over the entire accommodation.

A lot of the spade work on setting up the Department of the Environment had been done by Labour before we came to power. Harold Wilson decided to look at the reorganization of Whitehall and set up a committee. It came to the conclusion there should be two giant departments.

One was to be the Department of the Environment, combining housing and local government, public works and transport, on the basis that all were linked: planning decisions in one affected the others.

The other was a Department of Trade and Industry which combined the Ministry of Fuel and Power, the Board of Trade and the Department of Industry. The thinking here was that we needed a mighty department, such as the Japanese possessed, to give the commercial and industrial view on policy and counter-balance the influence of the Treasury. The new department would speak with practical authority on economic matters. Again, the policies needed to be closely linked: trade, energy and industry were interdependent.

As part of the usual pre-election talks with civil servants, we looked at these proposals. Ted Heath thought they were sensible and we should bring them in, if we won.

When we did win, it still took a few weeks to get the new departments established. The vision of a new department looking at the environment as a whole was exciting and I was lucky in having as my new Permanent Secretary Sir David Serpell. David and I became close personal friends as we proceeded to knock the three separate departments, all with their obstinate and sometimes valued traditions, into one.

Some of the decisions were unpopular. All the old departments had their own offices in the regions, but the firmly established practice was that the brightest and ablest people stayed in London, while the less able people worked in the regions.

David and I took the view that we would have much better decision-taking in Whitehall if the high-flyers first gained experience in the front line. We decided that in future the bright people would be sent to the regions. They would quickly learn that they needed to be a success there to win a top job in Whitehall itself. Quite suddenly we had civil servants of considerable ability running regions and more high quality decision-taking there. Ministry of Transport civil servants were identified as one of our weak links. Too many of them considered that their job was how to get traffic from A to B and nothing else, no concern for the environment or wider planning considerations, like the housing and economic activity which would follow. Talented people from other departments were drafted in to get a much wider perspective.

I regarded the new department as a success, largely due to the enthusiasm of the ministerial team and top civil servants. It was a mistake when transport was taken out of the Department of the Environment. It is so closely linked with housing, planning and local authorities issues. Perhaps there was a danger that the DoE could become too big and cumbersome, but I believe we avoided that by operating it regionally.

Regrettably, the policy of sending the brightest civil servants to the regions also fell into disuse after Sir David and I left the scene.

I accepted readily the case for local government reorganization. I knew from my own constituency that the smaller local councils could not cope. I had the borough of Droitwich with an electorate, at that time, of about 10,000 and the Droitwich rural district council with an electorate of about 12,000. Both had council officers and chief executives, but when Droitwich had to renew its sewage works, which had been put in in 1890, its ratepayers could not afford it. It would have meant the rates going up tenfold. Even the purchase of a new refuse vehicle was a blow to the Droitwich ratepayers.

All the old and ancient boroughs were too small to meet modern requirements. Instead I went for districts with 40,000 or 50,000 electors.

My guiding principle was to see that every function was as close to the people as possible. I consulted with the Minister of Education, Margaret Thatcher, in great detail on what should happen to education. We agreed that the typical district council was not big enough to provide the range of education services and they must therefore be administered at county council level. But conurbations or metropolitan district authorities were big enough and, against some opposition, we gave education to the metropolitan districts, while it remained at county level elsewhere.

I was accused later of damaging the counties by creating new counties like Avon. The truth was the opposite. I leant over backwards to keep all the existing counties and where possible the exact county boundaries.

One difficulty was what to do with cities like Bristol and Hull. Both were big enough to be good county boroughs, but if I took them out of the counties those counties would be seriously weakened.

I looked, obviously, with great care at Herefordshire and Worcestershire. I took out the parts of Worcestershire in the north of the county, which belonged clearly to suburban Birmingham. Herefordshire never had been viable and was in great financial difficulties. I decided if I created one county out of the two, I would keep the character of the best parts of Worcestershire and Herefordshire and it would be strong financially, able to resist any pressure to become part of a still bigger Birmingham conurbation. My thinking was correct. Redcliffe-Maud would have wiped out Herefordshire and the Liberals would have gone for regional government and amalgamated Worcestershire, Hereford and parts of Warwickshire and Gloucestershire.

Herefordshire Liberals used to complain about this 'terrible Walker'.

I would retort: 'These Liberals want a merger not just with Worcestershire, but with Warwickshire and Gloucestershire as well.'

But whatever the arguments in favour, my proposals won me few friends in my constituency. No one actually liked the merging of Herefordshire and Worcestershire. I got rid of the county borough of Worcester, I abolished Droitwich borough and rural district council and merged them into the Wychavon council.

Politically most reckless of all, I abolished all the aldermen, a system which meant seventy- and eighty-year-olds remaining in the job until they died. I also wrote to local authorities suggesting ways in which they could streamline their procedures and to industrialists urging them to encourage staff to take part in the new local government, giving them time off for council work.

In the short term, my idea of breathing new life into the system failed miserably. All the aldermen were selected for safe Tory seats and all the old chaps came back with no influx of young people.

The suggestion that the reorganization was responsible for a big jump in rates was a myth. What really happened was that inflation took off as the changes were coming in and hit rates along with everything else. As it happened, the two subsequent years were the only ones in which the staff of local government went down rather than up.

Local government reform has been hung round my neck like a millstone, but if I was asked, with hindsight, what I would now do to correct it, I would make only a few changes. It was a mistake to give responsibility for planning to both the counties and districts. I bowed to pressure from MPs and it was a compromise which did not work. The job should have gone to the counties.

Labour and the Liberals opposed my reforms, but offered only second rate and unconvincing alternatives. There was no real split in the Tory Party at the time. Only two Tory MPs voted for preserving their county borough.

Even on Rutland, the MP, Kenneth Lewis, who made an emotional appeal to keep it, agreed that it was nonsense to retain it as a county. He said that if I kept it as a district I would satisfy everyone. I kept it as a district. The Cabinet was totally in favour of the reforms without so much as a whisper of dissent and there was little difficulty in getting the proposals through Parliament. Even the press was in favour. Everyone said thank goodness, he has not gone for the Redcliffe-Maud Royal Commission proposals.

I had had John Redcliffe-Maud to lunch at Cowley Street and he told me that he preferred his plan, but the two-tier alternative I had spelled out to the Conservative Party conference earlier was perfectly sensible and would be a big improvement. In the speech announcing what I was going to do, I said that no one had reformed local government for a hundred years and no one in their right mind would reform it for another hundred years.

The one thing I could guarantee was that whatever went wrong with local government for the next thirty years would be blamed on this local government reform.

Now we are looking at local government reform again, I think it is important to keep the tradition of the towns and cities. My proposals did keep local government at the level of places like Worcester, Leicester and Coventry. If I had gone for unitary authorities at county level, all these historic towns would have had no council of their own. If I had put housing at county level, I would have ended up with more trouble. Hereford, in the new Hereford/Worcester, for example, would have had no housing remit.

If you decide to give all the powers to the districts, you end up with problems about what to do with roads, social services and education. If you try to cluster the districts to form a big enough council, you find the really big one, which can stand by itself, is in the middle of the cluster.

One fundamental mistake I made was in setting up the metropolitan county councils. I specified what they could do, but not what they could not do. I did not, for example, say that they should not go in for economic development. What happened was that the councils took on a whole range of new spending functions. It would have been wiser to have excluded these other activities.

I wish Michael Heseltine good luck in the review he is making. He will need it.

The Green Belt was critical in the local government reorganization. Every check was needed to stop the big urban areas spreading outwards. It was a major preoccupation with the Conservative Party. I seemed to be in hot water over the approval of the development of a brewery technically in the Lancashire Green Belt.

Suddenly, I was being threatened with protest at my decision from keen Tories at the Conservative Party conference that year. I took the attack to the enemy. I pointed out how bogus the accusation of irresponsibility was. The land was not as it had been described.

I described what the land was really like. It clearly had no Green Belt value.

I told the conference that, important as it was to retain the Green Belt, it was even more important to improve the lot of those who suffered from a bad environment. Too many of our people had to endure bad housing, bad working conditions, serious air and noise pollution.

The middle class was terribly articulate and good at organizing campaigns, as we had just witnessed, but where was this articulation in demanding improvements to the worst inner city areas where the residents were not able to put their case with such force? My first priority was to improve the bad environments.

They had given me a lovely wicket. They won early cheers decrying my decision. My reply was hard hitting and one of the best speeches I have made at a Conservative Party conference as I fastened on a bogus middle-class campaign. I was able to draw attention to the misleading reporting by the *Guardian*. Its report was illustrated with a photograph of a beautiful stretch of the countryside which was described as the area Walker was to ruin. The only snag was the countryside was three miles away from the site. When I pointed this out – and much more – I got one of the biggest ovations of my political career.

Closer to home, I was tested by a proposal to build a hotel on the side of the Avon Gorge. It was an outrageous idea and I turned it down.

I tried to resolve the controversy over the siting of the third London airport by coming down in favour of Maplin. The chosen site would cause less noise nuisance and would use reclaimed land. Most important, it would help bring prosperity to the east of London. One of the big advantages of London's West End was its closeness to Heathrow. Choosing Maplin would have meant providing superior roads and railway connections to the east of London. The theory was that as a consequence more people would want to locate their businesses and live in East London.

I considered I could give no greater boost to East London than to go for Maplin, as opposed to massive extensions to Heathrow, Gatwick and Stansted.

I appointed the board to carry out the Maplin project and it was going ahead. I also decided to go ahead with the Channel Tunnel.

The disappointment is that both schemes were stopped by Tony Crosland, the incoming Labour Environment Secretary. He was not opposed to them personally, but he was under pressure from a Treasury desperate to make cuts in public spending. He decided these were two things he could drop and produce immediate savings. Both were schemes nobody yet benefited from. If you stop something which people have never enjoyed, there is little political downside. If you change something which has happened or is happening, you invite last ditch opposition.

Dropping Maplin will, I am afraid, still prove to be a mistake. I was and am less certain about the Channel Tunnel.

The new Channel Tunnel is theoretically a private sector venture with the government only on the periphery, but the reality is that if the private sector cannot complete or there is some other difficulty, the Treasury will have to step in with public sector finance. I am still not totally convinced of the Channel Tunnel versus ferry arguments. At the end of the day, the best figures show that twenty per cent of traffic will go through the Channel Tunnel and the other eighty per cent by other routes.

The scheme was, however, something the Prime Minister and government were keen on as part of their European policy. And if it had been been implemented then it would have been more cost-effective.

Environmental issues cropped up everywhere. After all the hard work involved in setting up the new department and bringing in local government reform, I was reckless enough to take Tessa on a weekend break in Paris. As we arrived at our hotel, a message was waiting, telling me that a tanker had been damaged off the British coast and there was another threat of a *Torrey Canyon* type disaster. Every twenty minutes I was phoned about what should be done and was forced to return early on the Sunday morning.

What the incident did show, apart from the folly of thinking you could have a quiet weekend in Paris, was that our methods of tackling such disasters were still inadequate, even after the *Torrey Canyon*. We introduced new procedures to see that the emergency services were properly led to take swift action and that government departments themselves were fully co-ordinated.

My path again crossed that of Dick Marsh. After our early exchanges we became friends and I knew that for a period he was depressed by the whole political scene and cynical about the Labour Party and its leadership. I argued that he had made a good impression in the Commons and should certainly stay. Later he took over from Barbara Castle as Minister of Transport and we virtually agreed on which parts of the Labour Transport Bill should be cut out.

When the tables were turned and I became responsible for transport, John Peyton, my junior minister in charge of transport, came to me and asked if I thought it would be a crazy idea to make Dick Marsh British Railways chairman. I said he was able and I thought it would be a good idea. He could command the enthusiasm of railwaymen, but, at the same time, knew what had to be done. Ted Heath agreed that we should put the idea to him. Dick was fascinated and phoned me a couple of days later to say he would like to accept.

Not everything went smoothly in these early days in government and Paul Channon and Julian Amery had their awkward moments. Embarrassments came in twos, if not threes.

On the first question time for Housing and Local Government, we were fourth in line for questions and No. 62 was the first question we would be called upon to answer. I was told there was no question of it being reached. A Parliamentary Secretary should be there just in case something totally unexpected happened. Paul Channon was responsible that first day, but his private office told him, quite reasonably, that it was absurd to go to the House; No. 62 had never been reached. For some strange reason, it was reached on this occasion and Paul was not there at twenty-five minutes past three when question No. 62 came up.

The press made a good deal of the fact that the department led by this great whizz kid did not have a minister present when he was needed. Paul arrived ten minutes late and had to apologize to the House.

The second incident was more serious. It happened one weekend when the Duke of Rutland had invited Julian Amery and myself to shoot. On the Saturday evening I was summoned to the phone to be told that the *Sunday Times* was carrying a story accusing me of organizing the rigging of questions for Tory MPs to ask me in the Commons. I said this was rubbish and that my press office must issue a denial. My office said that it had made inquiries and though I was not involved, Julian was. He had sent a minute to a civil servant asking him to prepare twenty favourable questions for Tory MPs to put down before the GLC elections. Julian said he had probably done so after his PPS had suggested it. I said, 'Julian, civil servants must not be involved.' It was a sensational story. It was the first item on the television news and it ruined our weekend. There were enormous headlines: 'Walker Rigs Questions'.

Having seen the papers, I went to Ted and said I was sorry. It was something which happened all the time in politics, but civil servants should never have been involved and the only thing I could do was to apologize to the House. Whoever was responsible for the department must apologize and hope the House would be in a forgiving mood.

Sir William Armstrong, head of the civil service, and Willie Whitelaw were both in the room. Sir William said a minister could not do that. It was perfectly proper for the civil service to provide the service. There was an important constitutional position involved. Ministers had the right to ask for virtually anything to be done. If they asked for party political advantage, that was proper. I argued that if a minister wanted to take party political advantage, he should ask his research department or use his own political brain. He could not ask a civil servant.

But Sir William insisted that it would be constitutionally disastrous to apologize and set a precedent. I pleaded and argued, but Willie and the Prime Minister both came down in favour of Sir William. Totally against my wishes, I had to go to the Commons and defend the rigging as something that was constitutionally correct. Quite properly, everyone, on both sides of the House, was critical, so I got the most terrible press the next day, largely for arrogance in trying to defend the action.

But it was Sir William who insisted that it should be done. If I had apologized, everyone would have said he is a young chap and will never do it again. They like a politician to apologize. I would have got the blame when Julian deserved it, but that was part of the job of being boss.

For the next few days I was under a cloud of depression. Some days later when I was walking through a division lobby Dame Irene Ward stopped me and said, 'Peter, for the first time since I have known you you are depressed.'

I said the whole department had been going well and there was a good, happy team, which was trouncing the opposition, and then suddenly there was this ridiculous slip by Julian. I had been commanded by the head of the civil service not to apologize and asked to defend the impossible.

She said, 'Dear Peter, you are silly. You must remember that in politics these things are forgotten in a few days. I am sure in a week no one will remember it.'

I walked off not really believing her, but the next day I received a lovely postcard from her. It showed an enormous field and a man ploughing it with a hand-plough. She had written: 'Just to remind you that in politics you must always plough on. All my love, Irene.' I have had that card on my desk ever since.

She was right. It was forgotten in two weeks, but at the time it seemed catastrophic. The use of the word 'rig' made you look as if you were a crook and I hated it.

The pressure of the job stopped too much fretting. I had made it clear at the party conference that I was anxious to improve life in the inner cities. The government gave a high priority to the issue. I quickly came to the conclusion that the environment and inner city problems were interwoven and trying to tackle them through the councils was not working. You could pour money into the GLC or Liverpool and see no improvements. More often what you saw was deterioration. One of the reasons was that councils were not using a total approach.

If housing was bad, they would put more money into housing, but neglect job creation, communications and transport. If they put money into transport, they did nothing about housing. Nothing at all was being done about law and order, which was, and is, particularly important in inner cities. If there was a big increase in burglaries, firms moved out and a vicious cycle began. There was more un-employment and another increase in burglaries. When burglaries increased again, more firms moved out and more unemployment and then more burglaries followed.

I decided on a total approach, but first we had to look more closely at the problems. We set up six groups to analyse what was happen-ing in inner cities, three in inner-city conurbations and three in smaller, depressed, industrial towns. Each group consisted of three people: a minister, the leader of the council and the senior partner of a firm of outside consultants.

The civil service complained strongly. I must have a civil servant involved. Not for the first time, I said, 'No.' Anything the minister wanted his civil servants would give him, anything the council leader wanted his council officials would supply and anything the senior consultant wanted his firm would provide. Despite the objections, I set up these six groups. I took responsibility for Birmingham and my ministers took responsibility for other cities. Michael Heseltine, if I remember rightly, took Liverpool. I think all the council leaders were Labour.

I committed myself to publishing a report. Every three weeks I went to Birmingham and determined the work and the method of examination. We specifically looked at Sparkbrook in Birmingham, Liverpool 8 in Liverpool.

Unfortunately, when Geoffrey Rippon took over from me, he

decided he did not want to go to Birmingham every three weeks. Civil servants told him they did not think it was really a minister's job and should be done by civil servants, so what should have been an important initiative was allowed to drift.

It was not quite lost without trace. By the time my report was finished, we were out of office and Peter Shore was Environment Secretary. His civil servants told him that he should not publish the reports. They would mean extra public expenditure.

I was on the back benches, demanding to know when they were to be published. Finally, Peter did publish them, but without any press hand-out. Virtually no copies were available and few people knew they had been published at all. It was one of those unlovely, classical civil service operations in which Whitehall gets its own way in the end. Unfortunately, it was at the expense of people living in the inner cities.

The Liverpool 8 survey showed that with thirteen per cent of the population, the area had thirty per cent of the crime, thirty per cent of the unemployment. Handicapped people suffered too.

The explanation was simple. If you were running a Labour local authority you did not put money into your safe Labour seats. You put it into the marginal seats where new pavements or school repairs could win you crucial votes in the next local election. It changed because the Liberals emerged as challengers in safe Labour seats and the party had to rethink its strategy, but at that time safe Labour areas were being neglected monstrously because they could be taken for granted.

I believed strongly that to achieve impetus we had to create what were virtually new town corporations in the worst of the city areas. We needed dynamic leaders to move in and raise the standards of a range of services. When the standards were up to the national average, the services could be passed back to the local authorities.

Michael Heseltine got the closest to the ideal in Liverpool ten years later. London Docklands has done a great deal, but as a different type of operation.

The sad truth is that even now we do not have a really total approach looking at job creation, communication, education and housing. There have been some improvements in some towns and cities, but there are still ghastly problems. Inner cities should, for example, have the best teachers and highest teacher-pupil ratio. How often does that happen?

I would still use development corporations to tackle inner cities. There is a theory that you can encourage free market forces to do the job, but the free market, without powerful inducements, ignores the inner cities. You might attract a property developer to the most fabulous site in Birmingham, but that is the exception.

The reality is that many small and medium-sized firms have left, often because of the crime rate. If I had a medium-sized business in an inner-city district I would hate to have my factory broken into two or three times a week, my staff mugged on their way to work and their cars stolen. Life is too short to put up with this. You say, 'I am fed up: this is the third burglary I have had this month. I will look somewhere else.'

Part of the total approach must be stopping pollution. This requires legislation and enough inspectors. There has been an improvement. In air pollution, it has been substantial. I extended the Clean Air Act zones and imposed the first lead-in-petrol restrictions on cars.

What we discovered about car pollution was frightening. The chances of lead poisoning in urban environments were high. You could have heavy traffic flowing on both sides of a school. The potential for lead poisoning and brain damage to young children was real. Of course, ministers could argue they were on the right side of international safety levels, but these levels were too high for comfort. No children were showing brain damage, but I was aware we were getting to the point when some could be.

Sometimes the answers seem undramatic. Pollution could be cut dramatically by a widespread recycling of waste materials. But here governments have come up against commercial considerations. The cost of the recycled product is often much higher than that of the primary product. If I run a business and the recycled product costs a hundred pounds a ton and the primary product costs fifty pounds a ton, of course I buy the primary product. Even if, for higher motives, I wanted to buy the recycled product, I would not be able to do so because all my competitors would buy the primary product, and I would soon cease to be cost-effective.

If we are serious, we need international recycling agreements between, for a start, the United States, Japan and Europe. We shall have to tell manufacturers that for environmental reasons they must use twenty per cent of recycled material. It would be the same for every firm and you would not be destroying anyone's competitiveness. If we acted alone, our industry would be damaged.

When the Prime Minister phoned to say he wanted me to go to Trade and Industry, I was elated that my ability to run a big government department had been recognized. I was also sorry to leave Environment, because there was still much to be done and I was pleased with the progress we had made in such a short period.

It is daunting to look back at what we did in the first two years, apart from local government reorganization. We brought to the attention of the nation for the first time the problem of the inner cities, setting up studies which resulted in action being taken. We reorganized a water industry which had been neglected for fifty years and was in a state of decay. We introduced a river basin system which became the envy of the world. We restored the Green Belt policy which had begun in the 1930s as a reaction against the ribbon development but had been neglected in the post-war period.

Perhaps the most fundamental social reform was the housing rebate. Even Richard Crossman, a former Minister of Housing and Local Government, could scarce forbear to cheer. On my arrival at the department, I discovered that the government gave substantial sums to subsidize council housing up and down the country. It was dispensed as a grant to local authorities and no two local authorities operated in the same way. Some used it to reduce the rates, others put in a rebate scheme for the less well-off. A large number of local authorities had no sensible rebate scheme for poorer families. The private sector did not have a scheme of any kind.

People who were earning too little to pay rents faced eviction. I decided that if the government was putting in money to help the low income groups, we had to see that it was applied nationwide.

I brought in a new rebates system for local authority houses and rent allowances for the private sector. We became the first capitalist country in the world where no one could be evicted simply because they had not the money. At a *New Statesman* lunch, I told Dick Crossman, then its editor, of my plans and the principle on which I wished to act. Crossman said it would be the most Socialist measure to be introduced in housing. He had wanted to do something similar, but been turned down by a Labour Chancellor who said the country could not afford it.

If I could get that through a Tory Cabinet, I would have achieved the most fundamental housing reform in the twentieth century. I told him that if he studied history he must know that all the best

Socialist measures are brought in by Tory governments. We did get it through the Cabinet.

I embarked upon a massive programme of clearing derelict land where there had been coal mines and steel works. It was the biggest scheme of its kind in the world. In areas of fast-rising unemployment, I introduced *Operation Eyesore*, giving substantial grants to local authorities to clear up blots on the landscape.

I recognized that if I sent out a circular to local authorities, nothing would happen for a long time. Instead, I fixed a deadline. No grants would be available after a particular date. Even more important, I persuaded Hugh Cudlipp and the *Daily Mirror* to conduct a campaign saying that I was going to do this and asking readers to make sure I kept my promise by sending photographs of local eyesores which could be treated. The *Mirror* did it beautifully. Much of the front page and large slices of the inside pages were devoted to the challenge. Thousands of photographs and letters came to me. I divided them up and sent them to appropriate local authorities saying: 'Here are forty eyesores in your area. Please look at them.' As a result thousands of schemes took place.

In the depressed north east and north west, we decided to introduce road programmes to attract new firms and bring prosperity. The new road systems have helped to diversify the economies of the two regions, even if there is still a long way to go.

Looking at housing, we came to the conclusion that the problen was not so much the number of houses, but that so many had no bathrooms and no toilets, and needed improvements and major repairs. We launched a housing improvement programme. It had the bonus of helping the low income groups. My Labour predecessor had done well in legislating for this, but a poor job in seeing the improvements were carried out. We put a leaflet through each door, mobile film shows toured every street. Ministers opened exhibitions put on by the local councils. The number of house improvements trebled.

We also introduced the principle that the polluter pays for the damage he does to the countryside. At the time it was a fundamental change. We had cleaned up the rivers, acted against environmental pollution and improved the air and the housing stock.

I was called upon to conserve in unexpected ways. I discovered that all the London theatres were being bought by developers to convert them into office blocks. There was a danger that in a short time planning permissions would be granted and many London theatres would be lost for ever. The difficulty was that the London theatres could not be profitable unless they based rents on historic costs. I did not want London to lose its elegant theatres and visited them all personally, asking caretakers to let me see for myself.

I returned to my office to tell civil servants I wanted many of them protected by 'listing' that afternoon. My private office said it could not be done because all the applications had to be referred to an advisory committee. I said I did not need any advice. I had visited the London theatres and taken the decision. They said decisions were never taken without advice. I said they would be taken that afternoon without advice. The Permanent Secretary came in to say it would offend the advisory committee. I said no offence was meant. I had visited the theatres and come to my conclusions. If the committee later decided I was wrong, I would eat humble pie and listen to their reasons why some theatres should not have been listed.

I was determined to act speedily because planning applications were being made and properties were going to change hands quickly. I did not want to allow time for property developers to be alerted to what I was doing. They were all listed immediately and virtually all of them remain today. I could have been charged with using dictatorial powers in a way which should not be allowed. Of course, I interfered with the market place. It would, at first sight, have been better economics to have office blocks on the theatre sites, but this would have been a short-sighted view. I took into account the importance of the theatres to the prosperity and cultural life of London and the country as a whole. They were well worth saving by any criteria.

Wellington Barracks, near Buckingham Palace, also came under my protection. It was going to be pulled down, but I considered it to be one of the most elegant buildings in an important area and slapped a preservation order on it. It has since been rebuilt behind the façade. Now, when I pass the floodlit building at night, I take joy in the spectacle.

We also took pleasure in London's parks. As the proud possessors of a brood of young children and an Old English sheepdog, we visited the parks a great deal. I used to exercise the dog at the crack of dawn in Hyde Park. Tessa and I would take the children to Kensington Gardens and St James's Park to see the ducks.

We admired the display of flowers and trees and the way that the grass was kept. On becoming Environment Secretary, I discovered that I was now responsible for these glorious parks. I asked who managed them and was told how it was done. I asked if anyone thanked them. My officials displayed blank faces. Thanked them? Why, no.

I suggested we should invite some of the workers to the department to thank them for producing parks without equal throughout the world. We invited about a hundred of the staff of the Royal Parks and their partners to drinks and snacks at the department. They were an impressive-looking group, all sun-tanned, healthy and contented. I said that as someone who had the privilege of travelling round the world, I knew the most beautiful parks were in London and that it was due to them. A great many people appreciated and admired the parks, but did not know who to thank. I did know, which was why they were there. On behalf of all the visitors to London, my family and everyone else I wanted to congratulate them.

These people do a fantastic job, but because they are part of the system they rarely get any appreciation.

As well as the nation's housing problems, I found myself, with Tessa, taking decisions on housing for my family. When we were married we moved into 12 Cowley Street and I had a house in my constituency called The Old Parsonage, a small Elizabethan house in which my mother and father lived. We stayed there at weekends.

As children came along we wanted a separate place of our own. Martin Court, near Droitwich, came on to the market with a 300-acre farm and we bought that. It had belonged to a district council leader who was a friend. He restored it and then died. His widow said she would love us to live there: it was very much a family house. This was my first real experience of farming and the first time I learned the problems.

We had a marvellous gardener, well into his seventies. He was pretty hopeless about keeping the garden in order, but knew everything about nature, every insect, bird and tree. He proved to be a first-class teacher for the children and their parents.

8

SPARKING INDUSTRY

I was embarrassed by a spate of speculation that there was going to be a Cabinet reshuffle and that, following what was regarded as my success at Environment, I was to be moved to the Department of Trade and Industry. No word was said to me by the Prime Minister or anyone else. I found myself going to Cabinet meetings with John Davis, whom I liked, after extensive Sunday newspaper reports that I was to replace him. John had been criticized as the first Secretary of State of the new department. In my view, the criticism was unfounded. He was a good minister but slipped up on his handling of the House of Commons and party conferences.

One Sunday morning, Ted phoned to say he had decided to move me from Environment to the DTI. He was going to make the announcement on Monday morning at 9 a.m. He then asked me if I would prefer Margaret Thatcher or Geoffrey Howe as my number two. I said Geoffrey. It was a fateful decision. Who can say how it might have worked out if I had chosen Margaret?

It may sound sexist today, but I think I made the choice because I felt I would find it easier to deal with a man as number two. I thought if I had to congratulate or reprimand or issue stern orders, it would somehow be easier with a man there. Although I liked Margaret a great deal and there were no policy differences between us at this point, I felt I would be more courteous and understanding with her than I would be with a man. In my business life, I had always had male colleagues and in politics I had never had a woman junior minister. I can only plead that this was twenty years ago. Since then women have come to the top in every sphere.

Michael Heseltine was already at the DTI as a kind of advance party. I had recommended him to the Prime Minister as an outstanding Environment Minister and Ted had promoted him and switched him to the DTI. It was a happy accident that he was already in place.

I immediately put the running of the department on the same basis as Environment. John had had all the ministers to a buffet lunch once a week. Now they met every morning.

I was enthusiastic about my ministerial team, but ran into an immediate and unusual problem with my new Permanent Secretary, Sir Antony Part.

The first morning I arrived at my new department I thought he looked extremely ill. He appeared ashen and tired, I noticed his hand was shaking during our conversation and I became concerned about his health. I discovered from my private office that he had been under great pressure and had gone through an exhausting time. Criticism of the department had weighed heavily upon him, but, in any case, he was still suffering from an injury sustained in Japan some years before.

That evening I asked him to come and have a drink with me and told him that I had no idea whether Secretaries of State had any power to order Permanent Secretaries, but I was ordering him to have a holiday. He replied sharply that Secretaries of State had no power to decide when Permanent Secretaries had a holiday and that he had no intention of taking a holiday. I said that if I did not have power, I would find out who did, the civil service or the Prime Minister, because we had a great deal to do together and I thought a couple of weeks' holiday could make all the difference.

I had seen business people become ill through overwork. One of the reasons was that they never took a holiday. I am told he went and spoke to colleagues about this incredibly audacious suggestion of the Secretary of State and decided that he was fed up with the whole thing and would go on holiday anyway. He said that he would almost certainly not come back. I learned later he believed this new 'whizz kid' who was now Secretary of State wanted to get him out of the way so that he could appoint someone else.

Two or three weeks later he returned looking sun-tanned and much better and we worked closely together and became great friends. I remember a pleasant moment twelve months later when we had a drink in the early evening. He said that he had not said it to anyone, but my sending him away on holiday had probably saved his life. He was also generous when the February 1974 election broke up our partnership: he wrote me a letter praising my grasp of a wide range of industrial and commercial problems and the 'bravery which never failed you even in times of great and unreasonable stress'.

After he retired from the civil service, he had a distinguished career in the City; he was a talented man. I did have the privilege of reading the lesson at his memorial service some years later when many of his former friends and ministers were present.

The whizz kid title was something I hated, but had to live with. About this time speculation began to grow in newspapers, the media and amongst MPs that I could be a future leader of the Tory Party. It was no part of my thinking at that time.

As a young politician my great ambition had been to get into Parliament, not to become a minister. No scrawled ambitions on the back of envelopes. I suppose I thought vaguely that someone from a three-bedroom semi in south Harrow did not become a Cabinet Minister, let alone Prime Minister. I was thrilled when I became an MP. Then I was a rebel over our entry to the Common Market and went round the Commonwealth opposing it. It was young Walker saying that he felt strongly about the question and it was the job of an MP to speak out. That has always been my attitude. The immediate effect was to create hostility to me among those who could pull the strings of patronage.

The first shock realization that I might go further was when Selwyn Lloyd asked me to be his PPS. Here was a great Cabinet Minister, a former Foreign Secretary and Chancellor offering to tell me all he knew about politics. It started me thinking: 'Good heavens, I might be good enough to be a minister.' Shortly afterwards Alec Douglas-Home put me on the front bench and I was described as one of the star performers on the Finance Bill.

From then on, I thought I might be a minister. I moved my sights to the Cabinet when Ted asked me to organize his leadership campaign. Arriving as an MP only in 1961, I was in the Shadow Cabinet four years later. I had no desire to become Prime Minister with Ted in the job because I wanted him as Prime Minister.

The DTI team was strong and we quickly created a team spirit. Chris Chataway was the Minister for Industry. He was highly enthusiastic and intelligent and had great personal charisma. His running achievements and public persona as a television broadcaster meant he was known to millions and he got on well with civil servants and industrialists. He started putting into operation the workings of the Industry Act in which I had taken the power to intervene to help industry, a power I would use only after a high quality advisory board of top businessmen had looked at any proposition.

The important thing was to get high powered businessmen as advisers, and we succeeded. Gordon Richardson, who was then a banker and later became governor of the Bank of England, was persuaded to be the first chairman of the advisory committee on industry and virtually all the decisons taken by that body ended in success. It was a riposte to those who have argued since that government must retain an arm's length relationship or wreak havoc. We were wise to reject many projects, however.

Michael Heseltine was responsible for aviation. By this time we had become friends. I first came to know him when he was the new MP for Tavistock and I met his wife and young children.

On one occasion the friendship was almost extended too far. They invited us down to their Devon home for a weekend and we had a lucky escape which could have been disastrous for both families. Michael and Anne and Tessa and myself went swimming in the sea close to the spot where Lord Mildmay, the famous jockey, had been drowned a few months earlier. The tide turned and certainly Tessa and myself had some difficulty in getting to the shore. It was quite the most treacherous current I had experienced. Two ministers could easily have departed prematurely from the political scene and created two by-elections.

Michael was a high quality minister. You asked him to do something and you knew it would be done well and with enthusiasm. At an early stage he came to me and told me he thought we should merge BEA and BOAC. I examined his well-prepared paper and there was no doubt about the logic of his argument. It did, however, cause family strains. My father-in-law was then the treasurer of BOAC and there was nothing he loathed more than BEA. I feared my decision to merge the two airlines – with BOAC's concern that it would be dominated by the bigger BEA – would cause considerable family friction. It did. My father-in-law thought I was mad, but there was no real doubt that the creation of one strong British Airways was right. Michael handled the issue with great skill.

He has remained a good friend in all our years in politics, some when he has been in office and I have been out. When Margaret sacked me from the Shadow Cabinet, he wrote expressing his dismay and saying what a mistake it was. He was one of the few colleagues who, when I was out of fashion and Thatcherism was at its height, always expressed the view, behind my back, that I should still be in the Shadow Cabinet.

I knew this from what fellow MPs told me. I am afraid there were other colleagues who while I was in a top position were full of praise for what I was doing, but then stopped all contact the moment I was banished. Some were heard to say hostile things at those private dinner parties which are such a feature of politics in London. The exchanges were often reported back.

Geoffrey Howe, my number two, was an incredibly efficient and competent minister. He had the training of a very distinguished lawyer and probably more than any politician I have worked with accepted a brief and executed it with skill. At this point, he had no doubts about what some would have described as the interventionist policies of the DTI. The positive approach to regional policy had his support. Although he was unhappy about implementing price control, as indeed everybody was, he was in full support of the strategy. When decisions were taken to cut unemployment and to see the economy was not damaged more than necessary by the enormous leap in oil prices, the Cabinet, including Geoffrey, were united. Geoffrey was always charming, working long hours, coffee-drinking and chain-smoking as he did so.

Tom Boardman, who later became chairman of the National Westminster Bank, was responsible for day-to-day energy policy during both the oil and coal crises. He too had considerable charm and considerable ability. His one fault was that he worked too hard and worried too much. During the worst aspects of the energy crisis in 1973/74, I had great difficulty in seeing that Tom got enough sleep and relaxation at weekends. British politics lost out when he lost his seat in 1974.

In a frantic phase, the DTI attempted to rationalize and modernize British industry. The BEA-BOAC merger was part of that campaign. Support for firms which were likely to succeed was another aspect of the policy. Geoffrey Howe was responsible for a shake-up on the consumer front to give customers the benefits of livelier competition.

We took a positive approach to the prospect of finding sources of energy in the North Sea. As a result we were able to point to higher private investment in private industry, a substantial improvement in productivity and a big increase in the volume of exports. Manufacturing production rose to an all-time high. The performance was not matched again until the late 1980s.

The tragedy for us occurred when OPEC's sudden hike of oil prices produced inflation and an adverse balance of trade. Though it was not quite as bad as it seemed, the balance of trade was affected in the short term by an increase in the import of machinery and raw materials. This later yielded bigger exports. A study of the trade figures shows that if we had continued in power we would, by the final quarter of 1974, have made considerable improvements in the balance of payments. With our tough policy on incomes still in place, there would also have been a brake in inflation.

Alas, a Labour government got in and abandoned any form of wage restraint. Still influenced by its union paymasters, it allowed enormous wage increases and inflation burst to the high levels we saw from 1974 to 1979.

Inside the DTI, we studied the pattern of trade to see where we could make the most impact. The Far East looked good. Michael Heseltine and myself went to China to win orders and a new trade agreement. We timed it to coincide with the opening of a major British trade fair in Peking. A few weeks before the exhibition was to be opened we were given an insight into the way the Chinese economy worked. The Chinese ambassador came to see me and to tell me, with confidence, that our trading mission would be a great success. I said I hoped so. He replied it would be. The American trade fair had had 210,000 visitors. The Germans had had 260,000 visitors. The British trade fair would have 335,000 visitors. His prediction proved accurate.

I may say that most of the visitors came not to purchase our goods, but were sent from all over China to examine and copy the technology on display. Chou En-lai opened the exhibition and was excited by many of the exhibits. I had a phone call from his office after the opening to say he would like to purchase the exhibition as it was. I told him it was not my exhibition to sell. All the exhibits were in the ownership of the firms concerned. He said this could not be true since it was a British government exhibition.

I explained that there were differences in the way our two countries related to industry and I could not myself sell the exhibition. But I said I would circulate all the British firms asking if they wished to sell to the Chinese. I duly sent out the circular, but with the warning that whatever they sold was likely to be copied.

The opening of the trade talks also reflected the double-talk which can be characteristic of a Communist state. The Chinese minister opening the talks said that though we might wish to offer China credit facilities, the Chinese government was not interested in taking credit from overseas countries. He said that Chairman Mao had laid down that it would be contrary to the dignity, standing and independence of China if it became indebted to other countries. I nodded happily since I had no desire to offer credit facilities to China, but I was not to escape so easily. The minister paused and went on: 'But I would inform you we are very interested in deferred payments.' What, in fact, he was saying was that he wished to pay no interest.

The mission went well and Michael Heseltine sold aircraft as well.

I was intrigued by the whole Chinese scene and tried to create trading opportunities for British industry in China whenever I had the chance. We succeeded when I negotiated that the main oil concession in the China Sea should go to BP. BP were excited by the project. Early investigations showed there were good prospects for major oil finds, but, unfortunately, justifiable hopes turned to disappointment.

A dramatic change in the exchange rate presented a big opportunity for British exports, but I discovered even major firms were persisting in their out-of-date practices. They continued sending salesmen anywhere they had an established market, but there was no attempt to go after new markets.

I became frustrated at meeting a succession of businessmen who were not assessing the world opportunities. I decided we must make direct contact with the business community. If the DTI sent out a new circular it went straight into the waste-paper basket. I asked my ministerial team how we could make industrialists sit up and think. We discovered there were basically 12,000 exporting businesses responsible for ninety-five per cent of our exports. I said that I would personally invite all the business leaders to come to a one hour briefing and we would damn well tell them the difference the more favourable exchange rate could make. We would also tell them of the range of export services we offered. Only a handful of businesses ever used them.

There was the classic example of a service for which businessmen paid ten pounds a year and in return received information from our embassies all over the world about the demand for the goods they made. If you were making umbrellas, you registered umbrellas, paid your ten pounds and information on the demand for umbrellas anywhere in the world was sent to you. I thought it was a fabulous service and asked officials how many firms in my Worcester constituency were using it. There were four. I rang up the chief executives of all of them and asked if they found the system useful. They said, 'What system? We don't have a system like that.' I had to say to each of them, 'You do. You pay ten pounds a year for it. Your firm has actually had 320 pieces of information in the last six months.' They went away and all four came back to say that the information had come in, but they had not done anything about it. A clerk had simply filed it.

I said we would have to seek out the chief executives and tell them where they were going wrong. We would arrange a superb hour's briefing, partly on currency exchange rates and how these affected their exports, and partly on the range of services they could get from the department. I suggested early evening meetings in the regions. It was Michael Heseltine who came up with the brilliant idea of breakfast meetings. He said that if we organized those they would all feel they had to come. If ministers were ready to get up, the industrialists would think they should be ready to do so. Once the briefing was over, the only place they could go on to was their office. If you excited them, they would go straight back and do something about it.

I sent out 12,000 letters which looked as though they had come from me personally. We sent them round in white envelopes to stress it was a personal invitation. I said I wanted just one hour of their time. If they came at eight o'clock in the morning to the Mecca dance hall in Birmingham, I would promise they would be out at nine o'clock. Michael Heseltine did some of the presentations, Geoffrey Howe others. Some 9,700 businessmen turned up. In Birmingham it caused a tremendous traffic jam.

The result was impressive. Take-up of the export services of the DTI quadrupled in a month. You saw, suddenly, two months later, a significant jump in the export figures. It sounds unbelievable, but these businessmen had not realized that the exchange rate meant someone in Germany was paying 30 per cent less for their goods. Quite extraordinarily, business after business had not realized it. I gave the simplest illustrations. I said such is the exchange rate now that something you were selling in Germany six months ago for £1,000 would now cost £700.

MPs are criticized for their lack of knowledge of business, but this was a reflection on how unprofessional British industry was. I was shocked about how many major firms fell into this trap and how poor the management sometimes was.

I visited one of the most famous shipyards in Britain. Because it was the right time of year, we had both grouse and salmon for lunch. I would guess the grouse had been shot by the board and the salmon caught by its members. They were charming, but when I started to discuss the state of worldwide shipping I found they were remarkably ignorant. They simply did not know their subject.

As always when I went to visit a major industrial concern, I asked to meet the shop stewards by themselves. It was usually lunch with the board and tea with the stewards. On this occasion the shop stewards, though they did not know much about world shipping, did know shipping and were highly intelligent and aggressive. As we drove away, I remember telling the head of my private office, 'If only we could make the directors of that shipyard the shop stewards and the shop stewards the directors, we would have a perfect combination – a group of tough, pretty ruthless directors and a lot of charming shop stewards.' Instead, as in much of British industry, we had it the wrong way round.

We were seeing the adverse result of third and fourth generation businessmen. The great nineteenth-century tycoon had been a great entrepreneur. He had gone round the world, built in Argentina and India and done everything, including amassing a fortune. Unfortunately, his big desire was that his children should become gentlemen and ladies. It seemed a perfectly proper ambition. He bought a nice house in the country and the children were taught to ride, hunt and shoot. There was nothing wrong with that. What was wrong was he never trained the sons to run his shipyard. The sons inherited with no idea how to run the business. The gentlemen took over, while in Germany and Japan it was the professional players who were building up the system.

There are some exceptions, one of which was Great Universal Stores. Leonard Wolfson was, in a totally different way, as able as, if not more able than, his entrepreneurial father. We know that in that case the father took a great deal of trouble to train the son. In many firms this did not and does not happen and it is a major weakness in British industry.

It is changing slowly, but there is still a great deal of non-professional management in this country. The conferences of businessmen proved the point. With a big screen in front of them you saw them saying: 'What a good idea' and then going back to their offices to do something about it. 'Let's call in the salesmen.'

British Leyland let themselves down badly over exports to Japan. Donald Stokes, the chairman, came to me and said there were a number of ways in which the Japanese were stopping him selling his cars in Japan. I remember one of them. British cars arrived at the dockside in Japan only for a Japanese official to come along and say he was terrible sorry, but there had been a change in the rules about where the engine number should be stamped and they would all have to go back to the UK for the number to be put in the right place. There were some fifteen methods used by the Japanese to stop British cars. I knew that if I went through the Foreign Office nothing would happen. Perhaps naughtily I asked the Japanese ambassador to come and see me. I said to him, 'Here are the fifteen ways in which your country is stopping my cars being sold in Japan.' Would he please convey to his government that unless they all stopped within three months, I would stop all Japanese imports to Britain. He smiled, as only a Japanese ambassador confronted with such allegations can, and said that would be illegal since we were all members of the General Agreement on Tariffs and Trade. I said: 'You are quite right, Ambassador, it would be illegal and these are the fifteen reasons I would give publicly and internationally for acting illegally. I think the whole world would be fascinated by every one of these methods.'

He bowed and smiled and left. About six weeks later he returned to say his government had asked him to say that it had looked into the fifteen allegations and none had any foundation. I looked at him and he paused before adding: 'My government has also asked me to say that none of them will occur again.'

None of them did occur again. The Japanese said that while that year we had been able to export only a few hundred cars to Japan, they were confident that next year we would export 7,000–10,000 cars. It was a very sizable increase and when I told Sir Donald he said it was staggering and opened up the market just as he wanted. He would launch the new Jaguar range there.

I promised to arrange for me or one of my ministers to come out for the launch. It would emphasize to the Japanese government that we were keeping a careful watch on what was happening. The date was agreed and I sent Sir Geoffrey Howe, as he now was, out to Tokyo to attend. I should say Japan is one of the few other countries in the world to have right-hand-drive cars. Geoffrey phoned me the night before the launch to say, 'Would you believe it! They have sent six left-hand-drive Jaguars.'

I got on to Donald and said I could not believe what he had done.

He said: 'Well, it is not so easy. There is a big demand in Britain and we had a bit of a surplus on the left-hand-drive cars.'

I told him, 'I cannot believe it. You took a new range of cars with the wrong drive.' While I had my moment of triumph, British Leyland managed to destroy it.

Japan has always been a protected market. They have eased restrictions slowly and in a calculating way. It is a lesson to us that they have built up this enormous economic giant by pursuing a policy of protectionism against the threat of imports and advocating free trade for their exports.

Even in 1991 when there is a serious recession in America, the UK and other parts of Western Europe and these countries are cutting back considerably on capital investment programmes, the Japanese have decided that with everyone else retrenching, this is the moment to increase investment in Japanese manufacturing substantially. They are planning thirty per cent increases in new plant and machinery. They calculate that at the end of the recession, Britain, American and others will be way behind with new technology and Japan will have a further lead.

The Japanese government's industrial strategy is designed to see that Japan gets an even bigger share of the world market. We cannot say they are wrong to do this and to be protectionist. They have succeeded in the same way that France and Germany have succeeded. Both are countries which it is difficult for the outsider to penetrate. They have done it by government and private sector working together to defeat the competition. Britain has lacked this clear industrial strategy, which involves industry and government co-operating closely. Even the Americans do not leave investment to free enterprise. They have built up part of the West Coast as one of the great electronic areas of the world. There is gigantic investment by the Pentagon. They offer small firms a four million dollar development or research programme. Money is poured into American firms so that they can build up a big computer presence.

Dogma has stood in the way of our progress in recent years. It does not matter whether you support the theories of Adam Smith or Milton Friedman. What you have to do is to look at the practices of all your competitors. That is the only way you will succeed.

France has a system in which industrialists and civil servants interchange. They all know each other and went to school together. They control what happens partly through the nationalized banks. Crédit Agricole decides on the agricultural policy for France. There are massive hidden subsidies through the banking system. If they do not want you to come in, you do not. They stopped Japanese electronic goods by making them all go through one tiny, slow-moving port. The lamb war was another classic example. When the European Court found in our favour in the lamb war, a senior French civil servant contacted all the seven meat importers in France and said that ministers would not be 'amused' if they imported British lamb. I know of the threat because one of the importers was a subsidiary of a British firm. You cannot imagine any British civil servant doing that.

The French could sometimes be co-operative and sometimes aggravating. I had a brush with Valéry Giscard d'Estaing, then Minister for Finance and later the French President, during the Tokyo GATT round of talks in 1973.

We had an initial battle before we went to Tokyo over what should be the position of the EEC Commission in the negotiations, but finally agreed. I flew over the Soviet Union and through the day to reach Tokyo airport at midnight. Our ambassador met me at the airport with the unwelcome news that Giscard had changed his mind and now disagreed with the line to be put by the Commission in the negotiations. A Council of Ministers meeting was waiting to take place immediately. I drove to it tired and annoyed. Giscard explained that, on reflection, France wanted something different. I said it was outrageous that having made an agreement in Brussels he should throw Europe into disarray just at the moment the talks were to start. Ministers from other countries endorsed my stand. Giscard wanted to break off the talks, but I said we must stay until we agreed and we remained until 4 or 5 a.m. In the end, the French relented and we were able to offer a united European view.

At the opening session of the talks the next day Giscard came up to me and said he presumed I was pleased with my victory of the night before. He added, 'But, as you become more experienced in politics, you will realize such triumphs are momentary.' He then walked away, but later that day he dropped me a note saying he was sorry if he appeared angry and suggesting we should meet. We dined together and afterwards enjoyed a good relationship.

My quest for trade took me to Eastern Europe too. We wanted to export the 1–11 aircraft to Romania and were poised to agree a sizable order. The Hungarians were the most entrepreneurial of the eastern bloc nations and there was the possibility of doing more business there, too.

I asked the Hungarian Minister of Finance how he financed the farmers. He said his farmers were always unhappy. I said we had farmers like that. He said that last year they were so unhappy he had sent out the president of the Communist Party to placate them. He said to one of the farmers, 'What kind of year have you had?' Back came the reply: 'Medium. Worse than last year, better than next.' They had all the best anti-Russian jokes.

I was the first British Cabinet Minister to go to Romania. A month before, Harold Wilson had gone as leader of the Opposition. The Romanian President had given a great banquet in his honour and this received a good deal of publicity in Britain. I was going to do specific business and I was led to believe that the Romanians welcomed the visit of a British Cabinet Minister. The programme provided for me to meet the President, Nicolae Ceaucescu, on the first day; on the second he was to give a banquet in my honour.

When I arrived our ambassador informed me that I would not be seeing the President, he would not be giving me a banquet and I would be seeing only Foreign Ministers. I said we would leave. The ambassador said we should give them a chance and warn them of our intention. I was about to see the Foreign Minister and made our position clear to him. I said I was shocked about the change of programme. He said the President was electioneering in northern Romania. I asked how many candidates there were and he said one. I said there should be no great problem if there was only one candidate and the idea that he had not known this before I left London was incredible. A few weeks before they had given a terrific reception to a Socialist leader. Were they trying to contrast it with this poor treatment of a non-Socialist? I said I would tell the British public of what had happened. The credit facilities for the aircraft would have to be abandoned.

Rather like Disraeli in Berlin, I said that I had my own plane and I would be leaving at four o'clock that afternoon. At three o'clock the embassy was told that the President was returning and would be hosting a dinner the following night and would like to see me that evening at 6 p.m. We did the aircraft deal, but I cannot say I enjoyed the meeting when I did get it. You sensed the President's megalomania the moment you met him. The palace was ostentatious and he sat on what amounted to a throne. He was clearly running the whole government, with the help of his family.

Energy policy, in one form or another, occupied much of my time at the DTI. I took the attitude that, all right, OPEC was causing serious difficulties, but it had also had the other effect of opening up markets to us. I was not nervous about the adverse balance. Part of it was the oil balance. I did barter deals. Hushang Ansary, the Iranian Minister of Finance, came in for the biennial talks on the Anglo-Iranian trade agreement. I found such talks a waste of time. Civil servants did all the preparation before the talks took place. You gave him lunch. He gave you dinner. You issued a communiqué which was drafted before he even arrived and it was purely chatting up and pleasantry.

The Iranian minister struck me as lively, so I took a risk. I said it might sound terrible because I was delighted he was here, but we were to have a series of talks this morning, this evening and tomorrow morning when the work had been done already by our civil servants. Quite honestly, all we would say at the end of it was that we loved Iran and Iran loved Britain. It meant nothing. I said I would prefer to tell him what I wanted. Oil. I desperately wanted as much as I could have from him. If he told me what he wanted, I would arrange it for him. Instead of all this guff and platitudes, we could actually get down to business.

'You can let me have X million pounds of oil and I can let you have X million pounds of the raw materials, machinery and equipment you want.'

He uttered a sigh of relief and said it was a first rate idea. He had now been to five other countries for talks of this kind and they were all a total waste of time.

He accepted that we should cancel our planned meetings and

meet again for lunch with a list of the items which Iran wanted. His list contained some difficult requests. I called my Permanent Secretary, now Sir Peter Carey, and asked which were the best firms to supply them. He said we could not do this because it ran counter to the whole principle of the DTI and the old Board of Trade. The department never favoured one firm against another. On chemicals we could not contact ICI because other companies would ask why they had not been invited. We would be showing partiality. I said that was exactly what I wanted to show, partiality. I wanted the best firms in our judgement.

He predicted a tremendous row. I said that when I landed £300 million of exports I would go to the dispatch box in the House of Commons and apologize for being partial. I would take all the blame, but if there was any credit I would take it all. 'I order you to let me know who you think are the best firms. I will phone the chief executives and ask them to get down here this afternoon.'

Peter really loved it. He was quite rightly advising me on the traditional approach and the possible protests. When I ordered him, he entered into the spirit enthusiastically. It is probably what he had wanted to do all his life. We phoned all the chief executives. They all rushed to London. We tied up a deal within three days. Instead of the usual meaningless communiqué, we announced we were getting millions of pounds' worth of oil and giving millions of exports in exchange. Equally important, it was the forerunner of other deals in which we exchanged oil for exports.

One outcome was that I came to know the Shah well and arranged with Tony Barber to meet him to get further oil facilities.

The chemistry was right. I think he liked the decisiveness and our admiration of him. On one occasion, when I was dining in the palace in Teheran, he said he would like his son to attend because he would like him to hear the conversation. The son, aged about thirteen, was condemned to listen to the two of us conferring on the world's problems. I told him I wanted to do further transactions and it was in his interests. He agreed in principle and wanted to discuss the financial aspects. He asked if the Chancellor could go and see him at St Moritz.

There was a nervousness on the part of the Treasury. Should the Chancellor of the Exchequer be seen going cap in hand to the Shah of Iran to get financial facilities? I said that of course he should. It would be nonsense not to. Tony Barber wanted to strengthen the

British economy and it was only a two hour trip to St Moritz. He could be there for lunch and back again the same day. Tony and I discussed it with the Prime Minister and it was agreed he should go.

We went off together with the chiding of the *Daily Express* ringing in our ears. To have the Chancellor going to the ski slopes to ask for oil was not in the great British imperial tradition.

The excursion succeeded, though. We had lunch, another good meeting and, more important, another big deal on oil in exchange for British exports. The Shah was also concerned about the depositing of money in London. He was moving money round the world, a good deal going to the United States. We felt it would be good to have some of it in London and persuaded him of this.

These deals proved to be extremely good value. The price of oil came down and the price of exports went up, so that although the deal was designed originally as a balancing act, events outside our control gave Britain a surplus. It could have gone the other way, but it went the right way from our viewpoint.

I decided there were areas of the world where our export performance was appalling. Oil-rich Venezuela was an example. I tried to open it up, but did not succeed there. You would go out to Venezuela and reach trade agreements, but nothing would happen. You would write letters, but get no replies. In theory, we were supplying two per cent of their imports. If it had been ten per cent, we would have been in big figures.

We did, however, have increasing trade with China and Iran. We developed it with Europe by livening up the export trade facilities. The Foreign Office agreed to raise the standing of the commercial staff of our embassies. At the start, the commercial attaché was not even in the mainstream of diplomacy. You became commercial attaché, but never got further.

Alec Douglas-Home, who was Foreign Secretary at this time, agreed that Britain's future depended so much upon the commercial links round the world that the Foreign Office must change its attitude. The career structure was altered so that you were more likely to become ambassador if you had done well as a commercial attaché. Suddenly the best brains in the Foreign Office became interested in the commercial side.

I liked Sir Alec and had an immense admiration for him. As Trade Secretary I went to Council of Ministers meetings with him. I remember one in Luxembourg. We stayed with the ambassador and on a warm, sunny morning, before the Council of Ministers began, went for a walk in the gardens, next to the main road. We sat down in a couple of deck chairs and to my surprise Sir Alec took off not only his jacket, but also his tie and shirt. Here was the British Foreign Secretary, a full blown member of the aristrocracy even if he had disclaimed his peerage, sunbathing with the whole of Luxembourg passing by and looking at this man happily sitting in the sun. I think I took off my tie.

At this time the activities of the companies in the City were under scrutiny and Ted came out with his memorable phrase about the unacceptable face of British capitalism. I was trying to get much more disclosure of information by firms. Sir Geoffrey Howe had the detailed responsibility for the policy.

Then the Hill-Samuel-Slater-Walker merger was proposed. It was obviously something which the government needed to look at. I was in the embarrassing position of being the minister in charge. Though I had no vested interest or shares, my name was associated and there would be suspicions whatever decision I made.

I said to Ted that I could not handle it personally. I asked permission to make a clear statement that I would have nothing to do with the examination and this would be carried out by Geoffrey Howe.

In the Thatcher years the assumption was made by my detractors that I was against all aspects of the free economy. The reality is that in these years at the Department of Trade and Industry, I began the privatization process by offering Thomas Cook, which had been nationalized with British Rail, for auction. It was purchased by one of the clearing banks.

I also saved Rolls-Royce Motors from nationalization. The company got into difficulties as a result of the ruinous RB211 engine contract, encouraged by Tony Benn, and the government could have been left with Rolls-Royce Motors as a nationalized industry. I arranged for it to be floated off privately. I have always recognized the weaknesses of nationalized industries and was pleased to have started to move back the frontiers.

Tessa got into the news. Tony Crosland, a Labour minister, had caused controversy for accepting a silver tea-pot. The story broke the week before Tessa was due to launch a ship in a north-west dockyard.

The tradition is that when a woman launches a ship she is given a piece of jewellery, but the ministerial rules lay down that wives cannot accept such a gift. The form was that she took the present and then gave it back, or gave it to the Treasury to sell it, or personally paid for the present and kept it. On the two occasions she launched a ship, which was an exciting thing to do, I was not going to say she must give it back afterwards. I paid for the jewellery.

In this particular case, the present was a watch with diamonds set around it, worth quite a sum. I fortunately sent a cheque before the ceremony, and before the Crosland story broke.

The chairman got up at the lunch and asked Tessa to take the watch as a small token of appreciation for launching the ship, without, naturally, saying that I had paid for it. The press was clearly ready to write a story about another scandal. I said I was in something of a predicament when I suddenly discovered the shipyard was giving this generous gift. Should I be corrupted? I decided that it was such a nice watch and they were such lovely diamonds that I would be corrupted and wanted to announce the award of another contract to the shipyard. All the journalists looked starry-eyed, wondering what was coming next. The only specification, I said, was that it must be of a size that my five-year-old son could sail in his bath. Everyone laughed and that was the end of the story.

About three months later a parcel arrived addressed to Jonathan containing a wooden replica of the ship which Tessa had launched, made by the apprentices in the yard – for Jonathan to sail in his bath.

The steel industry provided another challenge. I discovered our steel was being produced at much higher costs than most of our competitors'.

The reasons were our outdated steel works and serious overmanning. Production was much higher under new methods. The Japanese, Koreans, Germans and Americans had all put in new steel technology and cut costs sharply. We had not done that. I agreed with the British Steel board that we must have a big investment programme to introduce new methods and make the industry competitive with the rest of the world. But this meant the closure of many existing old steel works and a considerable loss of jobs. I believed that if you did not do that, British Steel would melt away.

I did make a miscalculation. I made a perfectly good estimate about the potential of British Steel alongside our competitors, but without taking into account the fact that our competitors would be enhancing their investment programmes at the same time.

It is a quite common fault of governments and the private sector. A company might, for example, decide that do-it-yourself is the boom market and it will invest outside major cities, say Bristol. What it forgets is that other firms are opening do-it-yourself centres round Bristol at the same time. Luckily, the miscalculation would not have mattered too much if we had stayed in power. By the time I had made the closures and started on the investment, I would have seen that the worldwide demand for steel was lower than expected.

Obtaining Cabinet agreement for the steel investment programme was not easy. I prepared a paper on what should be done, only to hear Ted Heath open the Cabinet discussion by saying: 'The Secretary of State has come to us with proposals for a huge investment in British Steel. I am quite certain we shall not be foolish enough to accept them. Secretary of State, I ask you to introduce your paper.' I argued strongly that unless we acted there was no future for British Steel and its demise would have a damaging effect on the balance of payments and those industries which needed the steel. I said it was also nonsense to keep an overmanned and decades out of date industry.

The result was a bitter Cabinet battle with the Treasury and other ministers siding with the Prime Minister against this lone voice. We agreed to set up a Cabinet committee under the Prime Minister. At one stage, Ted told me I had got all my information from the board of British Steel. Why should the Cabinet accept its judgements? I retorted that if he thought it was a rotten board, he should sack them all and bring in the men of genius whom he thought much better. I said I had examined their proposals in great depth and commended British Steel's courage in going for a long series of closures. If he thought they were wrong, he ought to have the whole British Steel board before the Cabinet and discover for himself. I told him that was what I had done. He could do the same. Ted said that was precisely what we would do.

'The Cabinet will meet the board and we will do it next Friday morning,' he declared. In fact, the Cabinet met the chairman, Lord Melchett, and the deputy chairman, Monty Finniston. They came before Cabinet to face two hours of the most hostile questioning imaginable. Questions were prepared by the Cabinet Office. At the end of the inquisition, Ted said in a gruff voice, 'Well, I suppose you'd better get on with it' and walked out of the room.

He was not being as unreasonable as he might seem. Prime Ministers have a large workload and a huge volume of advice on every issue. If they have doubt about a recommendation, they will put it to the test by themselves strongly opposing it. If the minister presenting the proposal then folds up and admits that he has not thought of a particular aspect, perhaps offering to come back with another paper, they think, 'Thank God I did that. He had not done his homework.' If the minister fights like mad for it, the Prime Minister has to admit that perhaps his own brief is wrong and the proposal is accepted. Margaret and Ted used the same method.

The standing of ministers who retreated would almost certainly go down. I can think of ministers under both Ted and Margaret who, pressed by the Prime Minister, said they had got it wrong and came back with a new paper. This pleased the Prime Minister, but he would say to himself, 'I have to keep a watch on that minister in future.'

It was remarkable that during that Cabinet there was never, ever any disagreement on broad issues. Margaret and Sir Keith Joseph always agreed. Both went for big increases in public expenditure. There never was a moment in which the Cabinet was divided, on either foreign or domestic policy. It was some time before I realized that all Cabinets were not like this. It was a great surprise to find serious divisions arising in the Shadow Cabinet after we lost the General Election in 1974. This was bad, because it occurred between two elections only months apart, when we should have been concentrating on beating Labour.

Perhaps we should have realized slightly earlier that the seeds of dissension were being sown. In 1973 Keith Joseph, Margaret and Geoffrey Howe asked Ted to lend his support to fund-raising to set up a Centre for Policy Studies. As I recall it, he was told the centre would promote the importance of free enterprise. What it actually did was to advocate a particularly extreme *laissez-faire* policy, a view not shared by Ted Heath or a majority of the Cabinet. Under Mrs Thatcher the centre became highly influential. It will no doubt continue to provide lively reading, but, I suspect, without the influence it once had.

The steel modernization was not a split over a principle, but over the detail and magnitude of what I was proposing and I was being put to the test. Having won my point I decided I would go personally to all the steel plants to be closed and explain for myself. Labour opposed closures anywhere.

I explained that we were not being negative. We were to invest a substantial sum of money to have a modern industry. I went first to Cardiff, where I met the trade union leaders, the Lord Mayor and Jim Callaghan and George Thomas, local MPs, at the town hall. Outside, demonstrators were protesting at the closure of the East Moors steel works. They argued it was a good plant. I argued that it was outdated.

I drove from there to Ebbw Vale to be met by Michael Foot and the managers of the steel works there. There were no demonstrations and I had a most impressive meeting. Michael Foot said he wanted me to hear what the men had to say.

I spent the afternoon with shop stewards who came forward with their plan to cut costs, the labour force and improve productivity. I had to say that I would, of course, go back to the steel board and have their scheme examined in great detail, but I feared that their method of steel working would not be good enough. I recognized that Ebbw Vale was dependent on coal and steel and promised to do everything I could to attract new industry. I told them I would write giving full reasons if I rejected their plan. They were able and sincere and I could understand that after the recession of the 1930s they were passionate about keeping the industry going. Michael acted in a civilized way and I went away depressed that we were likely to keep only a tiny percentage of the workforce in Ebbw Vale. I was simply not going to be able to site a new steel works there. I had announced where we were to put the big new steel plants.

At Shotton in North Wales we had another excellent group of men with a no-strike record, but again there was no way in which we could keep the plant open. They staged an intensive lobbying campaign and I met them personally.

The tragedy was that the election came and we lost. Tony Benn added to his catalogue of errors in other directions by announcing that there would be no steel closures of any description. Nor, I would add, any modernization programme. What happened was that the capacity built up, inability to compete got worse and the losses escalated.

Eventually Labour decided it would have to make closures. I am told that Michael Foot said he would like the closures at Ebbw Vale to be announced before the 1979 General Election, so that we could start encouraging alternative industries, but the Labour Cabinet was against announcing anything as potentially damaging electorally before the election. The Ebbw Vale closures were announced, together with a package of money for the Welsh Development Agency to attract new firms.

Michael Foot was unpopular and encountered hostility from his steel workers, but he was absolutely right. I admired the way he handled my proposals and, later, Labour's own proposals. He was straight and honourable.

We did have another, happier point of contact. During my time as Secretary of State I had a great character as my driver, Winnie Dabin. When I went out and Michael became a minister, she went to him. Then when Labour lost the 1979 election and I was seen going to Downing Street, he phoned up Winnie and said Peter Walker was going to get office. He told her, 'I know you liked working for him and have phoned up Downing Street and told them that whatever else they do they must make you his driver.'

The sequel is that when he became Opposition Leader he was entitled to a driver and a car. He dropped me a note saying that Winnie was the most marvellous person in his political life. Could he possibly have her back? I replied that if she wanted to be his driver and there was the possibility that he might one day be Prime Minister, then of course he could have her back. But I could not order her. I was happy for him to approach her. She must decide. I told Winnie. She said, 'Dear old Michael. I will go and sort him out.'

I subsequently got a nice note from Michael to say that Winnie had been to see him and he realized she should stay with me.

When Winnie Dabin retired I wrote to Michael saying that Tessa and I intended to give her a farewell dinner and would he and his wife, Jill, like to come. He said he would love to and there was the extraordinary scene of a Tory Cabinet Minister and the Leader of the Opposition dining in honour of Winnie. She was extremely intelligent, a fine driver and a very determined lady. Had she had a different educational background, she would have been a Permanent Secretary and not a driver. If you were driving long distances with her, you could have any conversation in the world. If you wanted to rest, that was fine, too. Michael still brings her out of retirement if he has to make long journeys to Wales or elsewhere.

I think Michael's problem was that he emerged in politics as a left-wing, pacifist rebel, a committed Socialist, devoted to Nye Bevan. No one ever thought of giving him office because he was not that sort of person. Then he did emerge as a popular figure of the left and got into the Shadow Cabinet and later the Cabinet. He was a thoroughly competent minister, bringing liveliness to the conduct of his departments.

But when he won the leadership it was to the joy of Tories, because they knew that the country looked upon him as an anti-nuclear, anti-defence, Socialist figure. He tried to push his past allegiances into the background and made perfectly good speeches, moving to the centre of economic policy and avoiding nationalization, but he could not defeat us. The Falklands factor was too strong and people remembered his left-wing past. To be fair to him, he never wanted to deny he was a Socialist or pacifist. He was trapped.

When he decided to go, he did manage to organize who he wanted to be the next leader, the chap from the next valley, also left wing, also sharing his views on the nuclear deterrent and socialism, a young boyo popular in the tea room for his good humour and jokes. He arranged it so that this man, Neil Kinnock, could, quite extraordinarily, defeat seasoned Roy Hattersley for the leadership.

I do not think Michael would have been a good Prime Minister, because of his pacifism and his inbuilt passion to see Socialism succeed. The sadness for him was that his ideals were no longer relevant.

Energy, not steel, caused the first serious strains in my relationship with Ted: he said he wanted to take responsibility for energy away from the Department of Trade and Industry.

This happened when the oil and fuel crisis was at its height and every popular newspaper was saying there should be a separate Department of Energy. I believed he was bowing to unthinking pressure from the media.

The media case was flawed and pure gimmickry. If you had a Department of Energy, it would be a small department and small departments had small clout.

Everybody, Ted included, agreed my team was handling the oil crisis extremely well. I had the initial problem that the civil service team was not the strongest. One, under pressure, came close to a breakdown and Tom Boardman, Peter Emery and myself effectively ran it.

Much of the pressure came from oil companies who wanted petrol rationing. They gave me stock figures they said called for rationing. But I knew that the oil companies were not entirely disinterested.

Rationing would have suited them financially. We had a prices policy when other countries did not. If they supplied less oil to Britain, they would be able to get better prices elsewhere.

I stood up in the Commons and said that while I was issuing petrol coupons in case there was a future emergency, I was not going to ration petrol unless I was forced to. It is the only time I can remember sitting down after a Commons statement when both sides were totally opposed to what I said.

There was a good press cutting from the *Economist* the following Friday. It was headed Peter and the Wolves. It just listed one after the other, the editorial comments from the *Sun*, *Mail*, *Express*, *Telegraph* and *Times* on why I was off my head not to ration petrol. It made no comment, but at the end of the piece said if, by chance, motorists were again offered Green Shield stamps at the petrol stations, we should know that Peter was right and the wolves were wrong. The point was that in a genuine petrol crisis in which everyone was stocking up, the garages did not have to give Green Shield stamps. When they had ample supplies of oil, the stamps would return.

About three months later, I went to a petrol station and was offered Green Shield stamps.

What I did know was that I had done my homework on coal and on oil and that I was pursuing an effective, tough policy which was succeeding. Convincing others was more difficult. Part of the demand for a separate department arose because Peter Walker would not ration petrol. I did impose speed limits to reduce consumption, but knew that petrol rationing would be almost impossible to administer. It would have been monstrously unfair. What did you give drivers who lived in the countryside as opposed to those in towns? How did you discriminate between two neighbours, one of whom was a commercial traveller or had to travel a great deal for his business and the other of whom used his car at weekends for pure pleasure? What did you do between husband and wife? Of course, you could operate a crude system, but it was a potential disaster area. If you had to, you did it. We did not have to and I knew that if we showed a little constraint we would manage. The oil companies knew that, too. The trouble was they also knew that the less petrol they sold here, the better for their profits.

I saw Ted regularly and no warning cones were hoisted. Then I discovered that he had met Peter Carrington and Willie Whitelaw and they had decided to create a new Department of Energy with Lord Carrington in charge.

When Ted did tell me about this decision, I said he was wrong and he must not do it. I asked if there was any question about the way I had handled the crisis. He said there was not. I had handled it well, but the whole country wanted a separate minister. I said, 'Look. You are in the middle of a very major crisis. You say I am handling it well. I know the quality of the civil servants, the quality of the oil companies. I know exactly what I am doing and I am telling you that you cannot bring in anyone, yourself or any genius you like to name, at this moment of crisis to handle it as well. I think it is extraordinary you should come to this conclusion without discussing it with me. If you wanted to come to a conclusion like that, you should have called me in and at least asked me if I thought the change should be made.'

I could not care less personally. He could take away any part of my ministry if he wanted to, but it was dangerous to do it in the middle of a crisis. The new team would have to take time to learn about energy and would have to make judgements about civil servants and others when it did not have the background to do so. The only victor would be gimmickry and public relations.

If Ted had sought my advice, I would have been happy to make changes once the critical phase was over. Ted disagreed and I said that he should find a new Secretary of State for Trade and Industry. I was not going to sit by and let energy be taken away without a word of consultation.

I went to the length of minuting the Prime Minister, saying that I believed strongly that the setting up of a new department would have substantial disadvantages. Morale would be damaged seriously, work would be slowed up, the position of the regional offices would be difficult and there would be delay in the choice of nuclear reactors.

There was a major conflict. Ted said he still wanted to make the change, but had to go off to Washington. I should think about it further.

Willie Whitelaw was sent round to urge me not to resign. My resignation would bring down Sterling and damage the economy. I repeated that I was not empire-building, but the change at that point would be catastrophic.

'You have no idea of the people I am dealing with, how tough I am having to be,' I said. 'Peter Carrington whom I admire and like would make a superb minister of whatever you like. You can make him Secretary of State for Trade and Industry if you want, but this is not the moment to do it.'

Willie said that whatever happened I must not resign and he would have words with Ted when he came back.

He did so and it was agreed that we would not create a new Department of Energy until the worst of the crisis was over and oil supplies were adequate. This took two or three weeks and then the handover did take place. I briefed Peter Carrington as best I could, but he and his team made a series of mistakes. Patrick Jenkin introduced a touch of near-farce by doing his 'clean your teeth in the dark' bit.

They also made a terrible mistake on nuclear energy. It was not that they were not good ministers. It was just that their decisions were too rushed. I had been chairman of the Nuclear Advisory Board and about to go to Cabinet to argue for a switch to the Westinghouse reactor.

I had looked at three alternatives, including the AGR nuclear reactor. It had come as a great shock to me, when I became Secretary of State for Trade and Industry, to find myself chairman of the Nuclear Advisory Board of top government scientists, generating boards and outsiders. I could still remember my physics master writing on my report when I was fourteen: 'This is a disastrous result. There is no point in him taking physics again.' I never did.

I admitted that I did not understand the subject and asked for a teach-in. Top professors of nuclear physics came in. I applied an ice-pack on my head and did eventually become tolerably knowledgeable about nuclear physics. Victor Rothschild, who headed the No. 10 think tank, was a member of the board and I had heard all the arguments and then cross-examined witnesses. Sadly the AGR was not on. Westinghouse was the only reactor working well round the world and it was cost effective.

Despite the political objection to going American, we should go for it. Peter Carrington came in and decided that the politics of going American were wrong and we should opt instead for a British reactor. He was clearly acting without sufficient background knowledge.

He never implemented the policy. The General Election intervened, but when Tony Benn arrived he also chose the British way. Effectively what happened was that we lost the period from 1974 to

1983 in developing nuclear energy. It was not until Margaret appointed me Energy Secretary that I gave the go-ahead to Sizewell – with a Westinghouse reactor. In these lost years France busily developed its nuclear industry and we now import electricity from France.

Ironically, Peter Carrington paid a personal price. He left government over the Falklands and later became chairman of GEC. GEC would have built the Westinghouse reactors if he had decided upon that course.

It may not seem like it after the scrap over energy, but the Cabinet was basically happy. No member was disliked and we were ahead in the polls until the fateful combination of the coal strike and the OPEC crisis brought us down.

The energy skirmish did not damage my personal relations with Ted, either. These had always been uncomplicated. We liked each other. He genuinely felt that having decided to make the change, I would not be an empire-builder and stand in the way. Someone who was a good chum and friend and totally loyal would acquiesce. It may have been partly my fault that I had not gone to him earlier and explained the complication of somebody else taking over so quickly.

Ted's relations with people he thought were trusted friends were sometimes insensitive. He thought they would agree automatically. Charlie Morrison was a classic example. Charlie, who shared the flat with Ian Gilmour and myself and took an active part in Ted's leadership campaign, was a good friend. Ted used to go shooting and spending holidays with the Morrisons and knew Charlie extremely well. He appointed Charlie to be my Shadow Minister of Sport before the 1970 General Election and Charlie did the job terrifically conscientiously. He even went to the length making himself sick by agreeing, in the course of duty, to go gliding.

When Ted won the election and asked me to take on the Ministry of Housing and Local Government, I said I assumed he would make Charlie Minister of Sport. He said he was not going to because Charlie was a great friend and was one of the few MPs who would not mind being left off the ministerial list. He had a great many people who *would* mind. I said I thought he was wrong. Charlie had done the shadow job well and was liked in the sporting world. He could not say that because he was a good friend he would leave him out. Charlie desperately wanted to be a minister and deserved it. Ted said he knew Charlie and he would not mind at all. He appointed

SPARKING INDUSTRY

Eldon Griffiths and Charlie, having spent two years shadowing sport, got nothing, not even a phone call from Ted. I was horrified and Charlie was upset. Again it was Ted's judgement. 'This chap likes me. I am close to him. I don't need to give him a post.'

9

MISUNDERSTOOD

The tragedy for Ted Heath and, I believe, for Britain is that he did not have longer as Prime Minister.

His critics have tended to concentrate on his personal short-comings. He did upset people by cross-examining them and arguing against them when he thought they were wrong. He would not tolerate anything he thought was bogus or dishonest.

I knew this as well as anyone. At one point I advised Ted to spend more time in the smoking room since MPs were seeing too little of him as Prime Minister. I went into the smoking room a few days later to find he had taken my advice and was talking to a distinguished Tory. As I passed, I heard him say, 'That was a dreadful speech you made last Wednesday.'

Businessmen also got on the wrong side of him. They are sometimes arrogant and pompous people. Dining with him, they were surprised by his fierce cross-examination on their attitudes to their own companies and the economy. They expected courtesy and platitudes and got something entirely different. He did not think of himself as being ill-mannered, he was simply trying to have a lively dialogue with them. Some of the businessmen were not used to lively dialogues.

Underlying it all was a fierce loyalty to Britain, a great breadth of vision and a determination to improve the lot of its people. I remember him inviting President Pompidou and Willy Brandt to Chequers for a weekend discussion on how to advance Europe in the next ten years. The meeting was a success. All shared a vision of a Europe which was stronger economically and could exercise influence in the world. They were three popular leaders of their countries, all agreed

The young patriot.   *The young MP.*

Ted Heath (Shadow Chancellor) and the team that fought the
1965 Finance Bill.

*Developing my international interests: above, with the Shah
of Iran during oil negotiations, 1973; below, with Chou en Lai
to discuss the development of trade between Britain and
China, also 1973.*

The signing of an Anglo-Soviet trade and scientific treaty, 1973.

Beer and sausages in Bavaria with Herr Ertl, the German Minister of Agriculture, 1979.

Meetings with two Argentinian presidents, 1981. With President Videla, seated centre, above, and with his successor, President Viola, below.

The Boyhood of Young Conservatives"
Peter Brookes after Millais

AWFULLY WET

A cartoonist's reaction to one of my 'middle way' lectures.

With Jim Prior and John Nott at the Conservative Party Conference, 1980.

Early Thatcher years: I had already been branded as a rebel by the press.

The State Opening of Parliament, 1986: we await Black Rod's summons to the House of Lords. Left to right: John Wakeham, Sir Geoffrey Howe, Margaret Thatcher, Nigel Lawson, Peter Walker, Kenneth Baker.

Peter — a marvellous day in the Rhondda — Margaret

With Margaret in the valleys, March 1990.

*Nearing the end of my political career, but still a useful figure
for the cartoonists.*

on the vision, though they accepted there would be difficulties in achieving it.

Such are the twists of fate that a year later Pompidou was dead, Brandt had resigned and Ted Heath had been defeated at a General Election.

Perhaps one of the great unanswered questions of history is what Ted Heath might still have been able to achieve in Europe if Joe Gormley had been able to deliver the miners' vote and there had been no strike.

I think that if he had remained in power, there would have been a great enthusiasm about Europe. Progress would have been faster. As a result of Robert Carr's legislation on trade unions and the way he was surmounting the oil crisis, Ted Heath would have been seen to be an outstanding Prime Minister. We would have continued the fight against unemployment and struck the right balance between compassion and efficiency. He would have had a place of prominence among former Prime Ministers.

History may yet give him that place. Former Prime Ministers are defeated and in that moment rated as failures. When the period is looked at objectively, a different conclusion is often reached. Ted, though Prime Minister for only a relatively short time, started the reform of the trade unions, set up new structures in government, worked us into Europe and established an international reputation. I think he will be seen to have had a decisive input.

There are so many 'ifs'. The fall actually came after a partial success. We faced, in those final months of the Heath administration, a colossal inflation push as a result of the OPEC oil increases. During my twenty months at Trade and Industry, the cost of imported raw materials, for example, went up more than they had done in the previous 150 years.

It was a savage blow to the economy. Some argued that we should have gone in for a sharp deflationary policy. The unanimous view of the Cabinet, however, was that this would be a disaster. It would simply have ruined a large part of British industry and its competitive ability. Deflationary measures on top of a huge increase in the price of imported materials would have been too much to bear, so the economic strategy was right. But what we also wanted was maximum restraint in wages and prices and we tried to reach agreement with the unions to get this. We would have achieved it, but for the objections of two hard men.

The final meeting with TUC leaders at Downing Street when Ted, Tony Barber, Willie Whitelaw, myself and others met the TUC was a watershed. We offered a package of measures to help their members, in return for a period of pay restraint and saving jobs which would otherwise be lost. We were genuinely trying to be fair, reasonable and understanding. Ted, Tony Barber, Robert Carr and Willie Whitelaw had had many discussions with individual trade union leaders and everybody in that room was ready to co-operate, except two. One was Richard Briginshaw, the print union leader, and the other was Hugh Scanlon, of the engineering union.

What the TUC could not do was to be divided and say 'some of us will and some of us won't'. The government accepted that. Scanlon and Briginshaw both said they would have no part in an agreement. Briginshaw spoke first and Scanlon followed. If we had agreed a voluntary policy and the unions had fulfilled their part, it would have been a breakthrough for the economy. We were so close.

But even this was not the cause of the government's fall. The cause were another two, rather less known, trade unionists, so little known that few remember their names. When we knew the miners were contemplating industrial action if they did not get the pay increase they were demanding, I saw Joe Gormley and tried to persuade him that if their case was as justified as they thought, the new Relativities Board would make the award in their favour. I argued that surely, at a time when the OPEC crisis was hitting the nation and oil supplies were in danger, it was reasonable to go to the Relativities Board before taking industrial action.

I said I would ask the Relativities Board to consider their case immediately and urged him to try to persuade his executive, in the national interest, to go through the board mechanism. I thought they should accept the findings, but if they did not like them they could still take their decision on whether or not to strike.

He said that he would try, though the union was opposed to the Relativities Board and anything which smacked of incomes policy. He then came back and said the problem was that his members feared that if the Relativities Board recommended a high award, the government could still give a lower one. If I could promise that the government would honour whatever the Relativities Board proposed, he would deliver the NUM executive and there would be no strike.

122

I asked for time to consult and took the issue to the Cabinet. I said we did not have much choice. If the Relativities Board did make a recommendation and we said we did not accept it, it would undermine the board, put the government in an impossible position and probably win the miners the support of the whole country. The reality was that whatever the board recommended, we would have agreed in these particular circumstances. If a commitment to accept the board's findings enabled Joe Gormley to stop a strike, we should give it.

My colleagues were concerned that if we did it on this occasion, we would have to do it on others. I said we would simply have to admit we were making a special case of the miners. The Cabinet concurred. I could tell Joe Gormley 'Yes.' Joe Gormley expressed his thanks and went away very happily, but then contacted me a few days later to say he was very sorry, but the executive had decided to go for a ballot for industrial action.

He explained that he had been certain of winning by two votes, but had not taken sufficiently into account that there were two members of the executive up for re-election. The left wing had got at them and said it would do everything in its power to see they were not re-elected if they voted for acceptance.

Two people he thought he could count on had, without warning, voted against him.

The executive then had to argue for a strike and won the vote. They put on peaceful pickets and no one broke the picket lines, but we had a damaging and potentially ruinous coal dispute.

The awful thing was that the day after the election the Relativies Board reported and made its recommnendations and the miners accepted them and went back to work under a Labour government. If the Gormley-Walker formula had been applied, it would have worked out the same for miners and none of the political or economic consequences would have followed. There would have been no election, Ted Heath would have continued to govern and inflation would have come down rapidly.

It is also true that if Ted Heath had gone for the General Election three weeks earlier, he would almost certainly have won it. He almost did and there is broad agreement that the tide began to go against him in those last three weeks.

At this point there was no free market voice in the Cabinet. Geoffrey Howe actually carried out the prices part of the policy.

Keith Joseph later argued we should control the money supply, but neither he nor Margaret nor Geoffrey did so at the time. It was the unanimous view that we should go for a voluntary pay agreement and when that chance was lost, we should go for a statutory policy.

The free-marketeers later suggested that the attempt at pay and price control was always folly, that periods of wage restraint were followed by a flood of unstoppable demands and the dam eventually burst. That is not true. There was a burst in 1974, but that was because the incoming Labour government said to the unions that they were free to do what they wanted. We had a wage explosion and inflation shot up. If we had remained in power the miners would have taken the Relativities Board settlement and there would have been no wage explosion.

During the phase, the Labour Party expressed hostility to any form of incomes policy, but we did convince the majority of the trade unions, including Jack Jones of the Transport and General Workers' Union. We were offering a package, including rent rebates, which would have protected the ordinary trade unionist.

Some aspects of the dispute surprised us. When we went over to the three-day week, production in most factories remained the same. It showed the low productivity of British industry and its capacity to do better. Some firms actually produced more.

The other lesson it taught was the fickleness of some industrialists. Those who came to us at the start of the dispute and said we were absolutely right and whatever happened we must not give in were the same industrialists who returned a few months later, as their profit margins were squeezed, and said whatever happened the government must settle. The most bloodthirsty hawks became the most peacelike doves the moment it got tough for them financially.

I do think we should have gone for the General Election a few weeks earlier. We had the support of the British public, we were ahead in the opinion polls. The public thought it wrong for the miners to strike in the middle of the oil crisis when they were being offered a reasonable deal. They did not mind the measures, but, in my judgement, the more the measures bit, the more the public began to get faint-hearted.

If we had won the election, it would have been clear that the new government was in for five years and it would have become a popular government for having won. As it was, our position in the polls started to deteriorate. When we first went into battle all the polls were on the right side. We had actually improved our popularity and had a lead over Labour.

But then, as earnings were affected by the three-day week and profits slumped, the 'firm action' for which many had called initially became less and less popular.

My political instinct was to go for a quick election. Others genuinely believed that the public would interpret this as the government cutting and running in a difficult situation. The pros and cons were evenly balanced. I think the choice was discussed in Cabinet only once, but discussion went on outside. Like me, Jim Prior wanted an earlier election. Willie Whitelaw, as I recall, did not.

When we did go, we went into the campaign with an easily agreed manifesto. The party machine and the party in the country enthusiastically supported it. Party workers were strongly behind us.

Election day gave us more votes than Labour, but five fewer seats, with the Liberals holding the balance of power with 14 MPs. The crucial decision after the results were announced was whether we should try and link up with the Liberals to keep Labour out. The Cabinet met quickly and it was agreed we should approach Jeremy Thorpe, the Liberal leader, to see what the possibilities were.

Ted met Jeremy, who said he would support a Conservative government only if we would introduce proportional representation at the next General Election. Ted's honesty stood in the way of any shifty deal. He said, totally honourably, that there was no prospect of him being able to deliver his party on the issue. He might be able to deliver the Cabinet, but the whips would be unable to prevail upon Tory MPs to vote in one direction. Each individual member was conscious that he or she had been elected under the present system and might lose under proportional representation. It was asking too much to expect them to go into the lobbies to vote for their own extinction. He would be making a bogus promise to suggest otherwise.

Jeremy Thorpe decided that, without the guarantee, he could not back us. We had no choice but to go into opposition.

Soon after we switched to the Opposition benches, Sir Keith Joseph made the first of his controversial speeches on the need for a monetary policy and confessed publicly that he had got it wrong in the past. He reasoned that if only you got the M3 money supply figure right, all the problems of inflation would be solved. It was the first note of dissent since Ted became leader in 1965. The 1970–74 Cabinet had been united on every important issue. Suddenly there was this one lone voice in disagreement.

Margaret did not side openly with Keith, except to say she thought we should pay careful attention to what he was saying. Geoffrey Howe said he thought there were two sides to the argument and we should consider both. They were not passionately endorsing Keith's view. And the rest of the Shadow Cabinet were convinced that there was no magic which, with the wave of a wand of a particular indicator of money supply, could make your problems disappear.

Sir Keith made a second speech on the same theme and got tremendous publicity. Unfortunately, these two speeches, in the few months between the elections of February and October 1974, gave the impression of a divided party; it did not help in fighting the second election, which gave Labour a real working majority.

After the February election Labour took a series of actions to secure short-term popularity, though they were damaging in the longer-term fight against inflation.

The election went well enough for me personally. In Worcester we had one of the best results in the country. Ted had given me the defence portfolio and I was happy with it, able to consult both Ian Gilmour and Peter Carrington, who had been our defence team, and were friends. As a boy I had seen appeasement fail and was committed to a strong defence. The shadow post gave me the opportunity to confer with generals, admirals and a small army of other military experts.

In opposition, I found myself, once a ardent opponent of the EEC, making powerful speeches on the importance of the European Community: I was now convinced there was no other route.

I also spoke strongly about the need for profit-sharing. President de Gaulle was a source of inspiration. He had used the whole of the post-war period before he came to power to work out a social and economic strategy. He concluded that if capitalism was to succeed, it had to overcome tall obstacles, one of which was the failure of workers to feel they were an important part of the system. He brought forward radical profit-sharing proposals for

France, but was defeated on the issue when the French establishment opposed him.

The removal of de Gaulle had more to do with his passionate desire to change the capitalist system than anything else. He wanted companies throughout France to be committed to profit-sharing schemes. This struck a chord with me. I had always felt that it was essential to tackle the weaknesses of the free market system, if it was to last and prosper. Junior managers and employees had to be brought in.

These were not empty words. I had put my ideas into practice in a modest way. I had steadily transferred the equity of my own Walker Young insurance broker business, which at one stage I had owned outright, to other members of the firm. I saw that it had created a powerful team spirit and all the hard-working and key people felt they were participating in running the firm. If it worked on this small scale, I thought it had a good chance of working on a much bigger and wider scale.

Ted's appointment of Margaret as Treasury spokeswoman after the election did not cause any surprise or appear particularly significant. Ted knew that she had been interested in the economic side, she was a good performer at the dispatch box and he wanted to recognize her talent.

For my own part I had no ambitions for the Shadow Chancellorship. I had occupied the two big new jobs in government and I was shadowing another big department.

My relations with Ted were still warm, but different. Early on I had been the young MP who had organized his five-day leadership election campaign. Then I had worked closely as a Cabinet Minister, but I was no longer the young backbencher mobilizing others to support him. Instead it was a good personal relationship between a senior Shadow Cabinet Minister and his leader.

He came and stayed with us in Worcestershire for the Three Choirs Festival and events like that. The only serious row I had had with him was when he took energy away from Department of Trade and Industry, but I felt no rancour: just that he was wrong.

Margaret concentrated on a vigorous attack on the Labour government's new Finance Bill. Ted had obtained a high profile in attacking a Labour Finance Bill before he became leader; Margaret did the same. Her performance caught the eye of backbenchers and when

Sir Keith Joseph ruled himself out as a potential challenger for the party leadership, she stepped forward.

When Margaret made the startling announcement, we had to decide how to conduct the campaign. Ted concluded, with my complete agreement, that it should be run by his Parliamentary Private Secretaries, Tim Kitson and Kenneth Baker.

This was good sense. Ex-Cabinet Ministers like myself, who were close to a candidate, were not the right people to persuade backbenchers. A leadership campaign is about obtaining the support of backbenchers. If you have Shadow Cabinet Ministers and former Cabinet Ministers running the campaign, it suggests that they are the establishment on the run, anxious to keep their positions. Tim and Kenneth organized the whole of the campaign. All I did was to chat to people they wanted me to see.

I admit that campaign was difficult to run, but I think there was too much complacency. Supporters could not believe that a woman who had never been anything other than Minister of Education could defeat the current male leader who had just been Prime Minister. I think they failed to pick up the seriousness of what turned out to have been a well-organized campaign, led by the late Airey Neave and Edward du Cann.

I believe the Chief Whip, Humphrey Atkins, was also a Thatcherite and this did not help. You always expect a Chief Whip to be totally loyal to the leader of the party and I don't think Ted could have been getting adequate briefing from the whip's office on what was happening. It is the job of the Chief Whip to tell you if there is dissension or plottings. It never happened.

In the election itself, Humphrey made it clear he would be neutral. I found this strange for a man who was part of the team appointed by Ted.

I suspect that Ted was told from the beginning that he would win when this was far from obvious. With hindsight, I think his team underestimated the MPs who would vote against him for personal reasons. Every junior minister you have sacked is against you. To add to his sins, Ted had annoyed backbenchers by his refusal to hand out knighthoods without good reason. There had always been a tradition in the Conservative Party that after MPs had served in the Commons for X years they were given a knighthood. There were probably fifteen Tory MPs who felt – along with their wives – that they should have been dubbed, and blamed Ted for tightening the system. He thought honours were important and should be awarded with great care. If he had not been so punctilious, he might well have stayed on as leader. His campaign managers should have got down to this detail. You have to say that if Bill Bloggs is not saying which way he is voting, it is probably because he is in the group who have lobbied for a knighthood for the last four years. I felt this kind of research may not have been done as thoroughly as it should have been.

Tim Renton has been criticized for failing to keep Margaret Thatcher sufficiently informed of the threat against her in 1990 and for failing to martial her forces, but I do not think he was in the same position as Humphrey Atkins. If you are in government, the people who should keep you informed, apart from the Chief Whip, are the deputy Prime Minister, the Chancellor and the Foreign Secretary. I think they did know that Margaret's approach to Europe was wrong and told her so. That is different from being in opposition, when you do not have a Cabinet and are not seeing people every day. In these circumstances the Chief Whip's responsibility is to be the eyes and ears of the party.

I was in Ted's room when he was told he had lost the leadership to Margaret. There was a feeling of terrible depression. As I have said, I admired him and thought him an outstanding Prime Minister. Not only had he got us into Europe, but he had also struggled imaginatively and honourably with the OPEC crisis and the coal strike. If he had not taken the right decisions on the OPEC price increase, the economy could have been wrecked completely. He had also been far-sighted, as when he called that weekend Chequers meeting with Pompidou and Brandt to discuss the next ten years in Europe.

On a personal level, here was a man who loved being Prime Minister suddenly finding himself no longer even Leader of the Opposition, defeated by a junior Cabinet Minister on simplistic economic arguments which would not stand the test of time. It was a sad moment. He courteously thanked everyone for what they had done.

Ted Heath was always an enthusiast in whatever he was involved in. He was an enthusiast about politics. When he was Chief Whip he was dedicated to that task. When he negotiated in Europe he was dedicated to that. When I first came across him as a Shadow Chancellor and worked under him, he was totally committed to putting up the best possible opposition to the Finance Bill.

Those who knew him as a sailor said he was totally dedicated in that too, demanding and getting near perfection. His musical friends greatly admired his passion and enthusiasm for music, whether he was playing the piano or listening, admiring and understanding a piece.

I do not think he was or is aware of class. If there was a sailor, musican or politician of talent, he admired their ability. Nor was there any chippiness because he had not inherited an estate or great wealth. He had a wide range of friends, people from every part of society. The sadness was that with all his dedication, he never had anybody to whom he could go home.

On a day when things have gone wrong or on a day when we have had some small triumph, it is important to go home to someone who will put it in perspective. If you have had a bad day, they comfort you and point out that what has happened is not the most important thing in the world. If you have had a good day, they can bring you down to earth.

It is the small things that count. I can remember on one occasion enjoying a prolonged standing ovation at the end of a speech. Tessa had to stand whether she wanted to or not. As she got up, she whispered, 'Marvellous, darling. Only three split infinitives.'

Ted never had this. At the end of important days, he returned to an empty flat and I think this must have been a disadvantage.

But he had and still has many friends. You can encounter on two successive evenings a totally different Ted Heath. I have been at dinners where, to the horror of ladies sitting next to him, he said virtually nothing. On other occasions he could be the most sparkling and entertaining person at the dinner table, discussing the theatre, sailing or whatever the topic might be.

It is not true to say that he has no small talk, but he is either witty and enthusiastic in conversation or he is not in the mood and remained sullen. It varied from one evening to another.

I thought his enthusiasm for sailing sometimes went too far. He once asked me to Broadstairs on a Saturday to discuss tactics and look at some papers. He suggested that in the afternoon we should go sailing. I said I did not sail. He said I was being silly. Everybody sailed. We went out in a small boat and he shouted to me things I did not understand and started to become abusive. I actually fell in and when we brought this small boat to the shore he said we needed to clean it down. I argued since it had been in the water that afternoon there was no point. He said it was something to do with salt and I was left cleaning down this wretched boat while he signed autographs on the beach. When, some time later, he suggested that Tessa and I should go sailing with him, I said I would prefer to canvas in the most marginal seats on a wet Saturday afternoon than go sailing again.

You can ask too much of your friends.

10

IN THE COLD

The day after Margaret was elected leader, she called me in. I knew that I was on my way out. I had been close to Ted and argued more strongly than anyone else in the Shadow Cabinet against the simplistic monetary policy being put forward by Keith Joseph and now embraced by her. She was surrounded by new friends with new aspirations and it was right that I should go.

In anticipation, I had gone to the length of preparing a press statement to be issued after she had dismissed me, saying that I wished her well and how much I had enjoyed being in government, but that given our differences on economics it was proper I should go.

When I did meet her, she was nervous and tense. This was under-standable. She had before her a senior Cabinet Minister who had a high profile, was young and presumably still ambitious and she had to sack him. She also knew me from the Dartford days. Again, I had handed over the transport portfolio to her. She may have even guessed that I had a hand in her initial promotion.

She said, 'I think you will understand that I have to form a new Shadow Cabinet and must ask you to stand down, because I must try to get some younger people in.'

The awful thing was that I laughed. I did not do it viciously or nastily. As the youngest member of the Shadow Cabinet, it struck me as an absurd reason. She realized she had made a mistake. She said she did not mean younger people, but less experienced people. She must bring them in to get more experience.

I said I understood and that, in any case, we did have differences on economic policy. I hoped we would remain friends. The meeting ended. I duly released my prepared press statement.

Being out of office was a new experience. Soon after becoming an MP, I had been appointed PPS to Selwyn Lloyd, enjoyed success as the Shadow Transport Secretary, become the youngest member of Cabinet and run two large departments. The chance to look around was welcome.

There were some unpleasant aspects. People round me had been saying nice things. Suddenly I discovered that the same people I thought were friends no longer wanted to be seen talking to me. That was a shattering experience. The last thing they wanted to be seen doing was associating with this chap Walker who had been dismissed. Politics must be bigger than this.

I discovered from friends that even Shadow Cabinet Ministers who had worked enthusiastically with me were saying I was not all that I had been cracked up to be. I could understand them holding different views. I could not understand this personal hostility.

Within two days of my sacking, one close colleague who had been everywhere with me came and said he had been offered a job in Shadow Government provided he had nothing to do with me.

On the plus side, I was glad of the new freedom to float off ideas. I felt no bitterness. I could roam my wilderness at will.

My roaming did leave me free to criticize monetary theory. I was genuinely concerned at the concept that if you got one money supply figure right, all your problems would be solved, and I let that be known. I resolved to go on preaching the balanced concepts of Conservativism as I saw them. I thought we had to get right the balance between compassion and efficiency.

Friends helped to develop ideas. Denis Stevenson, whom I had appointed chairman of the Peterlee New Town at a young age, was one. Tim Price, who had been at Cambridge with Denis, was another. Andrew Neil, who had been in Conservative Research Department and was to become editor of the *Sunday Times*, was yet another lively mind who shared my thinking. Jamie Stevenson, Denis's brother, who was an economist and original thinker, also took part. We used to meet once a week, early in the evening, and have a glass of wine. If I wanted to prepare a major thoughtful speech, I would tell this little group and invite any thoughts or contributions.

What was quite important was that I was quickly seen as the

133

most senior backbench voice, putting the more liberal viewpoint and questioning monetarist policy.

The only other person who had been in Cabinet and was now in the cold was Ted Heath, and his position, in the ex-Prime Minister league, was entirely different from that of a young politician who had nevertheless had important Cabinet posts.

A group of Tory backbenchers did ask me to lead a group to propound these more liberal, traditional views. This I refused to do. Throughout my time at Westminster, I have been convinced that the Labour Party has suffered grievously from self-inflicted wounds administered by the many party groups expressing organized opposition to the leadership. So there never was a Walker-inspired opposition group. It is a pity that later groups were formed and there is now yet another to keep alive the spirit of Thatcherism. It can only be disruptive.

When I first came to the House and opposed our negotiations on Europe and again when I was in the wilderness after our second 1974 election defeat, I was always able to express my views, go to any Parliamentary committee, chat to other Tory MPs. If a group with the same objectives came together to organize opposition to a specific piece of legislation, that was fine. But to form groups who have a different creed, right, left or middle of the party, is lunacy for Conservatives. I would like to see the party get back to the position where there were no formal groups.

The groups do not even make sense from the limited perspective of the people who call them together. If I had bowed to the pressure to head a group during my days in the wilderness, I believe those who shared my view would have lost influence rather than gained it.

My strict attitude did have an advantage to the party when the Liberal-Social Democrat Alliance was launched and a number of more liberally minded MPs were tempted to join it. I was able to play probably the key role in persuading them to stay inside the Conservative Party. Had I been the leader of a group, the group could well have decided to desert to join the Alliance. The fact that they were individuals and I could see them one by one, sometimes for hour after hour, was important in checking a drift.

This may even have been important historically. A sizable group of Labour MPs joined the Social Democrats, but only one Conservative MP, Christopher Brocklebank-Fowler. Christopher came to me the morning he was announcing his resignation. He said he had not consulted me before because he felt it was wrong to get me involved. He had decided quite definitely to make the break and was attending a press conference at noon. I argued it was a mistake and asked him to put off the press conference, but he was adamant. He said he much respected the view I was taking, but was determined to go ahead. He was the one who got away. Christopher had no particular weight in Parliament and it did not matter too much.

If the fifteen Conservative MPs who were also thinking seriously of the move and consulted me had gone across at that time and joined it would have made the Alliance far more formidable than a group of ex-Labour MPs. It would have been a Social Democrat party of Socialists and Conservatives and it could have become a very considerable force in British politics. The pressure to join was considerable. It was happening in the wake of the depressing effects of the 1981 Budget and the steep rise in unemployment. The fifteen potential rebels, all of whom I saw, include some who are ministers today.

I thought about it again after we won the 1983 General Election. I walked along the corridor with David Owen to the Speaker's reception following the Queen's Speech. I said that I trusted by the time of the next election he would have formed one party instead of two. Going round the constituency, I had discovered that no one hated a Social Democrat more than a Liberal and no one hated a Liberal more than a Social Democrat. David had done well, but with a single party he would do much better next time. He said, 'If you ever looked in depth at merging with the Liberal Party, you never would.' I laughed and we went off to the reception, but looking back that was a significant comment.

Had they merged the two parties, he would have quickly become leader and there would have been a strong likelihood the Alliance would have replaced Labour as the main opposition.

There was a moment between elections when the Alliance could have come right through the middle. David Owen himself is personable, a good speaker, writes well and could have had a big impact. He does have considerable leadership qualities and he could have made a breakthrough in British politics. I am sorry it did not happen because, in my vision of British politics, it would be more healthy to have a democrat party as an alternative to the Tories. Labour has moved to the centre, but it still has two major drawbacks, the hard left-wing attitudes of many of its members and the link up with the trade unions. Even now Labour is influenced by the unions and still financed by them.

History may well judge David Owen and David Steel harshly for their joint failure, but I cannot personally. I was partly to blame. If I had persuaded a couple of dozen Tory MPs to leave with me to join the new party, it could have tipped the scales in its favour. I remain a passionate Tory, but I would like, in those short phases of history when there is a non-Conservative government, for it to be Liberal Democrat.

David Owen has rejected the idea that he might join the Tories, but I am left wondering. His public praise of John Major suggests that the jump is not impossible.

During my wanderings in the wilderness, the Tory Reform Group also approached me to form a Parliamentary group, but again I refused. I was in favour of the TRG as a research organization, holding conferences and meetings and discussing the more liberal ideas of Tory Party policy. We gave platforms for people at party conference to propound these views. That I considered was right. Forming a party political faction would have been wrong.

I had become involved with the TRG some years before. There was an earlier manifestation of it in the 1940s when Lord Hailsham and Peter Thorneycroft were members, but when we came into government in 1951 it disappeared.

Then something similar re-emerged under the name of PEST, an organization started by Michael Spicer, my neighbour MP for Worcestershire South and a former minister, when he was an undergraduate at Cambridge. He asked me to encourage these Oxford and Cambridge graduates. There was also a Tory Reform Group formed in Manchester University. The two decided to merge.

I was asked to become its patron, a nominal position, and was never involved in the details of its running. In fact, during this period it became an embarrassment to me. A lobby correspondent who was a TRG member was writing a paperback and was passionately opposed to Mrs Thatcher. As the TRG press officer, he would daily put out handouts attacking Mrs Thatcher and Sir Keith. Everyone then wrote that the TRG, whose patron was Peter Walker, was saying that Mrs Thatcher was dreadful. I had to tell the TRG officers I thought the attack on Margaret was a mistake. They were being personal, bitter and ineffective and it must be stopped. The press officer was relieved of his duties.

I stressed that the TRG must be positive, coming out with new proposals and research.

Willie Whitelaw and others were also on the top of TRG letter paper, but the organization was always run by the young people. I have never sat on the executive or attended a meeting. They are nevertheless a lively-minded group of young Tories whom I like and try to encourage.

Even during Margaret's ascendancy there was never a large, dedicated right-wing or Thatcherite group. This is little understood. The majority of Tory backbenchers loyally support whoever is the leader. They do not have deep commitments to particular economic doctrines; instinctively many shrink away from doctrine. But if leaders with the ability of Keith Joseph and Margaret Thatcher say the right course is to adopt a monetary policy, which involves the volume of money supply as defined by M3, they think they are clever, nice people and it may be right.

I made progress with writing *The Ascent of Britain* and made major speeches like the Kennedy Lecture and the Harold Macmillan Lecture in which I tried to put the middle way alternative, describing how Harold Macmillan had gone for the middle way and how his philosophy was relevant to modern day problems.

After one of the lectures, Harold Macmillan wrote to congratulate me on keeping alive the spirit of what he tried to do. In the same period, I received a surprising note from Matthew Parris, who later became an MP and is now the hilarious and perceptive Parliamentary sketch writer on *The Times*, after another speech. He wrote that he had never read a more moving account of the way forward for the Conservatives and one with which he so heartily agreed. 'I am hardened to letters about speeches from Members of the Public and have never before been stirred into joining their ranks,' he added. He wrote with feeling. At the time, he was dealing with the correspondence in Margaret Thatcher's private office.

I was a great admirer of Harold Macmillan, notwithstanding the Night of the Long Knives when he butchered Selwyn Lloyd, among others. I had read his autobiography and was affected by his book *The Middle Way*. Because of my initial opposition to the Common Market I did not think he looked kindly on me, but after he gave up he did ask me to lunch at his home, Highfield, and we got on well.

Rather later I suggested writing a book, *The Middle Way, Forty Years On* and he agreed that I should. He would write a foreword and discuss the book itself, chapter by chapter. Unfortunately when we won in 1979, I could not, as a minister, continue and he died before I could complete it. But it did give me the opportunity of long discussions with him.

He was an amusing man. On one occasion he told me, 'You know, Peter, this book is going to be a great success.' Macmillans were to publish it.

I said, 'I hope so.'

He said, 'It certainly will be. When we publish I will agree to go on television. You know I am a television star. When I was Prime Minister they all said how terrible I was on television and that I lost the party millions of votes. I never liked being on television, but suddenly I discover I am a star and they think I am marvellous. All I do, if they want a programme, is to bring them round here. I sit in my armchair with a glass of whisky and chat away in front of these cameras and it is yet another triumph. So when we publish your book, I will agree to do television and it will be an enormous success.'

On another occasion, he asked me if I had been at the party conference the other week. I said I had. Harold said: 'I watched it on television. Extraordinary affair. I have attended many conferences, normally sitting on the platform. We used to sit there listening to these extraordinary speeches urging us to birch or hang them all or other strange things. We used to sit quietly nodding our heads and when we came to make our speeches we did not refer to what had been said at all. They gave us good ovations and that was that. But watching her at the party conference last week, I think she agrees with them.'

He loved Gibbon's *Decline and Fall of the Roman Empire* and Trollope's novels. 'I read them and reread them and know them almost by heart, but the reason I have them at my bedside is that both authors wrote the most beautifully balanced English sentence. If you have balanced English sentences, they provide you with a marvellous rhythm to send you steadily to sleep.'

The speeches I was making during this period were described as anti-Thatcher, but began an important dialogue. All them were putting a totally positive view.

I decided I should look at past policies and see if they were correct.

As Minister of Housing and Local Government one of my first actions had been to look at housing in Brixton. I remember going into one room which housed a West Indian family of a man, his wife and two children. It was without windows, but immaculately clean, with Christian pictures and crucifixes on the walls. I expressed my horror and asked how much they paid in rent. When they told me, I pointed out that there was legislation to stop this kind of extortion. They said they had agreed to pay it and having done so it would be wrong to go and try to get it changed. Fortunately, this particular family were offered council accommodation shortly afterwards.

My freedom from office allowed me to spend time looking at inner city problems and to visit the West Indians in particular. I could see they were not getting the jobs or the education they needed and many were becoming involved in shoplifting, first of all for the kicks. When they were caught and put inside, perfectly nice, bright kids became an addition to the criminal class. I put together a proposal of what I thought could be done and decided that the best way to get it debated was to put it in a letter to the Prime Minister, Jim Callaghan. It was also published in the *New Statesman*, partly to reach Labour MPs. In my opening paragraph, I wrote: 'But while the Asian community have immense problems of housing, employment and education, their problems are not as grave or as extreme as those currently being suffered by 120,000 households of West Indian descent.'

Birmingham and London both threatened disorder if we did not take 'imaginative and effective action'. Housing conditions were getting worse, a high proportion of West Indian children were leaving school with poor literacy and numeracy skills. In some districts nearly half the West Indian teenagers were without jobs. Many areas had no hope.

I said the situation must be remedied. Failure to do so would bring misery not only to the black population, but also to the indigenous white population. Eventually action would have to be taken. I concluded: 'The question is: will it be done after race relations have deteriorated still further, hatred has been built up in the hearts of the West Indian community, hostility has been created by the white community's resentment of the crime and property damage that will have been attributed to the coloured community? Britain has a size of problem which is manageable. Britain does have the resources to manage it. I plead with you, as Prime Minister, to take the urgent action that is now necessary.' One of the things I felt strongly was that the difficulties were of a size we could tackle. We did not need many millions of pounds.

Jim has since told me that it stirred things up. I know he called in the Cabinet Ministers affected and warned them that more might have to be done. He replied with a friendly letter asking for more details of my research.

I was able to focus attention, but I think both parties made mistakes in not trying to deal with the unrest much earlier and in a more emphatic way. People were pouring into one town or city with lousy housing, high crime rates and few jobs. It was all self-perpetuating. If we had just taken the trouble to see that good housing was more widely distributed and there were adequate training facilities, it could have been different. I devoted chapters of *The Ascent of Britain* to the inner cities and racial harmony.

I also put forward the case for employee share ownership and more positive industrial policy, not relying solely on *laissez-faire*. The French, the Germans and the Japanese were all succeeding with a constructive industrial policy.

The media accused me of attacking Margaret's monetarist policy. Certainly my approach was different, but I did not attack any individual. I wanted an industrial policy which linked government with industry. Money supply was only one of the many factors in the economy.

As a backbencher, I could float off ideas. I floated the idea of getting rid of the council houses as well as various economic and profit-sharing schemes. In office I had decided we would give council house tenants a twenty per cent discount if they wanted to buy the homes in which some had been living for fifty years or more. We had launched a new campaign and it had gone well, but we had still sold only a small proportion of all council homes in Britain.

The best council houses had gone to the wealthiest tenants. Administration and repair of council houses cost a fortune. I obtained all the figures and discovered that the cost of administration and repairs was actually greater than the rents.

My proposal was that we should tell council tenants they could become owners of their council houses straight away. If they had been tenants for a long period they would get the house for nothing. That was a small proportion, however. Everyone in the press described it as a give-away. It never was that. If tenants had been in council housing less than thirty years, their rent would be treated as a mortgage repayment for the balance of the thirty years.

The scheme took into account how long a family had been tenants and made sure their payment would never be more than the old rent, but tenants did have to do the repairs. I thought most council house owners would be able to organize repairs with the help of relatives and neighbours. It might be part of the black economy, but it would happen. You would have dismantled this costly bureaucracy and an inefficient repair service. Everybody, from day one, would become an owner-occupier. The whole scene would be transformed. Professors and experts of all kinds came to see me, but none found a fault with the plan.

Hugh Rossi, the Tory MP and former minister, was called upon to chair a committee to prepare housing policy for the manifesto and I was asked to give evidence. I was cross-examined about my plans, but it was clear that Margaret was against it because she felt it would upset 'our people' who had struggled to pay their mortgages. Suddenly, these other people would be getting their homes much cheaper. But all you had to say to 'our' people was that 'these' people would have responsibility for repairing and maintaining their houses and this would save hundreds of millions of pounds in public expenditure. Our people would be delighted. Margaret's political judgement on this point was wrong. I knew I was right and eventually I persuaded her to adopt a very similar scheme. If she had still been leader of the party she would have gone hard into the next election with a variation on the proposals. I am confident John Major will do so.

We had an amazing debate on incomes policy in this period. Geoffrey Howe, the Shadow Chancellor, having said how totally he was against any form of incomes policy, found himself trapped. He could not follow the logic of his own statement and go on to say he was in favour of a free-for-all on wages. There were some contradictory speeches and even occasions when Her Majesty's Opposition did not vote in the Commons.

The point about incomes policies is that they are unsatisfactory, but, in certain circumstances, when the unions are being totally irresponsible, you have to employ them. We did and they did.

On industrial policy, we were equally inconsistent. When it came to the Labour Party saving a major industry, the Tory Party did not say, 'No. We want that industry to disappear.' Party leaders were being strong on the rhetoric, but when it came to the crunch they had to take a pragmatic approach.

It was one of Margaret's great mistakes that we were constantly representing ourselves as the great cutters of public expenditure. People came to believe it, even that we were cutting the health and education services when we were doing the reverse. John Major is even now having to kill the myth. We were boasting of the unpopular things and we were keeping silent on popular policies because they did not fit the hairshirt doctrine.

I did extend my criticism to Labour. As a member of the Shadow Cabinet, I would have been compelled to concentrate on attacking my opposite number. Freed of office, I was able to attack them all. Tony Benn, as the new Trade and Industry Secretary, was a prime target. I have nothing personal against him, but do believe his stewardship was nearly disastrous for Britain.

One of the things I thought we had done well at DTI was the working of the Industry Act. Section 8 enables governments to intervene and put money into companies which need it. We had this powerful advisory body of industrialist and bankers, including Gordon Richardson. Never once did I go against the advice of these advisers. They rejected dozens of applications. Even a politician like myself who had some feel for business did not have the industrial knowledge to take the decisions. The advisers I appointed sustained a high success rate, much better than the average merchant banker could have expected.

When Tony came in, he used exactly the same act, but he rejected the advice of the panel on numerous occasions and poured money into the most ill-thought-out co-operative schemes, based on idealism, but unrelated to their likely survival or viability. Scheme after scheme went bust.

I had suffered from his earlier excursions into government when I became Trade and Industry Secretary and had to pick up the pieces of his policy in the 1966–70 Labour government. One of the worst things he did was to push Rolls-Royce into the RB211 engine, which made the company bankrupt. He pushed them into the contract so that he could say he had landed this enormous order, but it was on terms which destroyed Rolls. He was not interested in whether something was viable under market rules. He was interested only in trying out Socialist theories. I thought he was a calamity. With my knowledge of the subject and having been at the DTI, I was in the position to say so.

Labour leaders came to the same conclusion. Just before the 1974 General Election I sat next to Harold Wilson at dinner. He talked about our creation of the two new massive departments and said he wanted to do the same. It was, after all, upon his original proposals that Ted and I had acted. I told him I thought he had been right to pursue the ideas. He said he was glad to hear it and if he won the election, he would keep the two departments.

But then, when he did win, he eventually broke up Trade and Industry into two, separating Trade from Industry. Ted had already put Energy on its own.

Some time later I was sitting next to Harold at another dinner and taunted him about what he had promised and what he had actually done. He replied, 'My dear Peter. Would you have given Tony Benn the whole of Trade and Industry?'

Closer to the General Election, I did have an approach from Willie Whitelaw, now Deputy Leader. He said that Margaret liked me and thought I was able and a professional politician. He was sure that she would have me back in the Shadow Cabinet as quickly as possible. The trouble was that I had never ever said anything in praise of her or what she stood for and this made it difficult. 'Surely you can approve of some of the things she stands for. Why can't you make a speech saying that, on consideration, you think she has some good policies?'

I told him I thought it would be totally bogus. I disagreed with her monetary policy because I thought it was wrong. I had not tried to embarrass her and I had not made any personal attacks, but, equally, I was not going to go out and start making speeches that I thought everything was wonderful simply to get back in the Shadow Cabinet. I was not like that. I told him he could be certain I would do everything I could at the General Election to see that we were elected. I was not being awkward or unpleasant or trying to undermine the regime, but neither was I someone who would make a toady speech in the hope I might get a post. Willie went away looking lugubrious and I heard no more.

Margaret Thatcher did come to Worcester for the constituency party's centenary celebrations. I wrote and asked her and she agreed immediately. She and Denis came down and spent the night with us. The speech I made at the centenary dinner praised the energy of the Prime Minister, but I also spelled out strongly the middle way of Toryism.

Newspapers were divided. Some said it was an outrageously critical speech to put before someone you have invited to dinner. Others said it was eulogy to the Prime Minister. What I did was try to describe the qualities of Margaret I genuinely admired and the traditions and ideals, as I saw them, of the Tory Party.

When the General Election was announced, Central Office asked if it could organize my speaking programme. I had always toured the country and spent little time in my constituency. I said I would divide my time the same way in this election as in others, two and a half days in my constituency and three and a half days speaking elsewhere.

To my surprise I was treated as a leading figure in the Tory Party and not as a troublesome backbencher, even a reluctant rebel. I suppose it ought to have given me a clue about what happened next.

11

CALLED BACK

I did not think there was any chance of being recalled to the Cabinet after the 1979 election. I was given VIP treatment in the election campaign itself, but being invited into a Thatcher administration was something which did not cross my mind.

The result of the election was clear on the Thursday night. It was not a nail-biting finish on this occasion. We were home with a comfortable majority of more than forty. If I had thought I would be involved in government-making, I would have gone straight up to London.

As it was, we stayed relaxed in Worcestershire. We went to bed on the Friday night and at 11.30 the phone rang. It was No. 10 to say the Prime Minister would like to see me at 10.30 the following morning. It produced a frantic rush. The children had to be got up early and a dash made to London.

I went in and Margaret said, 'You will come back into the team, won't you, Peter?' She complimented me on my campaigning. 'You obtained more media coverage than most of the Shadow Cabinet put together.'

She did say it had been suggested that with my wide experience I might become Ulster Secretary, but she had thought it unfair to ask someone with young children to do that job. Instead, she offered me Agriculture. After two important posts as Secretary of State, this was comparatively small beer, but I had no hesitation about accepting it.

As a result of my contacts with Leo Amery I had strong views about agriculture and was influenced by Leo's book *The Balanced Economy*. I also thought of negotiating a new agriculture deal with the Community. The job was going to be tough and would stretch me.

I was fortunately confident of the subject. My constituency interests had ensured that I was well informed. I had been extensively briefed by NFU experts in Worcester for eighteen years and was probably the best informed agriculture minister for a long time. On top of that I had a limited practical knowledge, running a farm of my own at Martin Hussingtree.

I had few illusions about the Prime Minister's motives. I knew Margaret was not going to give me a senior job. I was in the Cabinet because she thought I was safer in than out. She knew that I knew that was the reason. We were both Tories, however, and the idea of my saying that I would not accept unless offered a more prestigious post was unthinkable.

Even as one of a minority in the Cabinet, I was going to be able to contribute to all Cabinet discussions. I would be able to make my views known on foreign and economic policy and perhaps have an impact. Peter Carrington and I did, in fact, express strong views on Europe. Ian Gilmour, Jim Prior and I also took the same line on the economy.

Margaret said I could have whoever I wanted as minister of state, but would I consider Alick Buchanan-Smith, who had resigned earlier over devolution? I was delighted with the prospect of such an able number two. I had had a great respect for him in the Shadow Cabinet earlier and very much liked him, too. I always had the clear impression that Margaret would never make him a number one.

If there had been any justice he would have been a number one. He possessed outstanding qualities and would have made an excellent Secretary of State.

In a later reshuffle, Margaret said that she wanted to drop him. This was after he had done a superb job at Agriculture and Energy, where he looked after the oil industry. He had been so good that I treated the running of the ministries as a partnership with him. I told her that if she dropped Alick, she dropped me as well. I was not prepared to see him sacked after the work he had done. So he stayed. She eventually abandoned him when I went to the Welsh Office. I could not easily insist that a Scottish member came to the Welsh Office.

Alick's offence was that he had resigned two years earlier on a matter of principle over Scottish devolution. He had done it with great courtesy, never showing hostility to Margaret or the government, but she obviously considered that somebody who resigned was not fit to be a number one. She should have realized she had someone of exceptional quality. I have known her be generous to MPs and ministers behind the scenes on many occasions, but she could not forget that Alick would not bow to her persuasion on the devolution issue. She was not being vengeful. If she had been that she would not have had him in the government at all, but she was not having him in the Cabinet.

Robin Ferrers, in the Lords, was another excellent Minister of Agriculture, able and modest, to whom you could entrust any task. Both Alick and Robin became close friends and godfathers to my children.

I took over Agriculture after it had gone through a rough time. John Silkin, my Labour predecessor, was a pleasant man. The changeover was one of those rare cases when the incoming minister and his predecessor of another party were able to have a civilized talk about the department and which officials were good and which not so good.

But after examining the details of our negotiations with the Community on the Common Agriculture Policy, I came to the conclusion that, however much I liked and respected John, he had left a mess. Egged on no doubt by the Treasury, he had opposed increased farm prices, but done so in such a way as to put our farmers at a disadvantage with the French and others. We had a much smaller share of the CAP budget than we had a share of European agriculture. By the time I left we had eight and half per cent of the agriculture and ten per cent of the budget.

In trying to recover lost ground, I warned the industry to become more self-sufficient in dairy products before quotas were imposed. We were bad at making cheese and pretty bad at yoghurt. The Dutch, the Danes and the French were running ahead on dairy products, using their surplus milk on all these products and selling them round Europe. I had a go at the Milk Marketing Board and as a result we produced Lymeswold, the first new British cheese to be launched this century.

Critics said Walker increased milk production and then Britain was forced to have quotas. What they had not bothered to work out was that if I had reduced milk production sooner, we should have been given smaller quotas when these were introduced.

Lymeswold cheese was launched one morning at the Savoy Hotel in London with all the media present. In performing the ceremony, I remarked I had an Old English sheepdog, Bomba, who loved Lymeswold more than anything else. It so happens that it was one of those days when there was no news anywhere, at home or abroad. My dog became great news. Photographers came to my home to photograph him eating his cheese. Every television programme carried the story. We worked out we would have had to pay several million pounds for the publicity we received on radio, television and in the newspapers.

Unhappily, the board had only a small production of the cheese. The next day everyone went into the supermarkets to buy it and it became a black-market commodity. The board then made a mistake by releasing some before it was properly mature.

Achieving quality control of British cheese and getting it to go up-market was an uphill task.

I was blessed in the task by having Brian Hayes as my Permanent Secretary. Like Robin Ferrers he was modest, but the most talented civil servant I have encountered in all my time in Whitehall. I have never found anyone who could produce as good a minute as Brian Hayes.

John Silkin had told me I was also lucky to be inheriting the best press officer in Whitehall, Terry Dawes. This was an understatement. He had been press officer to every Agriculture Minister since 1960. Whoever was his minister, he worked hard for him and ensured the minister secured a good press.

I remember two things in particular about him. He was a great tennis player and captain of his local tennis club. He and his son went each year to a hotel with tennis facilities at Porto Carras in Greece, owned by a Greek shipowner, John Carras. One year he went and found himself playing regular foursomes for eight days against Giscard d'Estaing who had just stepped down as President of France.

He came back and told us what had happened and we all scoffed. He said he knew we would do that and produced photographs of himself and Giscard playing tennis. My press officer had been playing tennis with the immediate ex-President only shortly after bitter exchanges on the lamb war.

When Terry was eighteen months away from retirement he should have received an award in the honours list. He did not get it. I thought that there must have been some kind of slip up, but when he did not get it the next year I tried to discover why. I suspected that Terry Dawes was unpopular with Sir Bernard Ingham, the Prime Minister's press secretary, for refusing to give his first loyalty to No. 10 rather than the minister he was serving. I was told other press officers would be against Terry appearing in the honours list as they felt he had been involved in a leak to the press.

The alleged leak involved a document in Brussels. The journalist concerned said he would not reveal his source, but did say Terry was not involved.

I mobilized support for all the Ministers of Agriculture for whom Terry Dawes had worked, Labour and Conservative. The list included Fred Peart, John Silkin, Cledwyn Hughes, Jim Prior. All urged that Terry Dawes should be honoured for his outstanding service. We failed at our first attempt. In 1991 a number of Cabinet Ministers again asked for the case to be reviewed, but we were told there was no evidence that Terry had been refused an honour other than for a simple administrative reason, that in the two years he might have received it there was not an appropriate allocation to the Ministry of Agriculture. I know of few men who have been more dedicated to governmment service, for both Labour and Conservative governments, than Terry Dawes and it is a disgrace it is not recognized.

We had a good team and I look upon what we achieved with satisfaction. British farming improved its quality of marketing in meat, vegetables, apples and dairy products and we became more self-sufficient in food, exporting far more and importing far less. Food prices went up each year by less than the price index and all settlements were lower than both our rate and the European rate of inflation.

Negotiations were tough because every agriculture minister knew he would be held personally responsible for what was agreed. If the French minister made a concession, he knew that the moment he returned he would be attacked by his farmers and political opponents. You had to analyse what other countries wanted and what their priorities were and try to reach agreement in that way.

There were some international issues which became highly charged, like the importing of New Zealand lamb. We had been

New Zealand's traditional outlet and other countries wanted to stop importing New Zealand lamb altogether, so they could take over the market. We also had responsibility for the Caribbean sugar producers. Levies could have destroyed entire economies in the West Indies.

The central fight, however, was to prevent large increases going on products which were in surplus in Europe itself. We always settled at a long way below the European inflation rate on the surplus products. The object was to do it in a manner which did not mean your own farmers were clobbered. The lamb war with the French was inexcusable. The French were aware of the Community laws and knew we were entitled to export whatever we liked, but they refused us access. We went to the European Court and won our case, but they still refused. I was forced to take a high profile and tell the rest of Europe that if France persisted we should be compelled to put restrictions on a list of French imports. France, which had refused to negotiate, began to see that its attitude was doing damage to its position in the Community and its considerable sales to Britain. British consumers began to stop buying French apples to help me in the lamb war.

I got my first taste of what negotiating would be like at an informal meeting of agriculture ministers in southern France. I walked down a corridor to be stopped by an Italian minister, Signor Giovanni Marcora.

He put his arm round my shoulder and declared, 'It is a delight to have you here and let me say if you help me to get a few more million écus on olives, I will see you get a few more million on sheep.'

The job called for a tough constitution. Another great character was the German agriculture minister, Josef Ertl. He was a small farmer in Bavaria, but an important agricultural leader and delivered the farming vote in a miraculous way. I remember conducting some negotiations with him at his farm up in the hills outside Munich. He was dressed in Bavarian national dress. At ten o'clock in the morning I was offered a quart of beer and German white sausages.

As Minister for Agriculture I got to know two French politicians, both of whom subsequently became Prime Ministers of their country. One was Edith Cresson who was suddenly appointed agriculture minister by President Mittérand during my time in the job, and then caused another surprise in May 1991 by being made Prime Minister.

She was lively and able and took quick command of her ministry. Civil servants learned swiftly that they were being led by a minister with strong views on most issues. She was herself appalled by her treatment by French farmers. On one instance, she was ambushed by farmers blocking the road with tractors. She told us she had never known people behave like this before and made no secret of her frustration in trying to deal with them.

I was fascinated to read that as Prime Minister her first priority would be to stop the protectionism of Japan and then to strengthen the position of French farmers.

Agriculture will be a interesting scene. Mme Cresson was a tough negotiator, but respected toughness from the other side. Once we agreed the resolution of a difference, she fulfilled her part of the bargain.

We clashed early when it was my turn to be president of the council of agriculture ministers, a task which rotates between the member states. Europe's ministerial meetings were notorious for starting late, anything from one to three hours. I warned colleagues that during my six months' presidency every meeting would start on time and if ministers were absent the meeting would proceed without them. There was some surprise and speculation on whether I would be able to stick to my ruling.

The test came at the first meeting in Luxembourg which was due to start at 11 a.m. It started at 11 a.m. Four ministers, including the French Minister of Agriculture, were not there. Three came quickly in a state of shock. Edith Cresson did not appear and we moved quickly through the agenda to Item 5 which was of considerable importance to France. No Edith. We came to our conclusions on the item and moved to Item 6. Nearly an hour late, Edith Cresson arrived and protested that we could not deal with Item 5 in her absence. I said we had already dealt with it and that she had been warned all meetings were to start on time. A messenger had gone to her office ten minutes before the meeting started and again immediately after it began. The decision reached by the council must stand. The EEC Commission confirmed this was legally correct.

With only one exception, all subsequent council meetings started on time with the French in their seats. The exception was an informal meeting for ministers in Britain when Mme Cresson did not turn up for the opening dinner of a two-day meeting. When she did, she explained that important business in France had detained her.

Michel Rocard, the French Prime Minister she succeeded in 1991, became the French Minister of Agriculture a few months before our 1983 General Election. I had met him earlier and been impressed by his humour and command of English. It would be difficult to find a more congenial dining companion and one could see why he was the most popular of Socialist politicians.

If I was asked to gamble, I would put my money on Michel Rocard being the next Socialist President of France. His handicap was, and presumably still is, his bad relationship with President Mittérand.

The differences were partly over policy. France has always opposed Japanese imports and investment in France. Rocard decided this was a mistake and that it was stupid for Britain and other countries to be benefiting from this massive Japanese investment while France kept up the shutters. He launched an offensive in Japan to warn the Japanese that the Community would not allow all investment to go to Britain. It must be spread throughout the Community and France would welcome its share. This was a reversal of the policy adopted by Mittérand himself.

I would not be surprised if Edith Cresson ostensibly changes the policy again. She will certainly show hostility to the Japanese commercial approach. Britain should, however, beware of French subtlety. There is just the possibility that Mme Cresson will use her formidable rhetoric to browbeat the Japanese into investing more in France to soften domestic French criticism. We should watch what she is up to with great care.

In the end, we did get free access to the Community for our products, including lamb, and British agriculture started to acquire a real confidence in itself. I told the farmers that instead of complaining about prices they had to improve quality. Their marketing and quality control was lousy.

I set up four marketeers to help. One was John Sainsbury, another John Cross who is a fine farmer and head of a big co-operative in East Anglia. I said they should look into whatever they liked, apple growing or potato production and anything else. When they had completed an investigation, they could report to me privately or publish their findings. They did a supremely good job. John Sainsbury, for example, took full page advertisements in newspapers to say how bad British potatoes were. He changed the whole potato-growing pattern in Britain. We were growing potatoes which were easy to grow but tasteless.

The message I tried to convey was that people would pay a premium for a quality product. I arrived to find the British apple industry being destroyed by French Golden Delicious. The French apples were coming in in beautiful boxes, every apple the same size, every apple perfection. Next door to them would be an enormous heap of Cox's Orange Pippins, some maggoty, some bruised, all different sizes.

The apple industry came to me and said they would be out of business in a couple of years unless I gave them more money. I said I would not give them a penny. The quicker the apple industry folded up the better because it deserved to do so. They were horrified at this. I said that the Cox's was a much better apple, but because the French had good quality control and packaged their Golden Delicious they were sweeping the market.

If, however, they came forward with a plan to improve quality control and marketing, I might give them some money to launch that. They told the press outside that I wanted to destory the industry and must be in the pay of the French. About a month later they came forward with a plan which was all right, but did not go far enough. The money they wanted from me was minute and the scheme would have had no impact. This time I said that if they improved their plan and brought in a number of additional controls I would give them not £100,000, or whatever the figure was, but £500,000. I said that if they launched it properly they should never need another penny from the government.

They introduced the Kingdom Cox, which has always been at a considerable premium over French apples and taken a bigger share of the market.

The weakness the apple-growers showed in marketing was evident almost everywhere. At the Royal Show, attracting thousands of visitors, the food display was appalling. I said so and the next year they got Marks and Spencer to arrange it. All the other exhibitors had to come up to a high standard. Years later I had the same experience with the Welsh Show and it changed its practice.

We were able to achieve as much as we did partly because I had a close relationship with an excellent president of the National Farmer's Union, Richard Butler, 'Rab' Butler's son. Over the years I had been briefed extensively by my local NFU branch, so the NFU was no stranger. I told Richard Butler that my objective was to have a good and stable British agriculture. There would be many battles and one I did not need was with the farmers.

If I proposed a change, I would speak to him and explain exactly why I was doing it and why I thought it was right. If, at the end, we disagreed, then he would be free to launch whatever attacks he liked on me. I said what I did not want was a repeat of what the NFU had done in the past, issuing barnfuls of press handouts on current issues and undertaking intensive lobbying for extravagant claims. He could come and see me whenever he liked. He had my home telephone number and I hoped I could see him and his experts whenever I wished.

Where we disagreed, I would tell him why. When he disagreed with my experts, he would tell me why and we would try to get to the truth. I might say 'No' and that we could not have price increases in a particular sphere because the surpluses were too big, but we would see there was no prejudice against Britain in the way the EEC acted.

Alick and I were well briefed and built up what we were told was a unique relationship with the NFU. Instead of battling endlessly against each other, both sets of officials were made to justify their views. If the NFU said its costs were X and my officials said they were not – they had left out some factors – there would be a meeting, with officials on both sides putting arguments, and I would come to a conclusion.

Care does have to be taken in the support of farming. Some areas of agriculture would disappear if they did not receive help. One of the most important is the hill farms. They can produce only beef cattle and sheep and the cost of doing so in the hills is quite high. If you do not offer a subsidy, there will be no viable farming there. This would mean no viable farming in great areas of Wales, Scotland and northern England, leaving it to go wild and abandoned.

I did negotiate what was said to be the best sheep regime that British farmers had ever seen. It was based on the market. Housewives got cheap lamb and the subsidy was paid only when it was justified to get a guaranteed price for the producer.

If we look on farm income as a return on capital, it is nil or almost nil. The value of land is such that return on your farm land is small. If you rent, by the time you have paid your rent, your income is small. The income is for the whole family, both wife and husband working.

There are obvious pluses. A portion of the expenses of the farmhouse is discounted because it is partly a business.

If you are a big cereal farmer, the return can be good. Those in East Anglia with hundreds of acres of fertile land make substantial money. The difficulty is that when you bring down the grain price, you also hit the chap with his hundred acres, twenty acres of which are cereals. He is seriously affected and it is difficult to discriminate in his favour.

We have a traditional pattern of farming in Britain. If we want to keep it, we have to force farmers to market better, produce better quality goods, but there will always be areas which will have to have subsidy. The hills are a classic example.

The same close co-operation I sought with the NFU served me well in achieving my greatest success, when I negotiated the European fishing policy. Every country has a political problem with its fishermen. They are great individualists. Everyone sympathizes with the tough life they lead. They all want to take as much fish as they can and they hate conservation policies which protect their future as well as that of the fish.

Overfishing had reached the point where something had to be done. When I was a boy the working class ate herrings two or three times a week. It was a great staple dish for high tea. The fishmongers in Harrow had piles of herrings. But, as a result of overfishing, the herring had almost vanished.

We needed conservation policies, but it was no good our fishermen using restraint if the French or Danes netted all the fish. I argued that if we wanted good stocks of all fish, it could be done only by a European agreed fishing policy.

The moment we began to discuss it, we found that the demands for high quotas and virtually limitless fishing areas were so loud there was little prospect of agreement. I decided that nevertheless it was so important that we had to put in a huge effort to get that agreement. Alick and myself had talks with every fishing minister in Europe. We warned our colleagues we all faced disaster unless we had such a policy. Of course, there would be tough negotiation, but it would be worth it.

I had the problem of what to do about the demands of the British fishermen, the biggest group being from Scotland. I called in their representatives. I told them the policy would entail quotas and international controls, stopping people poaching, but, as the conservation aspects took effect, there would be more fish. In the long trawl, the industry would be expanding instead of contracting.

For once there would also be security in fishing, so that investment programmes could be planned. I said I knew that they would want to make enormous demands. The Danes would make the same demands, as would the French and the Dutch. There would have to be compromises to see everyone got their fair share.

I proposed to have them and their representatives in an outer room at every negotiation. Everything which I negotiated would go to them for approval. If they did not approve and the talks ended, so would the chance of having an international agreement. They would have total power to veto. They were all astounded by this. The leader of the Scottish fishermen, who died in 1991, Gilbert Buchan, a tough old fisherman and a shrewd negotiator, said, 'You don't mean that.'

I said, 'I do mean it. You, Gilbert, will be in that room every meeting I have on fishing. You can decide how many people you bring and the smaller organizations can bring their president and general secretary and experts. So far as we are concerned, we can have fifty of you in Brussels or Luxembourg. I want every organization to be represented and every organization to have the right of veto.' If a group in south-west England was to veto the whole package that would be the end of Scottish aspirations as well. 'If I think it is a good deal, I will try to persuade you to accept it, but if you decide "No", that is it.'

They were amazed. Up to then they had complained about everything. For the first time, they were part of the negotiating team and had to think constructively. They knew what the prize was and they knew what they were doing if they stopped negotiations. They knew I would announce that the Scottish fishermen would not accept and I could not continue negotiations.

For all those months of negotiations in Brussels or Luxembourg, we had between twenty and sixty fishermen in the negotiations. When there were all-night talks, they stayed up all night in an outside room. I would go to them at 1 a.m. and say that we had reached a possible agreement on turbot. Did they agree? They would all say it was not enough, bloody awful, but could they have half an hour to consider. At the end of the half-hour, they would say they reluctantly agreed to the quota. So it went on.

I had great assistance from the French maritime minister. It was my first experience of a French minister being collaborative, totally objective. He and I agreed how to handle the other countries.

Towards the end of the negotiations, the most awkward country was Denmark, which had big interests. The Danes fished on a huge scale to make fertilizers. Among the fish they caught was the pout. This was easy for me to remember because Tessa's maiden name was Pout. The Danes were taking thousands of tons of pout, but these were in the breeding grounds for other fish. We had to agree to the 'pout boxes', the only places they were allowed to take out pout. It did not stop there, however. The Danes wanted large quotas of everything, including the North Sea herring.

We could not agree, but I then discovered that the Danish minister had a long-cherished ambition to shoot in England. He told me he loved shooting. I phoned Joe Nickerson, who was a great seed-breeder baron and said to have the best shoot in England, in Lincoln-shire, and explained that I had these crucial negotiations. Could he possibly give the Danish minister a day's shooting? He said graciously that he would do anything to help. The Danish minister went up to Lincolnshire and I followed the next morning. A late night vote kept me in the Commons till then.

The first slight embarrassment was the Danish minister's clothes. They were not those we would ever wear for shooting. Joe said, with great diplomacy, that we had these warm jackets and covered him with additional clothing. Next we were surprised by the gun he produced, which was not the kind conventionally used in British shooting.

The beaters made the first drive and hundreds of fat pheasants came over. It was towards the end of the season and they were flying low and slowly. There were just four guns, Joe and his wife and myself and the Danish minister. I am not a good shot, but there were so many pheasants I was getting lefts and rights. They were falling all round us, but we discovered to our horror that the Danish minis-ter was hitting nothing. There were big bags for Joe and his wife, a reasonable one for me and hardly anything for our guest. Joe kept on trying to help by saying they were flying very high and very fast. If the minister did hit something, he said, 'What an excellent shot.'

We need not have worried. The Danish minister did not seem to be embarrassed and said he had thoroughly enjoyed a memorable day.

I think the reason for his limited success may have been that in Denmark shooting is usually on the ground. You wander through fields and if there is a bird on the ground you shoot it.

I do not know how much goodwill our shooting expedition created, but when we came to the end of the negotiations, I had the whole of Europe lined up behind an agreement: only Denmark was still resisting. I persuaded everyone to put pressure on her for holding up the most important agreement in the history of fishing. The Commission and Prime Ministers were called in to build up the pressure on the Danes.

Late one night we reached the final agreement and I took it to my fishermen who were outside. There were some changes in the North Sea quotas they did not like, and I had to say that they could still veto the deal, hoping against hope that they would not. The agreement covered every pound of fish to be taken from the sea and Denmark was now concurring. They asked for another half an hour and then said that if there were no further changes they accepted it.

The celebrations were fabulous. The seamen bought me champagne. I still get Christmas cards from Scottish fishermen and when Gilbert Buchan died I was contacted and told the sad news. Whenever I have been in Scotland for election campaigns since, I have received the warmest receptions.

To enforce the agreement we set up a European inspectorate with powers to go on any boat to stop poaching. Since then there have been other negotiations to change quotas, but actually to put in place a European agreement covering all the seas round Europe was a real achievement. Alick, who has fishing in his constituency, played a most important role in bringing it about.

We did have problems subsequently from French and Spanish trawlers who were caught poaching and arrested. I phoned the French minister to tell him of the arrests and he said they had been warned and must take the consequences, so there was no hostility between governments.

The two things I am most proud of during my time at Agriculture is getting a European fishing agreement and saving the Cox's Orange Pippin.

Immersed as I was in fishing and agriculture during that period, I was also caught up in much more domestic political considerations. It was a moment when several of us in the Cabinet were close to resignation.

We were particularly divided over the 1981 Budget. By this time the recession was becoming marked and what came to be described as the 'wets' were alarmed at the steep rise in unemployment. We believed that the government should be doing more in the regions. Ian Gilmour, Jim Prior and myself were clearly identified as 'wets', but others like Peter Carrington, Christopher Soames and Willie Whitelaw took a similar viewpoint.

What aggravated our feelings on this occasion was the practice of telling the Cabinet nothing about a Budget before the Tuesday morning it was delivered. Usually the only people to know in advance were the Chancellor, Prime Minister and probably the Chief Secretary. You went along at ten o'clock in the morning and the Chancellor told you the details. You then quickly left the room so that it did not look as though a great argument had taken place. The Budget was presented at 3.30 p.m.

On this occasion we did have a glimmer of what was proposed before we went into the room. Jim Prior had picked up an idea of what was in the package. He told Ian Gilmour when they both attended the same official dinner on the Monday evening. Ian phoned me and the three of us had breakfast together and discussed whether we should resign.

At the Cabinet, the Chancellor outlined the tough policies he was going to follow and there was serious criticism. An important proportion felt the Budget was too deflationary with a recession setting in. Ministers accept that they do not always get what they want at Budget Cabinets, but this one was different. The Chancellor had underestimated the effect of the recession and his proposals would plunge us into deeper trouble.

Afterwards a number of us discussed again what we should do. We were faced with an impossible dilemma. If we decided we could not accept the Budget and must resign, we had to take into account the damage this would do to Sterling and the economy. If people like Ian Gilmour, Jim Prior and myself had decided to go, Sterling would have collapsed. You had to ask: Is it worth it? If you did it, you knew it was unlikely the government would change the Budget. It would be too late. The statement was at 3.30 p.m. and the Prime Minister was not going to say that because three Cabinet Ministers had resigned she was going to go into full retreat. Margaret would try to get Tory MPs behind the Budget and carry it through, but the government side would be seriously divided. The downside risk for the country was considerable.

Immediately after the Budget Cabinet, in the hallway of No. 10, a number of us chatted for ten minutes. I had a longer conversation with Ian Gilmour, who was a close personal friend, but there was no formal group. You simply knew that a large proportion of the Cabinet was troubled and hardly anyone had expressed enthusiasm for the Budget.

We decided we could not get it changed, and resignation would do more harm to the economy.

As a result of what happened, an important constitutional change did, however, take place. A number of us expressed individually the view that it was totally wrong to expect the Cabinet to come in at 10.30 in the morning and hear of the strategy for the first time. We could not expect details of the Budget in advance, but we should know its broad thrust. Margaret agreed that in future there would be a special Budget-strategy meeting of the Cabinet some weeks before the actual Budget was produced. The Chancellor would produce a paper saying what he thought. Colleagues would have the opportunity of putting forward their ideas for an alternative strategy. Although future Cabinets may be surprised by detail, never again should they be surprised by the strategy.

Margaret has called a special Budget-strategy Cabinet every year since 1981 and I am sure that John Major will go on doing it.

Alas, in my judgement, the critics were proved to be right. The Budget was over-deflationary. We went into much greater recession than other countries in Europe and when we recovered more sharply later on it was because we had gone down much further. We had a bigger loss of jobs and production than was needed. Manufacturing industries went out of existence when some of them could have remained. These are not easily replaced. You do not build a new factory and put in machinery after you have lost your market. The foreign manufacturer who has stayed in business keeps the business he has won. You have sucked in imports from elsewhere.

Treasury ministers do tend to underestimate the speed of recessions. They look at the latest figures and inflation is still too high, retail sales are perhaps too high, and they conclude they have not yet given enough of the medicine. If you look at the statistics of recessions, the figures first level off and then they start going down increasingly rapidly. The Chancellor did not take into account the speed with which production was falling. That Budget delayed recovery.

Of course inflation has to be tackled and of course you need tough measures, but you also need infinite care in deciding how tough you need to be to get the balance right. If you underdo it, inflation continues and you lose business and trade. If you overdo it, you lose manufacturing. They are difficult judgements to make.

The row over the 1981 Budget was symptomatic of a deeper criticism of the way that Margaret ran her Cabinet. Ten years later it was at least partly responsible for Sir Geoffrey Howe's resignation and his Commons speech which precipitated Margaret's slide from power. It had already been responsible for Michael Heseltine's earlier resignation.

The first irritation over her approach came early in her first government when I read in the newspapers that we had abandoned all exchange controls. It was a major decision. At the Cabinet which followed Michael Heseltine and I both demanded to know how it came about that we were phoned up by journalists in the morning to be asked what we thought of the decision and had to say, 'I did not know it had taken place.' Michael said he was not arguing whether the decision was right or wrong. It was an important decision and members of the Cabinet should surely have been asked their views.

Margaret said that exchange control matters, moving interest rates or fixed exchange rates, were not discussed in advance by Cabinet because of their market sensitivity. I said that given it was market-sensitive, the Cabinet could have discussed the principle of whether at some time in the future we should abandon exchange controls in their entirety or not. I thought there were strong arguments for keeping the mechanism of exchange control which you might need in an emergency.

She did develop a system of taking decisions by groups of ministers rather than the full Cabinet. I do not think she did it to exclude those ministers who had different views, though some believe this is precisely what she did on economic issues. That was a false accusation. She frequently put me in groups when she must have suspected that I would challenge the prevailing line. She did it to get the ministers who were most affected by an issue to come to a conclusion quickly.

A failing in the system was that if you read of a decision in which you had taken no part, you had no sense of the Cabinet's collective responsibility. If someone asked me about a policy of which I knew nothing before it appeared in the newspapers, I would not say that it was marvellous, but that I was rather surprised to read it. It quickly got round Whitehall that ministers were not consulted. Ted Heath's method of having every Cabinet committee report to Cabinet meant that everything came to Cabinet. He kept the main committees – economic affairs, economic strategy, home affairs, defence and overseas. Everything was done through those. They all reported each week to Cabinet. If there was something from home affairs and I did not serve on it, I could question it at the Thursday Cabinet. Normally the reports were accepted, but sometimes they did open up fresh discussions.

Again, if there was a disagreement in one of those Cabinet committees in Ted Heath's day, the Cabinet itself would resolve it. Say two ministers out of eight disagreed with a proposal, either one of the dissidents or the chairman of the committee could insist that the decision went to Cabinet. If this happened, a paper setting out the issues was presented. Under Margaret, that process had gone. There were some occasions when issues went to Cabinet committee and then to Cabinet, but not the majority. It was an important change constitutionally.

Life was nothing if not varied, switching from domestic to international issues and back again. In 1981 our ambassador in Argentina suggested a visit from a British minister could influence the future of that country. There was the possibility that the military would give way to a democracy and if so the process should be encouraged.

The visit was delicate. If you sent the Foreign Secretary you would build up great expectations and hostility at the recognition being given to a military dictatorship. If the Prime Minister went, it would be worse.

Some lesser figure: that would be different. The visit of a Minister of Agriculture to what was and is primarily an agricultural country would not attract a fraction of the attention and would not be considered politically significant. The minister could quietly have a wide range of discussions.

I agreed to do it. The Argentines themselves were excited by the prospect of a visit by a British Cabinet Minister to confer with the military. Naturally, they made the most of it and saw it as a sign of recognition. I was given the most incredible VIP treatment. I met President Videla and the whole of his Cabinet. The Cabinet gave me dinner, the key members lunch and I stayed with establishment figures.

At the centre of all exercise was the Argentine Minister of Agriculture Jorge Aguado, who was clearly more important than the Minister of Agriculture in Britain.

I was told in confidence of a plan that President Videla, who was popular, should retire and hand over to the next president. That president, a good friend of his, would remain for two years and then announce Argentina was to become a democracy. In the meantime, Videla would have set up a new political party led by civilian personalities. In political approach this new party would be a non-Socialist, Conservative party, capable of defeating the Peronists in an election. To succeed it was critical to defeat the Peronists. There was no other political party. Given two years, with able politicians and a popular ex-president touring the country, the new party could become a real force.

I reported this to the Prime Minister and the Foreign Secretary and it was agreed the visit had been important and the contacts should be encouraged. I arranged for Argentines to come to London and, among other things, showed them round Conservative Central Office, in Smith Square, giving them an introduction into how party politics worked in Britain.

The Argentine president did retire and I went out again. I met the new president, whose name was Viola, and was given the same treatment as before. We had civilized talks about what was to be done and everything seemed to be moving in the right direction.

Unfortunately, President Viola had a heart attack and General Galtieri was appointed in his place. Galtieri was not part of the plan. Apart from anything else, he was a serious alcoholic. He is said to have been under the influence of drink when his admiral persuaded him that instead of the annual naval manoeuvres they were about to undertake, Argentine forces should seize the Falklands. The plan which was to have brought peace and democracy and in which I had played a small part went up in smoke.

Interestingly, the Falklands issue was not raised during my visits. I was carefully briefed on what to say, but in my discussions with the Argentine president, the Foreign Secretary, the Finance Minister, the Agriculture Minister, all the Cabinet in fact, no one raised it.

In the end, I had to do so. I acknowledged the problem, but made it clear that no British government could hand over the islands against the wishes of the inhabitants. It was not because we had imperialistic desires or made great fortunes out of the Falklands, but we were responsible for the people. If the Falklanders said they would love to join Argentina, there would be no problem. They said, however, just the opposite. They wanted to remain British.

We would like to establish a happy relationship between the Falklands and Argentina. If, as a result, the difficulties dissolved, that would be fine. I suggested the two countries should discuss what joint ventures could be established. Fishing was clearly one, oil another. If British and Argentine oil companies took part in joint ventures and the two countries had ten, twenty or thirty years of doing things together, then there might be a more receptive atmosphere. They said it was a historic problem, but approved the idea of joint ventures.

I think that when the war came the Argentine diplomatic service was unaware of the military intention. Galtieri became an unpopular president, the economy got worse, inflation and unemployment went up. What I believe happened was that his admiral persuaded him he could become popular again by taking the Falklands.

The argument must have been that the British had no military force in the area and could do nothing. We would not send out a great fleet to rescue sheep farmers on a remote island thousands of miles away. There would be protests, but these would die down and El Presidente would become a hero of the Argentine people.

I was saddened by the war and am now working to improve relations again. I see the Argentine ambassador and Argentine ministers when they come here. I shall go out there in the next few months. It is the most Anglophile country in South America, by a long way. In the first thirty years of this century, we were great trading partners. It is a tragedy that in the second half of the century our relations have slipped so badly. There was no need. They have oil and agriculture and we should be friends. I am glad we have now restored diplomatic relations. They have sent a good ambassador to London and we have a good ambassador out there. Trade is increasing again and I hope it grows.

When Argentina decided to privatize, I suggested to British Gas that it should go and look at the possibilities. There was and is a political risk, but that was true almost everywhere in the world. British Gas did buy oil wells and is in partnership with an Argentine company. Tim Sainsbury, the Trade Minister, has led out an important trade delegation. We must work hard to help Argentina become a successful South American democracy.

12

FIGHT TO THE FINISH

After the handsome 1983 General Election victory, I was prepared to step down from government. I thought that if the Prime Minister did ask me either to continue at Agriculture or take on one of the other smaller jobs in the Cabinet, like Transport or Energy, I would tell her, without acrimony, that I would prefer to return to the back benches.

I discussed the prospect with Alick Buchanan-Smith, still my deputy, and said I would rather have the freedom of returning to the back benches to develop themes on wider issues. I had had four years of hard, tough negotiations in Europe as the agriculture minister, a period in which I had laid down a broad structure of British agricultural policy and helped to transform the market approach of our agriculture industry. Another four years of constant haggling in Brussels was not appealing.

Energy and Transport were not appetising either. Both were parts of the bigger jobs I had done at the departments of the Environment and Trade and Industry. I did not think that having carried out the agriculture job for four years I could be accused of failing to support Margaret and the party if I did step down.

If one consequence was that she decided to promote Alick as Minister of Agriculture, I would be delighted. This was perhaps the one way she would give him a number one job in the Cabinet. Everyone knew he had performed well in agriculture and he was popular.

I was phoned by the Prime Minister on the Friday after the election and went to No. 10 to see her. She began by saying she was full of admiration for the way I had performed my duties as Minister of

Agriculture. As a result, the party's standing among the agriculture community was probably higher than it had ever been. Was I being softened up? She said that when she went to rural communities during her election tours she was told I was the best Minister of Agriculture since the war.

She went on to say she wanted me to tackle another job. I could see it coming. Transport or Energy? She said she would like me to go to Energy, but before I could make my carefully prepared declaration, she added that she wanted me there because she believed the government was about to be challenged in a major battle with Arthur Scargill, the miners' leader. He had of course confronted her first government and because of the low stocks of coal the Cabinet had been compelled to meet his demands. David Howell, the Energy Secretary of the time, had inherited low fuel stocks from the Labour government. The government decided initially that it would fight, but then had to give way.

Since then Arthur Scargill had made at least three attempts to win his members' approval for strike action, but he could not get the two-thirds vote he needed. I thought the Prime Minister was right to expect a showdown with him during the lifetime of the new government.

She was properly nervous of the harm a miners' dispute could do to the economy. She had been with me in Ted Heath's Cabinet in 1974 and seen the damage done then. But the 1981 humiliation when she was Prime Minister was clearly scorched on her mind. She said she felt there was no one in the Cabinet who could conduct the battle with Arthur Scargill as well as I could. She thought I would have the political knowhow and the communications skill to explain the government case to the public. This was essential in a major conflict of this kind. Industrial unrest in the coal industry was probably the greatest threat to her government and I was the best person to see it did not happen.

This particular approach was a surprise and presented me with a dilemma. Put like this, the overture was difficult to resist. If I persisted in saying that I wanted to return to the back benches, it would be said privately that I was running scared of a scrap with Arthur Scargill. With some reluctance, I took on the post and told Alick what I had done. She had asked me if I wanted Alick to stay with me as minister of state. I told him that I would understand if he wished to take a different course, but luckily he said he would move across with me. It was all the more clear to me that the Prime Minister was never going to give him the Cabinet post he deserved.

My first action was to examine Mr Scargill's background. I looked at all the press cuttings available over several decades, obtained copies of the speeches he had made to Labour Party conferences and elsewhere, and pamphlets and leaflets with which he had been involved. I probably did the most thorough read-in anyone had done on the NUM president. And I quickly realized I was dealing with a person with a close and friendly connection with the Marxists. Communist Party literature which had not had wide circulation brought this out with crystal clarity. Perhaps the most significant was the leaflet he produced with an American Marxist, Peggy Khan, in which they presented the case against worker participation in industry. He acknowledged that if it succeeded the workers would become happy participants in a capitalist system and difficult to detach from it. The whole objective of Marxist philosophy is to overthrow and destroy capitalism.

My research brought out his strong connections with other Communist Parties, particularly the French, and the Soviet Union. It left me in no doubt at all about the nature of my opponent. I decided that in order to defeat him I must see there was no possibility of him winning a vote for industrial action. He needed sixty-six per cent and had failed to get it on a number of occasions. He was not popular enough without having a good case. He must never be given this case.

Arthur Scargill was, however, working at ways of avoiding the vote. Up to then, the NUM had never taken industrial action without a ballot. To me it was inconceivable that this great union would discard such a long-established tradition.

I looked at the scenarios in which he could win a ballot. On pay there was no problem. Productivity was improving as a result of £800 million a year capital investment and there was no reason at all why some of the benefits should not be passed on to the miners. Pay settlements in the future would improve the standard of living of the miner and reward him properly.

One potential problem was the level of redundancies which would have to follow pit closures. A large number of pits were uneconomic. The coal was not required because we now had a surplus and substantial coal stocks. With modern machinery the better pits could produce, on a cost-effective basis, all the coal required and could also satisfy export markets, if these were ever developed. We had to close the bad pits and invest in the new, where there were good seams and better working conditions.

If I was to avoid a strike, I must work out a policy in which there were no compulsory redundancies. They must take place only if miners volunteered. That meant offering exceedingly attractive terms so that a substantial number of miners would be happy to take advantage of them. I prepared a scheme which allowed the older miners retirement pensions on incredibly generous terms and also a considerable capital sum.

I felt genuine sympathy with the miners. I had been responsible for energy as part of my Trade and Industry brief and been down a number of coal mines and found the coal-face conditions horrific.

Those on the face itself contended with heat and dust and dirt and filth, often having to crouch all day. I thought face workers should be well paid and have early retirement. There are industries where the physical conditions of the job call out for the workers to be offered early retirement. I regarded an early retirement package as civilized and reasonable. But I had also to provide for younger miners. If a pit closed, they would be offered alternative work in other pits nearby whenever this was possible, but it would not always be possible and I again suggested generous redundancy terms.

We gave a capital sum for each year a man had worked down the mines. Most miners started work at the age of sixteen so those in their mid-twenties had ten years' service and would get a ten-year capital sum.

The policy had six main points:

* Not a single compulsory redundancy
* Early retirement provisions for miners over fifty which were more generous than those offered in any other industry
* The offer of a job at another pit to any miner whose pit did close
* Younger miners who did not want to transfer would receive handsome terms for voluntary redundancy
* A £800 million a year investment programme, far above that of other nationalized and privately owned industries and calculated to turn them green with envy
* A pay award which would reward those who produced more coal

Eight years before, the Labour Government had agreed a 'Plan for Coal' which envisaged spending six billion pounds over ten years, but the four per cent increase in productivity, which was the other part of the equation, did not take place. Improvement could be obtained only by concentrating on the better pits. We had already increased the level of investment.

I believed it was critical that these proposals should not leak and become part of a speculative story. In the past there had been heavy leaking.

I told the Prime Minister I wanted to prepare a paper outlining my proposals and wanted it discussed without a leak. If I circulated it round all government departments, I was sure it would quickly appear in the *Guardian* or some other newspaper and would certainly be in the hands of Arthur Scargill. She agreed I should prepare the paper and see the ministers she wanted involved for private briefing before it went to full Cabinet.

This was precisely what happened. It must have been one of the few occasions on which a major Cabinet paper did not do the rounds in the normal way to each department. I visited each of the ministers, gave them a copy to read through, explained the points and issues and gave them the background they required. We then met under the Prime Minister's chairmanship and my paper was approved.

As a result of the careful analysis, I was confident that we could not lose any struggle with Arthur Scargill. It was total nonsense to suggest, as some on the left and in the Labour Party did, that the Conservative government wanted confrontation, but if it was forced upon us we intended to win.

I was convinced the Cabinet had given me all the resources I needed to guarantee that there would not be a successful ballot for industrial action in the foreseeable future. I was right on that. There never was a successful ballot. The only way he could get industrial action was, despite the rules of the NUM, by avoiding a ballot completely.

He engineered a strike without a ballot. At the same time, a number of regions of the NUM decided they were going to abide by the normal traditions and have their ballot. These ballots demonstrated he had no chance whatever of winning through the time-cherished method. Nine areas balloted. Only Northumberland had more than fifty per cent in favour of a strike, and then the figure was only fifty-two per cent. The results of all the ballots were as follows:

Area	% for strike	% against
Cumberland	22.2	77.8
Derbyshire	49.9	50.1
Leicestershire	10.7	89.3
Midlands	27.1	72.9
Northumberland	52.00	48.00
North Wales	31.7	68.3
Nottingham	26.5	73.5
North Western	40.8	59.2
South Derbyshire	16.4	83.6

The dispute turned nasty with the introduction of paid, violent pickets. They were paid for each day they picketed and given car and travel allowances. We know substantial sums of cash were paid out over a period to the mobs who tried to close working pits and stop the distribution of coal by violent methods. The Yorkshire NUM executive voted to send pickets to other areas. Pickets were essential to the Scargill strategy. Their first targets were pits which were continuing to work. Coach loads of pickets arrived and there was violence and intimidation. That the strategy failed was a tribute to the courage and bravery of individual policemen. Over the entire period, 1,399 police officers were injured.

Month after month went by and the NUM leader failed to close a single pit or steel works. One of the crucial tests was at Orgreave where there was a small coke works in the heart of Scargill militancy. Thousands of pickets arrived, to be led by Arthur Scargill himself. The media, which had been tipped off to watch what happened, saw Arthur Scargill lead the protest and be arrested.

The picketing went on for eight consecutive days, but every load of coke from Orgreave went off to its destination. Mob power had failed.

In the Commons Tony Benn, one of Mr Scargill's backers, predicted confidently that the government would be defeated. Arthur Scargill tried to convince the miners with totally inaccurate facts about the level of coal stocks. In February he said there were only eight weeks' supplies at the power stations. At the end of March he said there were only nine to ten weeks' supplies. Towards the end of April there were eight to nine weeks' supplies. The fact was that the government was never in the remotest danger of running out. I was able to tell Margaret that we had at least a year's supply and, later, two years.

I became increasingly concerned about the attitude of Neil Kinnock, as Leader of the Opposition. He came from South Wales and the South Wales miners were deeply unhappy about what was taking place. They had always called for and obeyed a ballot. On the other hand, they had always supported the leadership of the NUM. Emotionally, they wanted a ballot, but, in the best traditions of miners, they thought they must back the leadership of their union. They would not, however, countenance mob picket lines. They told Mr Scargill they would organize the pickets and do it in the normal, peaceful way.

I thought Neil Kinnock could have an important influence in stopping violent picketing elsewhere. I asked a Labour MP to tell him I thought it would be in his interests to say publicly that his party supported the miners, but they must follow the TUC guidelines on picketing. These laid down there should never be more than six pickets at a gate and they should picket peacefully. He could so easily have told Mr Scargill publicly that he was sure that if miners obeyed the guidelines, no one would break the picket lines and there would be no violence. Unfathomably, the leader of the Labour Party never did publicly ask Mr Scargill to stick to the TUC guidelines. I regarded his performance as pathetic. He was failing totally to stand up to Arthur Scargill.

I tried again to elicit the help of Neil Kinnock. I proposed, through a Labour MP who acted as an intermediary, that Mr Kinnock should endorse Mr Scargill's request for a change in the union rules – to allow industrial action to be taken with a majority of only fifty-one per cent, instead of sixty-six per cent. But this should be agreed only on condition there was a ballot on the new rule. I knew that if there was a ballot, Mr Scargill would lose this, too, and the strike would have folded. Neil Kinnock endorsed the rule change, but made no public request for an immediate ballot.

Here were two opportunities for the leader of the Labour Party to be seen trying to stop the violence and almost certainly clearing the way for a return to work. He neglected both. Instead the observer saw a man who could put a pleasant face on events, but lacked political courage.

I was not asking him to do anything which was in any way detrimental to himself or the Labour Party. I was asking him to do something in the national interest. The question has to be asked: why did he not do either?

I believe the reason was that he was worried about the power of Mr Scargill and the NUM and the trouble he might run into if Mr Scargill attacked what he was recommending. That is, in my view, the only explanation for his silence.

It did leave me wondering whether Neil Kinnock, if he became Prime Minister, would be prepared to stand up to a union leader like Arthur Scargill. To me, his response was not that of a potentially great leader. When he did make a speech on picket violence, he said he hoped violence both by pickets and police would stop. To say this when the police had not created violence but suffered serious injuries was, to my mind, the height of irresponsibility.

The ostensible cause of the start of the strike was the mishandling of a Cortonwood pit. It was used by Arthur Scargill to call for immediate industrial action and backing from the other trade unions before a ballot took place. I personally believe the incident could have been handled better, both at local colliery and National Coal Board levels, but it was certainly not a justification for a nation-wide strike. Mr Scargill took advantage of an opportunity to create the strike.

From the start of the dispute, I presided over a series of 8 a.m. meetings of officials from the Ministry of Transport, DTI, to give details of the industrial impact, the Department of Employment, the Home Office, who advised on police movements, and the National Coal Board itself. One was the NCB official responsible for the distribution and marketing of coal, Malcolm Edwards. He, more than anyone, deserves the gratitude of the country for the way he performed. He was extremely skilful in getting supplies to industrial and commercial users and circulating coal throughout the system.

Every day I phoned the Prime Minister at No. 10 and told her what was happening. Throughout the dispute I had a close relationship with her. If anything developed suddenly, I would always phone her and tell her and advise her how to handle Commons questions and press conferences. She backed me totally.

This backing was important. Early on I was conscious of a feeling inside the Cabinet that having a 'wet' in charge was likely to lead to weakness and compromise. I think that Norman Tebbit and others on the right of the party probably held that view. They were anxious to use immediately the legislation we had passed to stop secondary picketing at premises which are not the pickets' own.

I advised strongly against it. I explained to the Prime Minister and the Cabinet how I wanted to handle the negotiations. It was true that the NUM was using secondary picketing tactics and it would have been possible to bring writs and, indeed, individuals did so. There were two snags in the government bringing writs as Norman wanted.

One was that when you were fighting Mr Scargill, the legislation was unlikely to work. I warned the Cabinet that if we brought an action against the NUM while they were, for example, picketing a dock, the union pickets would be replaced by 500 pickets who said they were from Sheffield Trades Council or some other organization. I would then have to seek a writ against the Sheffield Trades Council. The prospect of an award against the council for, say, a million pounds, when its balance sheet showed a surplus of only £325.50, was slim. I said that Mr Scargill would quickly organize picketing which he would claim had no connection with the NUM. The government would be made to look a fool and people would say the legislation was unworkable.

The other consideration was that I wanted other unions to keep their distance from the NUM leader. The railwaymen called one day strikes in support of the miners, the TUC called days of action and the Transport and General Workers' Union expressed sympathy, but not once during the dispute did Arthur Scargill succeed in getting the full backing of the other trade unions. If I had turned it into a battle involving Tory trade union legislation, it could well have provoked other trade unions, if reluctantly, to join in the dispute. Arthur would have loved writs from the government.

Margaret accepted this advice and when some of my colleagues argued the other way she stood by my analysis.

The other main player in the dispute was, of course, Ian Mac-Gregor. I inherited him. I understand the original choice was Sir Robert Haslam, now chairman of the NCB, but he had been ill and this apparently deterred Nigel Lawson, then Energy Secretary, from appointing him. Mr MacGregor was appointed instead.

When I first met him I liked him and thought him able. He had ended the dispute with the steel workers successfully, but the coal dispute was a totally different proposition. To ensure we worked closely, he had all my home telephone numbers and I had his. There were reports that when he visited pits, he was well received by the miners themselves. Unfortunately, this good will evaporated as the dispute dragged on. Working miners began to regard him as a liability. In the end, they argued the fight against Arthur Scargill would be easier if Ian MacGregor went himself.

Mr MacGregor came into the Energy Department regularly, sometimes three or four times a week, and was free to come to our morning meetings, though he sent his representatives there. I said that he should tell me if he was concerned about anything I was doing and vice versa. We would work as a team.

My first doubts were raised when he told me the date at which he thought the strike would end. I asked him why. He said that was when the steel dispute ended. It was the time it took for the strikers to start running short of money. For a period they had cash from a few weeks' work and wives and children drew social security. After that, they went back to work.

I said that they might in the steel unions, led by Bill Sirs, a decent, civilized man without political motivation who did not countenance violent picketing. The steel men called a strike after a ballot.

Scargill was different. You could not treat this as just another dispute. Mr MacGregor said, 'Well, note the date.'

Then there were complaints about his public relations. Once he was caught holding a bag over his head. As the dispute went on, there were protests that he was bad on television, bad at press conferences. The media began to condemn him as a poor communicator. He was getting on in age and a dispute of this dimension, with the media against him, including Tory papers like the *Express*, the *Sun* and the *Daily Mail*, must have taken its toll.

I was concerned that the industrial correspondents tended to get most of their information from the trade unions during the dispute, so I phoned several editors almost every day, and had in journalists like Paul Potts of the *Express* and George Jones of the *Daily Telegraph*. Editors of the quality of Sir David English were passionate to see that the nation recognized the reality of this dispute and my regular conversations throughout the dispute with key editors such as Sir David meant that, in the main, we were successful in bringing to the British public the truth about what was going on.

I did persuade Ian MacGregor to take on someone to be the spokesman. He appointed a warm Yorkshireman, Michael Eaton, who loved his industry and did not want it destroyed by Marxism. I was astounded a little later to discover that Michael Eaton had not been permitted to attend a crucial meeting between the Coal Board and the NUM. This was the man who was supposed to be communicating with the media and he was being denied first-hand knowledge of what was going on. When I raised the question, Ian MacGregor explained that top Coal Board officials were jealous of the high profile acquired by Michael Eaton and had said they would not attend the meeting if he did.

We also had differences over the board's treatment of NACODS, the union of colliery supervisors. Tory MPs were worried that the union, which was running the pits, was being increasingly hostile to the board. Mr MacGregor again said there were personality difficulties, but the union was making a lot of noise which would come to nothing.

He was wrong. In September, the union voted to ballot members on a strike. I urged the Coal Board to do a direct mail campaign to all NACODS members. The field was being left open to those who wanted a strike. And a strike would be of great encouragement to Arthur Scargill at an important time.

When more than eighty per cent of NACODS members voted for a strike, Ian MacGregor changed his tune.

NACODS asked to see me and I agreed. I have always been ready to meet unions in industries connected with my department, so there was no new principle involved. I was not prepared to negotiate with them. That was the job of the NCB, but I was ready to see that their views were understood by the NCB and government. Agreement was finally reached between the NCB and the union two days before the strike was due to begin.

Cabinet colleagues did ask me if we should find a new chairman. I said that would be damaging because Arthur Scargill would say that the change proved he was right and chairmanship of the NCB was at fault. Few things would please him more. What we had to do was ensure that Mr MacGregor remained tolerably cheerful. I would brief him constantly and when there were developments we would agree exactly what should happen. She accepted my advice and we did not discuss his removal again.

We did have more problems with Mr MacGregor. NCB officials who saw me every morning told me they were alarmed about a role being played by a Mr David Hart. I had never met Mr Hart and still have not. The only contact I had with him was when he phoned my office from Claridges, saying he was speaking on behalf of Mr MacGregor. He said he was the adviser to Mr MacGregor and we must meet to talk about several aspects of the dispute. I told him I did not know who he was, but Mr MacGregor saw me several times a week and if he wished to discuss anything with me he could do so then. I said I had no intention of running the coal dispute with someone in Claridges. That was the end of the conversation.

There was another distraction, this time from the Bishop of Durham, the Rt. Rev. David Jenkins, who used his enthronement ceremony to attack the government and the NCB over the strike and call for the dismissal of Mr MacGregor. I wrote to him saying that we must share many concerns and hopes. As an Anglican, I certainly shared the wish that the spirit of Christianity should prevail, and concern about poverty, misery, violence and despair.

'My personal approach to politics has always reflected a definition of patriotism which desires that every person born a citizen of our country rejoices in that birthright. This therefore demands social and economic policies that eradicate poverty and despair and give all families reasons to rejoice,' I wrote. As Environment Secretary, I had been pleased to improve the environment of miners in his diocese.

I added that the government had never tried to defeat the miners, but wanted to see they were victorious to a degree unsurpassed in the history of mining. I pointed out the government was investing more than Labour proposals. In spite of the NCB's insolvency, we were providing an extra £3,000 million investment in new collieries. In 1970 we had inherited a situation in which hundreds of pits had been closed, far more than was being contemplated now. It was for that reason we had directed economic aid to the North East, to bring new hope to the area. I said our plans to give miners and their families a better future deserved the support of Christians.

'Perhaps neither you nor I can analyse accurately his motives. But if you have embarked upon a study of Mr Scargill's written and spoken words over many years you can only come to the conclusion that he has always favoured conflict as opposed to participation, because he believes it is by conflict with the existing system that his utopia will be achieved.'

My objective as a Tory was to get the correct balance between efficiency and compassion. The trouble with compassion devoid of efficiency was that it never provided the means to exercise compassion. The trouble with efficiency devoid of compassion was that it created a society so divisive that efficiency itself was destroyed.

If Mr MacGregor had any intention of destroying the mining

industry, I would have dismissed him. 'Perhaps your observations
on Mr MacGregor were based upon his image as portrayed in propa-
ganda rather than upon the genuine aspirations or faults of the man
himself,' I concluded. The bishop thanked me for a reasoned and
compassionate letter, but argued that the government did not seem
to care.

We kept a close check on coal stocks which were being maintained.
One of the funniest and nicest incidents was being phoned at home
on a Sunday evening. A man said that I would not know who he
was, but he was in a signal box outside a particular station in Nottinghamshire. He said the chap who did the other shift was a Communist
who stopped all the coal trains coming through. 'What I will do, Mr
Walker, is to phone you every Sunday evening and tell you when I
am on shift for the coming week. You send all the coal trains through
then.' He did, and the coal trains all went through on that particular
route.

Stocks built up well. We were being given longer and longer estimates of the time we could survive. That ensured we would win,
but I did have emergency plans to move coal from pits which were
on strike, employing police, and to import it. If necessary the docks
would have to be controlled by the services. Winning the dispute
was that important to the future of democracy and British politics.

The most tricky moment of the dispute came when the TUC asked
to see me. My colleagues were hesitant about entering discussions
with the TUC. For a variety of reasons, I decided I should meet
them. I could understand their anxiety about the horrendous things
which were happening and I had a respect for Norman Willis, the
TUC general secretary.

Norman came to see me privately at my home in Cowley Street
to say it would help if I would see the TUC council. I discussed it
with the Prime Minister and argued that refusal would give the
impression that the government was being obdurate. I considered
we had a superb case and welcomed the chance to put it again.

We had a worthwhile meeting. I said that having been down
mines I was sympathetic to the miners, but knew when I took on
the job that there would have to be closures. I loathed what was
happening to them and I had a deep respect for trade unions. I was
the son of a shop steward and respected my father's attitudes.

I explained that I had persuaded my colleagues to offer the miners
a pay increase well above the national average and anything they

would be able to negotiate for their members. Other trade unions would also be envious of the early retirement measures on the table. If members of the TUC had been able to negotiate such terms, they would all be heroes. No miner was to be sacked, but there would also be generous redundancy terms for younger miners. I made them go through every detail of the offer. I pointed out that forty per cent of miners had decided to ballot against the advice of their leadership and seventy-eight per cent of those who had voted were against industrial action.

The TUC council came back and suggested that Norman Willis should try to agree a formula to be put to the NUM, without undermining the government's position. I agreed with Mr Mac-Gregor the principles which must be in such an agreement and that there must be no shift in policy. I asked him to prepare a draft and said I would discuss it with him before it was put to Norman Willis.

Two days before he was to meet Norman, the draft had not arrived, so I asked for it. He said it was on its way. The next day it did not come and I was getting seriously concerned. I stressed that we must agree the wording. The draft actually arrived only minutes before the meeting was due to start and was monstrously worded.

It would have allowed Arthur Scargill to claim he had won. Phrases in it were capable of being interpreted in either of two ways, one to satisfy MacGregor and the other Scargill. It was a fudge of the worst possible kind, allowing Arthur Scargill to say, 'This is what it means.' There were loose phrases like pits being 'deemed exhausted' without making it clear who would do the deeming. It mentioned a new independent body in a way which could have delayed pit closures indefinitely.

The meeting with Norman Willis was to take place in Ian MacGregor's flat and I phoned him immediately to say that he must not present the draft to the TUC leader. I said I would denounce it if he did so. I would damn it publicly as a fudge. I phoned the Prime Minister with his phone number and asked her to call him with precisely the same message. No. 10 did as I asked.

The next day I drafted the wording and it was that which was then delivered to Norman Willis.

That was not quite the end of the story. The TUC asked to see the Prime Minister. We agreed and after seeing the Prime Minister, Ian MacGregor, his adviser Tim Bell, David Hunt, my energy minister, and I went for lunch at La Capannina, a London restaurant. We discussed two minor drafting changes and Ian MacGregor readily accepted these. I said I would be in my office that evening before the TUC arrived, so that he could contact me. We arranged that I would be able to keep in touch with him, through Tim Bell.

The arrangement went wrong. Tim Bell arrived at the office to say Ian MacGregor had changed his mind after speaking to another adviser who had convinced him I was trying to reach an agreement while the Prime Minister was in Washington. That adviser was suggesting that Ian MacGregor should stick to the original wording and delay until after the Prime Minister returned.

Fortunately, the Prime Minister had not left and I was able to contact her. No. 10 again contacted Mr MacGregor to tell him the Prime Minister wanted the agreement based on our lunch discussion.

The TUC meeting was a success. A final version was agreed the next morning, together with a covering letter.

I was staggered therefore when that afternoon my press officer, Romola Christopherson, told me four journalists were working on a story that in discussions with the TUC I had wanted to make a long list of concessions, but Ian MacGregor refused. One journalist claimed to have received his information from a MacGregor aide.

As luck would have it, I was at that moment having a meeting with Ian MacGregor in my office. I asked Romola to come in and hear from Mr MacGregor's own lips that the story was totally untrue. He denounced it and she was able to say that Mr MacGregor had personally denied the story. It was easy to see what would have happened if the journalists had not checked. Four papers would have carried stories saying that Mr MacGregor had stopped me making concessions to the TUC.

Norman Willis then went to the NUM with the agreement and Mr Scargill turned it down.

The attempt, however, did not delay a settlement and the TUC and moderates in the Labour Party were made to see the objects of Mr Scargill.

When the dispute ended, Mr MacGregor desperately wanted to get into print with his version of what happened. I imagine he wanted to appear the toughy, fighting Scargill. In his book, I was presented as plausible, but with no backbone. He knew that my view and the view of the Prime Minister were different.

The timing of the publication of Ian MacGregor's book was unfortunate for him and left a sour taste on the very day he left. He was coming in to say his goodbyes and I put the book on the table in front of where he was to sit, making it clear to him that I had read it. He sat uneasily in front of it. I said that I had read it and found it extraordinary that in the whole period we had worked together he had never made any criticism to my face. He was silent for a moment and then said, 'Well, we write these books', trying to brush my remark aside. I repeated I thought it was a pity that he had never made any criticism to me personally. Now he had written a book in which he implied he was the wonder man and I had not got it right. If this was what he thought, he should have pointed out where he thought I was going wrong at the time.

I had the head of my private office sitting in as a witness and it was not the happiest of farewell drinks. I think Mr MacGregor must have been pleased to leave.

Police action was critical to breaking the strike. The police set up an operations room in Scotland Yard. Each of the forces had to provide so many men. They were moved wherever it was considered necessary and no politician was really involved. I only once visited the operations room, just before the end, and that was to say 'thank you' for the incredible job they had done.

Questions were raised about the principle of having a national police operation. But the Home Secretary had to advise the Cabinet how to deal with violent picketing and it would simply not have been possible to leave it to individual forces. Nottinghamshire police could not, for example, have been left to organize the control of pickets in their area, and the same was true throughout large parts of the country. You had to have an operations room to co-ordinate forces and arrange mundane things like the sleeping and feeding of the police. You had to identify where the convoys of violent pickets were coming from and where they were going.

Steadily miners drifted back to work. The first few who went back were brave men. They had to go through the picket lines, but the numbers returning increased daily.

The majority of miners wanted to go back. This is why Arthur Scargill constantly sought talks. If he could get these fixed for three weeks ahead, the return to work would slow down. Miners would think that if it was going to be settled in three weeks, they would stick it out. I had to get Ian MacGregor to say there would be no talks unless the closures were accepted.

As the numbers of miners working built up, so did those coal stocks. Arthur Scargill had repeatedly given his own NUM members untrue estimates of the time coal stocks could last. Even in June he predicted the power stations would cut back in August. None of this was ever remotely accurate.

The South Wales miners really ended the dispute, marching back proudly with their bands. You knew then it was over.

The first thing I said to my colleagues was that there must be no gloating. The miners were decent, honourable people. We took the view that we had not defeated the miners, but Arthur Scargill. The important thing was to return the mining communities to comparative prosperity. I refused to make any statements or speeches and my colleagues did the same.

We did, however, feel a huge sense of relief that a Marxist sympathizer for whom the ends justified the means was unlikely to have any real standing in the trade union movement again. He never has.

13

SID TAKES A BOW

The resolution of the miners' strike did leave me basking briefly in the sunlight, with talk of me being the next leader of the party. I had not, frankly, thought much of it since my days at the Department of Trade and Industry when there was similar speculation in the press. At that stage, with Ted in charge, I had not wanted it. With Margaret in charge, I was surprised to find myself even in the Cabinet, let alone a prominent figure. I thought this was psychologically a bad patch when the Tory Party was going to swallow all this monetarist stuff, but we should return to a more traditionally pragmatic approach again, as is happening now.

Now there was again widespread comment that I had handled the NUM threat with skill and this intensified speculation that I might succeed Margaret as the next leader. Opinion polls showed Norman Tebbit and I were the most popular choices among the electors if the leadership did become vacant. Ladbrokes made me the favourite!

An interview that David English did with me in the *Daily Mail*, giving two pages to the exchanges, was a pointer to the seriousness with which I was apparently being taken. The message was that this man has exceptional quality, he has handled a potentially dangerous situation with deftness and must have a future at the top of British politics. Liberally minded MPs came up and told me I must make sure I was the next leader. I laughed at them for saying so.

Privately, I held the view that the Prime Minister would go on and I was not in the business of making a challenge. I have always thought challenges do immense damage to a party. To those close to me, like my excellent PPS, Stephen Dorrell, I said, 'Yes, if there is a leadership election, I probably would stand to represent the more liberal traditions of the party.' Even in those days I was also conscious of the pressure of the Prime Ministerial job and how difficult it would be to do the job and stay close to the family.

My immediate preoccupation was not always with Labour policies or Arthur Scargill, but the policies of my own party. I fervently believed that we had been digging ourselves into a hole as a result of Margaret's continual references to cutting public spending when we were often increasing it. After the Cabinet row over the 1981 Budget, Nigel Lawson, who became Chancellor two years later, did go out of his way to emphasize that Y millions were going to go into public expenditure as well as Z millions into tax reductions. I tried to insist in subsequent Budgets that we stressed even more the increases in public expenditure.

If the Chancellor and Prime Minister did not do it, I did.

During this period I attracted frequent headlines suggesting I was breaking ranks or rocking the boat. I was always pursuing exactly the same theme. All the party conference and Tory Reform Group speeches and the Harold Macmillan and Iain Macleod Memorial Lectures repeated the same message of One Nation Toryism.

The 'dries' wanted to say how beneficial the tax reductions were and to forget they were increasing spending substantially in areas like health and education. The message did change gradually. More and more, Nigel Lawson drew attention to the public spending side.

Election pressures underlined the need. Suddenly the Prime Minister herself became worried by the allegation that she was destroying the health service: she exploded at one press conference with a passionate exposition of how much we were spending on nurses and health care of all kinds. It was the first time she had gone up front to say, 'Look how much we are spending on the health service.'

Even then it was not totally convincing. Too often in the past she had made tax cutting and reductions in public expenditure The Great Theme, when, in fact, she was also agreeing big increases in spending.

It was only during an election campaign, when there were reports that Labour was making ground on issues like health, that she forced herself to say what the position was. It was almost as if she suffered from a congenital block which prevented her from saying 'spending', except when accompanied by 'cutting'.

Yet the argument for sensible spending was overwhelming. Later, she allowed me to increase public expenditure in Wales and the result was better value for money. The policy represented a net gain to the Treasury, but you never heard Margaret say this because she wanted to maintain a purist doctrine.

I argued that the biggest battle of the period should be on unemployment. The cost of the jobless to public spending was enormous. The Treasury had to find unemployment pay and social security benefits and it lost tax receipts. I would guess that an unemployed man or woman today costs the Exchequer £11,000 a year. You have several billions of pounds going to pay three million people for doing nothing. Unemployment is not the way to cut public expenditure: it massively increases it. When the Chancellor cut unemployment from three million to one and a half, the saving to the Treasury was massive.

I urged the Treasury, when it was looking at regional programmes or job creation schemes, not to say that the policies were going to cost us ten million pounds, but that they would save us five million. The Treasury never, ever want to look at the net result.

The issue came up acutely in my time as Energy Secretary. I remember one public expenditure round in which the Treasury demanded a slashing of the capital investment programme of the nationalized industries. My view was that public investment was too low and had fallen behind other countries as a result of the neglect of earlier Labour and Conservative governments. It was absurd to try to bring down public spending figures by cutting the capital investment programmes of the nationalized industries. Gas and electricity industries needed large-scale investment if they were to be cost-effective.

The Chancellor was right to have criteria laying down the return they must achieve. That was good commercial practice which would be followed in the private sector. But then the Treasury came along and said the government had to cut back across the board and every department must find its share. The only spending the Energy Department did was the capital spending of nationalized industries.

I said I would not do it. If the Chancellor wanted extra money, he could put a five per cent tax on energy, but I was not going to pull back on capital investment programmes. I did not threaten resignation on the issue, but I would have gone if cuts had been forced upon me.

We were at an impasse. Then I discovered that the corporation tax paid by the utilities to the Treasury counted as public expenditure. The Central Electricity Generating Board was in profit and paying large sums of corporation tax.

I called in the CEGB and urged them to ask their accountants to find ways of deferring the payment of corporation tax in that particular year. Their accountants did find ways and I saved millions of pounds which was being paid in corporation tax. This, incredibly, met the Chancellor's objective of cutting public spending. The Treasury actually got £110 million less, but Walker had cut public spending by this amount and that was all right. It was absolute nonsense, of course.

The Treasury just want a crude balance. The whole public expenditure process is riddled with illogicality. Every year we have this Cabinet meeting to agree in principle the figure for next year and that means big cuts. Each department is called upon to make its contribution and the Treasury suggests what each department should save. This is always more than is possible, but ministers then negotiate. What should happen is that the Cabinet should decide priorities and the Treasury should start its round by saying that public spending cuts should be in specific areas. In the present climate one of those areas might be defence.

I know that there was talk about this time of a Heseltine/Walker alliance to get our own way in Cabinet. There never was any such alliance. We were both in Cabinet and we shared similar views, but that was it.

One thing we were agreed upon was our opposition to the poll tax. As long ago as 1972, when I produced a White Paper on local government finance, I told the Cabinet there was nothing wrong with the rating system except that the burden being placed upon it was too big. Any tax is subject to the same rule. You can tax up to a limit. Beyond that limit you have to fund large rebates. At that time I proposed we should give local authorities the revenue from motor vehicle licences in their areas and the right to levy an addition to petrol tax on a county-wide basis.

The petrol tax did fit, crudely, with the needs of local government. There is a relationship between the number of cars and other vehicles and areas of high spending. Both licence and petrol taxes would also have been 'buoyant'. Treasury ministers were implacably opposed, however, and I learned quickly about the ability of the Treasury to win its case. It simply told every other minister that if Walker took away revenue in this way they would have to find it out of their budgets. I still think it was a sensible idea, but, at the time, found myself in a minority of one.

My 1972 White Paper rejected emphatically a sales tax, local income tax and a poll tax. When Michael, now Environment Secretary ten years later, produced a Green Paper he advanced the same objections to the poll tax. This was not really surprising. He had contributed to my White Paper.

I recall that Willie Whitelaw was also asked to head a Cabinet committee to look at the alternatives to the rates, but failed to come up with an answer.

The poll tax was eventually given life by the revaluation of rates in Scotland after Michael had left in dramatic style. Revaluations are always electorally disastrous and there was trepidation about the reaction in Scotland. George Younger, the Scottish Secretary, proposed we should change the system. Willie, who had a border constituency, shared the apprehension about revaluation and legislation was rushed through, to the relief of the Scottish Office who thought it had saved the day. How wrong it was to prove to be! Initially, we had no intention of introducing the poll tax to the rest of the country, but we faced the certainty that if we chose another system for England, Wales and Northern Ireland we would be acknowledging that we had it wrong in Scotland.

Margaret was also a major factor. She felt strongly that each individual should feel he or she could influence the level of the charge and was attracted to the principle that everyone should pay something. I could understand the attraction of the principle. The trouble was that it did not work. She did not want to hurt the poorer groups and allowed them more in benefit to compensate for the poll tax payment, but even this did not work. They spent the extra twenty per cent on food and clothes and there was still nothing left for the poll tax.

In the early poll tax discussions in Cabinet, the chief opponents of the scheme were Michael Heseltine and myself. After Michael had made his exit, it was just P. Walker. Nigel Lawson now says that he was opposed to it. I am sure that this is right and that he argued privately with the Prime Minister. Had he come into the open, then the Treasury and P. Walker might have swung others. I do remember that Margaret, at the time of critical decision-making, was supported by her Environment Secretary, Kenneth Baker.

By the time the poll tax legislation was ready, I was Welsh Secretary and determined that, having opposed the tax, Wales would not suffer from it. I said I wanted a grant for Wales as large as it would have been under the old system and I made it clear I would not accept anything less. We were able to negotiate a grant, leaving the poll tax figures for Wales forty to sixty per cent lower than for Scotland and England.

I played only a minor part in the drama which led to Michael Heseltine's resignation and the Westland crisis. In the end, he went not on the arguments about Westland, but on what, to the outside world, must have seemed a technical point. It was a battle over whether the helicopter company should become part of a European venture or be sold to the American Sikorsky. Michael, as Secretary of State for Defence, and Leon Brittan, then Trade and Industry Secretary, accepted that the arguments needed to be conducted in a calmer atmosphere and that if either of them was forced to say anything it should be cleared through the Cabinet Office. Quite reasonably, Michael said there must be an exception if ministers were asked to confirm something they had already said. He offered a list of the things he had said. If the media asked for confirmation of something which had already been stated, ministers could not delay an answer for hours while consulting the Cabinet Office. Margaret said, 'No. Everything must be cleared.'

Michael said this was ridiculous. He would not spend his time telling journalists he would have to clear his remarks first with the Cabinet Office. He said he would not tolerate it and would go. Margaret started to say, 'Well, this is the way I want it . . .' when he got up and walked out.

I regretted later I did not go to him at the door and ask him to come back and thrash it out. I am sure he would have done. If the Prime Minister had said, 'Just sit down and don't be silly. Let's talk about this,' I am sure he would have done so. Everyone was so staggered to see him walking to the door, we remained breathless.

Events conspired against us. As he walked out of Downing Street, photographers were waiting for something else. They filmed him and he said he had left the Cabinet and would be issuing a statement later. If the cameras had not been there, one of us would have phoned him and asked him to come back and talk it through, but it happened so quickly there was no time for second thoughts. I am absolutely certain that at the beginning of the meeting, Michael had no intention of resigning. Equally, I am certain Margaret had no intention of forcing him to quit.

I knew a great battle was taking place. Michael did disagree with the Prime Minister on the importance of having a European rather than the Sikorsky American deal for Westland and he did think there were attempts to stop him deploying his arguments, but at that particular meeting both sides seemed determined to produce a rational solution.

The likelihood of a struggle with Arthur Scargill was only part of the brief the Prime Minister gave me when I agreed to take on Energy. She said it was also important to bring forward a major privatization. I was always in favour of this. I did the first of the privatizations, Thomas Cook's, and put Rolls-Royce back into private hands. I was against nationalization and in favour of what she wanted, but I was determined not to get into the same mess others had found themselves in.

Margaret said she wanted proposals for privatization of one of the industries by a certain date. I think it was a couple of months. I said I could not do that. I explained that I was enthusiastic about privatization, but that having watched some of the privatizations which had run into great difficulty, like British Telecom, I wanted to do my homework properly. If you were going to do a privatization of one of the biggest industries in the country, you must do it the right way.

It had been easy to say we would privatize British Telecom and to ask civil servants to prepare the legislation. Only then did we discover the problems. How did the regulator work? Did you break it up into regions? How did you deal with the monopoly aspects of it? What would be the management structure? I told Margaret she had the lifetime of the Parliament to carry it out. I would do one in this Parliament and move on to the next one. She accepted the campaign plan straight away.

The next candidate was gas. We had to decide precisely how it would be done. I set up a team led by Derek Davis, a bright civil servant. The members of the team were chosen not because they knew particularly about gas, but because they had good brains. I would guide on what they should examine in detail and they would report back to me. They went round the world looking at other privatized gas concerns. They were asked to look at regulatory systems and see where these had gone wrong and to draw up a list of the different ways of carrying out the privatization.

I then called in Sir Denis Rooke, the Gas Board chairman, and told him that I understood his opposition to privatization, but I wanted it to go ahead. I could either do it with guess-work from the outside or he could give me, from the inside, all the information I wanted. If he did co-operate, my decision was likely to be of a better quality than if he did not. He was persuaded that he would prefer me to know all the facts and details.

So my team was given full access to British Gas, to talk to staff and gather information at all levels. I did promise that when I had worked out what to do I would come to Denis Rooke and give him the opportunity of saying where he thought I was wrong.

The Prime Minister's deadline slipped by, but several months later I produced what I considered the best paper to be presented on privatization. There were seven choices. One involved breaking the industry up into regions, another breaking it up into distribution and retail sides. I listed objectively the advantages and disadvantages of each. The paper discussed the regulatory systems, where they had been successful and not successful. I sent it to the Prime Minister, Chancellor and the Secretary of State for Trade and Industry.

Before it reached a Cabinet committee, Nigel Lawson told me that the method I was suggesting, which involved keeping the industry together, was totally unacceptable. It would continue a monopoly when he wanted competition. I replied that the person who had stopped competition in gas was a good right-wing Tory, Robert Peel. He had done it because competing gas companies in London were digging up the same street and then undercutting each other to force the weaker to go bankrupt. The public was left with a monopoly in any case.

Peel had passed legislation to stop that kind of competition. None of the privately owned gas undertakings in the world faced the competition Nigel was advocating. If the gas industry was split up into regions, the south east and north west would still not compete. He argued that if regional companies were created, everybody would at least be able to compare the performance of one with another. I asked who was to make the comparison. The distribution of gas in London was entirely different from in Cornwall. They were two totally different problems. Consumers in the north west were not going to compare their gas bills with those in the south east. It was not like that.

Under my proposals there would be competition. Oil and gas companies would be able to come in and provide, for example, ICI with the gas it wanted.

I said that I had done my research thoroughly. He had not, even when he was Energy Secretary and had the opportunity. He should now choose anyone he liked from the Treasury, as tough as they came (and there were plenty of those in the Treasury), and send him to spend a few weeks with me to look at the alternatives in depth, examining all the facts and figures. They could then report back to him that the Treasury was right and Walker was wrong. He chose an official who was at that time involved in the public expenditure round. He arrived, spent weeks talking to my officials and Gas Board officials.

I can only presume he went back to Nigel Lawson and said, 'Dammit. Walker's right.' I was suddenly phoned up by Nigel and went round to No. 11 to be told he wanted to get on with the privatization and agreed to do it by my method.

When it came to the legislation, I insisted there should be no shoddy drafting. I did not want the bill to attract hundreds of amendments in Parliament. I told my officials they were to allocate whatever resources they wanted to the task. I also consulted top outside solicitors and they suggested hundreds of amendments which were, mercifully, made before and not after the bill was published. When the bill actually came to Parliament it suffered fewer government amendments than any other piece of legislation I can remember and as a result there was much less trouble getting it through committee and other stages in both the House of Commons and the Lords.

The central figures in British Gas realized that I had decided the breaking up of the corporation was lunacy and that I wanted a powerful British company which could compete round the world. Here was the biggest gas utility in the world, and it was not allowed to operate outside the UK. With that size and those skills it should be able to compete abroad.

Nor could the corporation pay proper salaries. The government imposed salary levels. Many of the bright people left and it was difficult to recruit others.

Sir Denis Rooke realized that though British Gas had worked well and been profitable as a nationalized enterprise, privatization would mean an end to interference and the long meetings in Whitehall. He was going to be able to make his own decisions and fix his own capital investment programme. From being genuinely opposed to privatization, he and the top managers, with one or two exceptions, changed their attitude and collaborated enthusiastically. Denis must have been relieved to be rid of government and particularly Treasury intervention.

On another occasion, Nigel informed me I must put up gas and electricity prices to produce revenue to help the public expenditure round. I said I was not going to do it. Gas and electricity were both profitable and did not need extra profits. If the Treasury wanted extra money, it must tax the industries. That would be a decision for the Chancellor. The industries judged they did not have to put up prices and the Secretary of State for Energy agreed with them.

The Treasury then played into our hands. Quite unbelievably, it kept briefing the political correspondents that bloody Walker was being awkward and refusing to put up prices. Newspapers wrote articles describing how Walker was fighting against price rises. Of course, the whole of the British public was on Walker's side and against the Treasury. For weeks, I had newspaper editorials praising my stand. The Treasury told me I would be taken to the Star Chamber of senior Cabinet Ministers, who resolve disputes between the Treasury and spending ministers. I said fine. I would go to the Star Chamber, the full Cabinet, wherever they liked.

Gas and electricity boards did eventually make some increases to keep up with their fixed return on capital, but I refused to budge on the Treasury argument that they should contribute more to help the public sector borrowing requirement.

The clashes had their ironical side. Denis Rooke was the type of chairman the Tory Party was always supposed to want, in theory. We said we wanted the nationalized industries run as private businesses with good managerial control, making profits. In practice, of course, the chap who ran it as a business, wanted to be totally independent of the government, argued with the ministers and refused to be interfered with, was exceedingly unpopular. It was interesting to see Treasury reaction when they had a nationalized industry chairman who said he was going to run it as a business, double his investment this year, borrow money at nine per cent to give an eighteen per cent return. That did not fit into Treasury thinking at all.

Whatever the theory, this was not what the Treasury wanted. It wanted chairmen who would happily comply when told to cut their investment programmes by twenty per cent. If they did not, then the Treasury was bloody-minded.

There is no doubt that relations between Nigel Lawson and Sir Denis Rooke were extremely bad. Nigel took a decision that British Gas's North Sea assets should be floated off. He interfered in a number of ways. Sir Denis complained that he was running a profitable business, making a good return and his North Sea ventures were sensible. Any sizeable gas industry in the world would do gas exploration as well as gas distribution and it was wrong to stop him.

Denis Rooke was the best nationalized industry chairman I met. He was as tough on his executives as he was on intruders. When he went into the private sector, it was easy for him to adapt. He could devote all his time to running the business.

I must admit to one difference with Sir Denis myself when I vetoed British Gas's purchase of the Norwegian Sleipner gas field. The theory was that if British Gas could get much of its supplies from Norway, it had less need to get them from the North Sea. Big oil companies, like BP and Shell, felt this weakened their negotiating position in obtaining the best gas prices out of British Gas. It was a matter of straight financial interest and I do not blame them for it. Lobbyists were saying that if vast quantities of Norwegian gas were bought, it would slow up the development of the British potential in the North Sea, making it less profitable and less able to attract investment.

I did not take that attitude because I do think British Gas has to have large, long-term supplies available. It has to plan its gas supplies for the next twenty years. What I objected to were the financial terms being asked by the Norwegians. I believed they were asking a variable price which was too high. Although I was guilty of straight government interference in a commercial decision, something I criticized when it was done by others, this decision was on such a scale, affecting a nationalized industry and my financing, I had to take a view.

That view was that I would not approve a price above a certain limit. The Norwegians demanded more and Sir Denis warned that if we did not go higher we would lose the chance, but I said, 'Too bad. I stick to my view that we should not go beyond the figure we decided was reasonable.'

The oil companies were delighted and believed that Walker had been influenced by their lobby. Sir Denis was displeased because he wanted to sign up. I do not claim any skill on my part, but, as it happened, I was shown to be right. The prices came down substantially. If the price had been agreed, it would, eighteen months later, have been seen to be a bad deal.

We then had to conduct a 'beauty competition' of bankers to determine who should do the gas privatization. Rothschilds won. The advertising agents, Young and Rubican, came to me with the first draft of the promotion of the shares. I shocked them by telling them the material was terrible and that they had got it wrong. I said we were trying to interest millions of people who had never bought a share in their lives before. They would not understand any of the 'guff' which was being presented.

Of course, stockbrokers and those in the City would understand, but we were not selling to the City. We were selling to ordinary customers of British Gas. I wanted them to be able to fill in forms easily when they applied for shares. They were putting forward a higher middle class presentation of which the City would approve, but which would be meaningless to the ordinary bloke in a three-bedroom semi-detached house.

They went away and came back with 'Sid'. My deep embarrassment was that my brother is called Syd. I could see trouble if I said I could not have it because it was my brother's name, and more trouble if people thought I had named it after my brother. I thought it was a good name and decided not to tell anyone my brother was called Syd.

Sid worked well for British Gas and produced the biggest application for shares in the history of mankind.

14

NEW BREED OF RUSSIAN

Mikhail Gorbachev has a near impossible task. He has to change attitudes, fight suffocating bureaucracy, modernize his industry, introduce a more market-orientated system, meet the demands of large parts of his country for independence, hold the military in check and soothe away the resentment of ordinary Soviets who expect Western standards overnight.

For the West to say how appalling it is that he should do this or not do that displays a frightening ignorance of the size of his task. I do not know whether he can, against the odds, introduce a more Western-style economy and way of life, but I do admire his bravery in attempting it. Mikhail Gorbachev and the Soviet Union need help and loads of understanding.

I was lucky enough to get to know the Soviet president when he came to Britain as a comparatively unknown Russian minister in 1984, leading a trade mission. We were seated together at a dinner in Lancaster House and, to my good fortune, the minister on the other side of him was preoccupied, so I had him to myself for virtually three hours. Sitting between us was an interpreter who translated simultaneously and the conversation went almost as quickly as if we had both spoken the same language.

It was a revelation for me. He was so different from any other Soviet ministers I had met. He had a strong sense of humour and an interest in ideas. I asked what I thought were penetrating questions about profit and investment. He said nothing which would have left him open to criticism that he was deviating from the Communist line, but he was so lively you knew he was quite out of the ordinary.

At the end of the dinner I asked the Soviet ambassador to let me have copies of speeches Gorbachev had made. The ambassador responded with enthusiasm, sending volumes of paper and keeping me up to date with his latest speeches as he made them. I must have become the best-read authority on Gorbachev in the Cabinet. When he became leader of the Soviet Union I wrote to him saying how pleased I was at his success and wishing him well.

Shortly afterwards, Margaret was to go to Moscow for her first visit. As one of the ministers involved in the earlier trade talks with the Russians, I saw her Foreign Office briefing. I thought it was too cautious and pessimistic. The theme was that the Soviet leaders were Communist, had always been Communist and they were not going to change. Britain needed to explore possibilities, but we should not expect anything to alter.

You have to be fair to the Foreign Office. It had been struggling with a recalcitrant Communist regime since 1917 and was unlikely to say that the new leader was a new breed and that everything was about to change. My own judgement of the man was different. I phoned up No. 10 and said I would like to have a private chat with the Prime Minister about her visit and, as always, she agreed immediately.

I explained that I had talked to him for three hours and since then had studied his progress. Some of the more exciting comments he was making were not in the Foreign Office brief. We discussed her coming visit for a long time and I gave her the draft of the chapter on Gorbachev in my book, *Trust the People*, which was to be published a few months later.

When she came back she thanked me for the briefing. She said it had been immensely useful. She would never have been able to raise some of the issues but for the briefing. She also said she thought my analysis had been right.

As Energy Secretary I went to Moscow myself shortly afterwards and met Boris Scherbina, whom Gorbachev had appointed to be Deputy Prime Minister in charge of all energy in the Soviet Union. Until then the Soviet Union had separate ministries for gas, electricity and hydro-power, and nuclear energy. Gorbachev had sensibly put one man in charge of the lot. It was a good start. Scherbina was in the Gorbachev mould. He also had a highly developed sense of humour and appeared able and energetic.

On the first occasion I met him Gorbachev had just prohibited the drinking of alcohol. I asked him how he liked being part of the temperance movement. Scherbina laughed and said, 'I was having dinner with my son the other day and told him, "You are the person I feel sorry for. I have had my share."'

We got on well and agreed potential joint ventures. Russians would be invited to look at things we thought we were doing well and we would see if we could help in capital investment in the oil industry.

Just a week after my return to England the Chernobyl disaster occurred. Scherbina was, of course, in charge. I am afraid that he went straight to the explosion and was badly radiated. He has had terrible health problems ever since and is a brave man.

I went to see Margaret and said that the whole of the West would condemn what had happened as incompetent and demand compensation. I pleaded with her to do the reverse, to contact the Soviets and offer any help they needed, medical supplies or engineers, anything, and to avoid condemnation and criticism. She agreed and told the Foreign Office this was to be our approach.

I phoned Mr Scherbina to express sympathy and said we would help in any way we could. We sent medical supplies and engineering equipment and he was appreciative. I said publicly that this was not a time to attack the Soviet Union, but to assist it.

We followed up our exchanges by sending a letter pointing out that there would be intense international interest in knowing what had happened and we would like to discuss how this interest should be met. There was clearly a right and wrong way of doing it. I flew to Moscow and told Mr Scherbina he could attempt a cover-up, argue that it was not serious, only a technical fault, but no one would believe him. Or he could decide to disclose all the details and seek, with us, new international standards to see it never happened again. The Soviet Union could be the initiators of international standards of safety and inspection for nuclear plants. Instead of being negative and inviting wide condemnation, which was what had happened to the Soviet Union over the last forty or fifty years, he could give a positive lead. We could call an international conference and get agreement. I urged him to at least consider this as an idea. He took the idea to Gorbachev and together they decided that was the route they wished to go.

They produced a detailed report disclosing every fault in technology and management. The hazard of the reactor we already knew. The Central Electricity Generating Board had looked at the

Chernobyl reactors some years earlier and produced a highly critical report.

It emerged that not only was the reactor unsafe, the manager was also to blame. He tried an experiment of his own and when it started to go wrong, he did not know how to stop it. He drove off in his car and was not caught for about four days. This was a human failing that could not happen in any nuclear establishment in Britain. We have a series of failsafe mechanisms. The Chernobyl reactor had none.

A conference to lay down new international standards for nuclear reactors was called to take place in Vienna. Mr Scherbina agreed a joint approach. He would speak first and I would follow. We would make some proposals and they would make others. I would try to carry the West with me, he would try to carry the Communist bloc.

We dined together before the conference, going over our tactics, and achieved everything we had set out to do. The conference agreed to a system of international inspection. Out of disaster we at least plucked the consolation that the world would be a safer place in future. Before Gorbachev, this would never have happened.

I was given the doubtful reward of being told I would be the first non-Soviet citizen to visit Chernobyl.

A few months later I made the trip, flying over the area and the totally deserted town and seeing many brave men working again on a nuclear reactor within fifty yards of the one which had blown up. It was all operating again, with new safety devices. It was a remarkable achievement by the Soviet Union to bring it under control so quickly. The bravery in sealing off the exploded reactor was staggering. Lives were lost as men moved in. The Russians used space technology, including remote control equipment, to get close and do the job. Concrete was dropped by helicopters to seal the top of the reactor and miners tunnelled beneath to provide a concrete base. It was the only way to succeed, and they succeeded.

I stood next to the reactor which had blown up with my own geiger counter at work. I had two. My visit caused some anxious debate before I went. Our nuclear people said that I had better take a geiger counter, have it in my pocket and look at it occasionally. If it went above a certain limit, I had problems. When I got there the Russians pinned theirs on the overalls they gave me. I did, from time to time, compare theirs with mine. Fortunately both measured the same.

Chernobyl did raise questions about the future of nuclear energy generally, but I have no doubt about its merits and its long-term future.

When I first took office, I had a thoroughly objective look at all sources of energy. Coal, gas and oil were obvious, but I also looked at wind, tidal and solar power. I came to the conclusion that one of the safest and best was nuclear power. I hold to the view that we shall solve the energy problems of the next century only by energy efficiency and more nuclear power. Solar, wind, tide and water do not work well enough to provide the amount of energy which is needed.

Back in Britain, I was left wondering about Gorbachev's other, wider problems. It was impossible to envisage how any man could shift this massive bureaucracy. Nobody under the age of seventy knew any other way of doing things. It was and is a dreadful, appallingly inefficient system, which has created a marked disparity of living standards between the elite and the rest of the country. Vested interests fight to keep their privileges. Bureaucrats with their nice houses and cars and comparatively high living standards resist change.

Another question mark rests against the mighty Soviet military machine, soaking up a large part of Soviet resources. Will it still use some excuse to intervene? It may already be exercising restraint on Gorbachev and the pace of change.

But the change that has already taken place is extraordinary. The first sign it would come was the speed with which Gorbachev began to get rid of the old guard and bring in his own people. When I went to see Mr Scherbina, the ministers were nearly all Gorbachev men of a younger generation. The old guard would have stopped him getting as far as he has.

Some of the bureaucracy has gone. The Ministry of Overseas Trade, for example, was highly effective – in stopping all trade. Gorbachev scrapped it. Instead he told each industry that they could spend so much abroad, depending upon their performance. They would have to decide what they bought.

The old system was hopeless. If you were in the electricity industry and wanted to buy a piece of machinery costing £50,000, ten bureaucrats from the Ministry of Overseas Trade would first crawl over the proposal and demand to know if it could be produced in the Eastern bloc. After months of dithering, they would ask if it was urgent. Years later they might decide to give you permission. By that time, the machinery was probably out of date. I suppose the military could still try to reimpose the old system, but this seems unlikely.

It is sad that the changes have brought so many problems in their wake. It is clear that the great majority of the people want a different social and economic order. The difficulty is that they have exaggerated expectations of an immediate improvement. They look at West Germany and what has been achieved there and say the market system must work. They then expect Western standards and a rash of Marks and Spencer stores all over Russia within six months.

The danger is that not only will they fail to win the better living standards they want, but that conditions, in the chaos caused by change, could actually get worse.

Questions rush into the mind. The West Germans have given Gorbachev credit for three billion dollars' worth of food-processing machinery in order that he can offer the Russian people more in the shops. At a lunch in the Soviet embassy in London in 1991, I asked Soviet ministers who was going to instal the German machinery, who was going to manage it, who was going to provide the materials and then who was going to distribute it? They were unanswered questions.

It may be best to invite a number of German companies to come in and carry out the whole operation, training up Soviets to take their place eventually. The truth is that at the moment the Russians do not have the distribution and management. Machinery, by itself, is not enough when you want an entirely new management structure.

I have retained my contacts with Soviet leaders. When I was the Welsh Secretary the Soviet Union sent over the Deputy Prime Minister in charge of economic policy, much to the chagrin of the Foreign Office, to look at what was happening in Wales under Peter Walker. He came to Wales and stayed at my house at Abbots Morton, near Worcester.

After that the Soviets set up a secretariat to work on the privatization of small and medium-sized businesses. When I left government, they asked me to see a team from the secretariat and I spent a great deal of time with them.

The issues were complex. The team wanted to set up a first-class management consultancy in Moscow to advise firms on privatization. They were going to privatize 16,000 firms immediately. The team leader had been president of the scientific and technical co-operative which had several hundreds of firms. These were to be privatized straight away. I asked what he meant by privatized. Who would own the ten million pound factory? He said the workers would. Was each of the thousand workers in a factory to be issued with shares? It transpired that the managers would be the proprietors. What would happen if the management of six executives decided to sell it next week?

The detail had clearly not been worked out. I explained that it was important. If the state was to remain the owner, this would put a different gloss on what happened. What were the managers to do about paying themselves? Were they to pay themselves American-type salaries?

Thousands more firms were to be privatized through the Soviet equivalent of Chambers of Commerce and I was asked if I could set up a management consultancy. They would pay, but I asked what would they pay. The pay would be the equivalent to that paid to good people in London, but it would have to be in Russian currency. Office accommodation would be provided by the state.

Perhaps they need more professionalism, but the country may also be too big to make the transformation smoothly. My success in attracting foreign investment and cutting unemployment in Wales was possible in a small country. In Russia it must be difficult to know who is really influential and can make progress, and to grasp the complexities of the industries.

If I was in charge of a city or town in the Soviet Union, I would bring in joint ventures. The rebuilding of post-war West Germany is a classic example of what can be done. The Deutsche Bank decided that the only way Germany could compete was to jump to the most advanced levels of American technology. The bank's chairman spent more time visiting American factories than in Germany. He reached agreements for German firms to have the royalty on a particular plant. Suddenly Germany leapt to the technology and management techniques of America, which was then ahead of the rest of the world.

If, by some magic formula, I was to have a say in the running of the Soviet Union, I would want someone to go round the capitals of the Western world doing deals which involved them in training my staff. They would receive a good return by being able to sell in the

Soviet Union. Later I would be able to produce my own goods and products.

Joint ventures would be helpful. It is important to do everything on a relatively small scale. If, for example, you were responsible for Georgia, you could invite international food distribution companies to come in on the basis of a phased buy-out. In ten years you would own the company, but by that time the food companies would have made good profits.

15

WELSH FERVOUR

The big attraction of the Welsh Secretary's job was that I was told that I could do it my way.

For the third time, Margaret Thatcher entrapped me when I thought I was about to leave government. She called me on the Friday afternoon after the 1987 General Election victory and began by telling me she appreciated the job I had done at Energy. Winning the fight against Scargill had been critical. She was phoning me before contacting any other member of the Cabinet because she was going to ask me to do something I might think rather strange and she wanted me to think about it carefully before she met other Cabinet colleagues the next day.

It was an intriguing start to our conversation. She said the party had done well in the General Election in England, but badly in Scotland and Wales. In the new Parliament, we had to put that right in the interests of the unity of the United Kingdom. Malcolm Rifkind had settled in Scotland and now had some experience behind him and she was going to ask him to continue.

There was, however, a problem with Wales. She did not have anybody who was ready for the job, but she believed that with my wide experience of agriculture, industry, environment, I could make a considerable impact.

I replied that I had now had a long period in Cabinet and was happy to stand down for younger people. It was crazy to ask me to take on Wales when the Principality had high unemployment, bad housing and a range of social problems. I said, 'You know how I would tackle it and it is not the same way as you would tackle it. I would want, for example, to increase public expenditure and take a number of other initiatives.'

She responded, 'You have always been awkward, Peter, but perhaps I need someone awkward in Wales.'

I said, 'Margaret, if you think I am going to spend the next five years arguing with you and the Treasury, I don't want to do it. Life is too short. If you are saying that if I went to Wales, I could do it my way and have the full and enthusiastic support of the Prime Minister, instead of arguing, I would be interested.'

'So we have come to an agreement.'

'Yes, if you are saying that I can do it my way, I will do it.'

We had no further conversations and I became Secretary of State for Wales. I was allowed to do it my way with a range of interventionist policies and I always had her backing. Whatever differences I might have had with the Prime Minister, she was as good as her word.

The agreement was put to the test in the first public expenditure round. I said I wanted to increase the budget of the Welsh Development Agency and spend on other projects. John Major, then Treasury Chief Secretary, said my bid was unrealistic. Everyone was cutting expenditure, but I was asking for an increase. He said he might consider keeping expenditure at the same level as last year, but the whole Cabinet had agreed we should hold down public spending and I must play my part. I said I had taken the job on an agreement with the Prime Minister. I was not going in for extravagant expenditure, only what was needed. If the Prime Minister, the Cabinet and the Chief Secretary did not agree, that was fine. They would have to find a new Secretary of State for Wales. I said, 'I don't want to argue with you on detail. I think you should check with the Prime Minister that I came into the job as a result of an agreement. I will fulfil my side, but this is how it has to be done.'

John said goodbye. The next day the Treasury contacted me to say he had agreed my figures.

The increase in public expenditure was relatively small, a drop in the UK budget, but the way in which it enabled us to bring down unemployment and increase inward investment was remarkable. Net savings on unemployment and social security and the increased tax revenue from people in a job, rather than out of one, turned out to be a bargain. It was not a question of the government making sacrifices to help Wales. The result was a positive economic story in which the Treasury benefited handsomely.

In the three years I was there, Wales, with five per cent of the population, got twenty-two per cent of all the inward investment in Britain. Exports from Wales rose sharply because all the new firms not only produced for the UK, but also for the whole of the European market.

The increases in public spending were all used for economic advance. We increased the derelict land clearance grant, getting rid of all the slag heaps; we pushed up the road building to provide links for economic development. The Welsh Development Agency had a dynamic programme with good teams attracting inward investment working in Japan and America.

If American or Japanese businessmen were interested in a site in Wales, I personally took them to visit it and gave them the option of putting up their own factory or leasing one from us. If they leased it, they would have the option to buy the freehold after five years.

At the same time, we established a terrific relationship between the trade unions and local authorities.

It started with the jeers of the media ringing in my ears, an Englishman come to conquer Wales. I think I got away with this taunt rather well. On the first day of my appointment, I was asked on Welsh television if I did not believe it wrong that an Englishman should be appointed Secretary of State for Wales. I agreed that it was 'absolutely appalling'. The fault lay with my mother who was still alive, I explained. She had made this terrible mistake. I should have been born in Wales. Alas, she had given birth to me in England and I was terribly sorry.

They thought this was at least a good-humoured approach and it defused the situation. When I was asked if I would learn Welsh, I pointed out that some years ago I had tried to learn French and it was an insult to the French language. To insult a language as ancient and important as the Welsh language would be unforgivable. Of course, I would not do it. I knew what a lovely language it was and the quality of Welsh literature, but for me, at the age of fifty-five, to start fumbling out a few words of Welsh would be recognized as a gimmick and I did not go in for gimmicks.

We did encourage Welsh speaking by setting up a Welsh Language Board, all enthusiastic Welsh speakers, to promote the language. We argued from the start that it would be wrong to impose the language. That would be the one way to guarantee hostility. Far better to encourage children in English-speaking areas. The extreme Welsh Language Society wanted a hard statutory requirement to learn Welsh and the English speakers thought I was going too far in the other direction, but I received a great deal of support from leading Welsh speakers who saw the value of a voluntary approach.

Local authority co-operation was critical to the success of my plans. I met all the leaders of the local councils, invariably Labour, and trade union officials to tell them I wanted to work with them and form a team. I think they trusted me and I had an excellent relationship with them. I explained to the trade union leaders that I had investors looking at sites and they would probably want single union agreements. I asked them to meet them and to say how keen they were on productivity. They readily agreed. Everybody who came to Wales got a warm welcome.

For many, the welcome started before they got to Wales. I used to travel down to the Principality on the morning train from Paddington each week. The chief steward was and probably still is a grand man called Peter Murrin. If I was taking down an American or Japanese businessman or a German tycoon, my private office would phone British Rail the day before and say that I was coming down with Mr So and So. Peter would be on the platform at Paddington in his full livery. He would bow, say, 'Good morning, Your Excellency' or whatever was appropriate, and show us to our seats. When we came to breakfast, he would explain that the Secretary of State was partial to a 'kipper', a smoked fish we enjoyed in Britain. He would ask them to try the kipper and, if they disliked it, have one of BR's excellent grills. We got magnificent service and when we got to Cardiff, Peter would jump out, hold the door for us and say how honoured BR was to have such a distinguished visitor. They arrived in Cardiff having been given the full VIP treatment. I am glad to say Peter got into the honours list while I was still Welsh Secretary and I presented him with his BEM, which he wears on the train each morning.

It was not simply the warmth of the Welsh welcome. We streamlined the planning application process. I explained to the councils that if we were competing with other parts of Britain and Europe, we did not want to tell prospective industrialists that they would have to wait for a decision on their new factory until the council's planning committee met next month. I wanted them to call special meetings and to be able to say they would act quickly. The councils loved it. They thought they were part of transforming the Welsh economy – and they were, an important part.

Wales is relatively small. You quickly discovered the good and bad industrialists. You could ring up the good ones and say that you wanted to take a guest round their factories and to hear what an efficient work force they had. Suddenly, the atmosphere changed.

The other thing I think I was able to do, as an Englishman, was to shake them out of their depression. I had a classic illustration of this quite early on.

In my first year as Welsh Secretary, the Welsh Office came along with a selection of six Welsh views from which I was to choose one as my Christmas card. The only thing they had in common was heavy black clouds. I said I was not going to send all round the world pictures of Wales with black clouds. I wanted blue skies and sunshine. 'The trouble with you Welsh is that you always like gloomy landscapes,' I told them. Timothy, my thirteen-year-old, had taken a photograph of the Welsh landscape on a brilliant sunny day. I said we would have this as our Christmas card. For the first time ever in the history of the Welsh Office, it had a Christmas card without black clouds.

We had gloomy paintings in the waiting room at the Welsh Office, too. They went as well. I visited Mountain Ash comprehensive school, in the heart of the valleys. The headmaster was excellent and so was the art section. Paintings were lying around the classroom, not on the walls. I suggested that the best should be collected for an exhibition in the Welsh Office in Cardiff. We framed them and had the competition, but I bought six or eight of them and hung them in the Welsh Office in London.

I told them I was not going to go round the world describing Wales as depressed when it had such magnificent landscape and other attractions. We had to say we were clearing all the derelict land and slag heaps which still existed. We had to say we were going to provide attractive modern housing.

This last item was a problem initially. The Labour councils had not given planning permission for private housing for years. They had built council houses, many not very good. Applications for private housing seemed to be rejected as a matter of Socialist principle.

In discussions with the council leaders I pointed out that I was trying to bring in businessmen, including middle and top management, all of whom wanted pleasant private housing. If they found that the local council was not allowing the building of decent private housing they would go away again. Instead of obstructing private housing, they should give a number of planning permissions to get them built. It would not cost the council anything directly. It would actually relieve rates.

Barratt's picked up the thinking and approached me about a development on derelict land in the Rhondda. They doubted if it would be viable and we gave them a grant towards the project. They built the houses and sold them immediately at a good profit. It was the end of any subsidy for private development, but was valuable for proving that the demand for private housing was there.

It had a ripple effect. Other councils realized that if the Rhondda was providing good private housing, it was likely to attract more inward investment. They began competing with each other to allow first-class private development.

Quite separate was the Valleys Initiative.

I said we were going to have to clean up the valleys and adopt a range of measures. To announce them individually was silly. What we should do was to look at what we could and needed to do over the next three years, putting all the plans together in one document, so that people could see what was going to happen and when. Derelict land clearance, road building, new schools, new hospitals were to be listed. I pulled together the details of what each section of the department thought it could do and wrote the document myself.

It showed what we would do with the current level of public spending and what we would do with more money, covering housing, tourism, everything. We were specific down to the name of a miners' institute. I think it might have been a unique document. It presented party political problems for Labour, which could no longer say, at least with any conviction, that the commitments were vague and there was no new policy. Newspapers, many of them Socialist in outlook, could see for the first time exactly what was going to happen, and they applauded.

The private sector was asked to help on particular projects. I went to the two largest breweries, Whitbreads and Welsh Breweries, a subsidiary of Bass, and said that if I was to clear up the valleys they should act, too. Both were considering action. I asked them to produce plans to show what they would do in the next three years. They gave me a commitment to spend nearly forty million pounds on cleaning up the pubs in the valleys. I asked the ten biggest industrialists for their capital programmes over the next three years.

It was not just a question of what the government was doing. Everyone saw that over three years the valleys were going to improve substantially. The gradual decline was to be halted.

What was exciting was that during the period I was in the Welsh Office, unemployment fell faster than in any other part of the United Kingdom. Unemployment in the valleys fell faster than in any other part of Wales. The leaders of the Labour councils knew it and praised it privately, but could not publicly for party political reasons.

David Hunt, the new Welsh Secretary, is continuing the Valleys Initiative. When it was set up as a rolling programme, we announced that it would go on for at least five years, but we left the detail to David, who is making a great success of the job. It has transformed the whole attitude of the valleys.

What was true was that the government had been spending a great deal of money for a long time. Obviously, the road programme for the valleys was not entirely new expenditure. Nor was the education programme, but there was a lot of new spending. I had increased substantially the budget of the WDA and for derelict land clearance. The important point was that until then no one had taken a look at the full picture. We set up advisory services throughout the valleys to encourage new businesses and suggest locations.

The full Valleys Initiative covered the Welsh economy, education and training, tourism and the arts, roads, the environment, voluntary effort, health and social services and housing. The programme included:

* New schemes to assist small businesses
* Research projects to promote new opportunities for Welsh firms, such as developing the clothing industry and joint purchasing and marketing by small firms
* Export advice
* A new centre for Quality Enterprise and Design
* A Welsh Technology Development fund to help firms translate new ideas into sales
* Plans for the 3is, Investors in Industry, to invest at least £2.5 million in the valleys in a single year, two thirds more than in previous years
* A trebling of spending on an advanced factory and workshop programme
* A new campaign to improve the standard of retailing

* New links between business and schools in each valley
* A training commission to carry out a 'skills audit' and identify the skills likely to be needed by existing and potential employers
* A marketing scheme to attract more visitors to the valleys
* An enhanced road improvement programme
* UK2000 to promote more practical projects to improve the environment, provide training and create jobs
* Increased funding for the Prince of Wales Committee
* Funding of two valley health centres and twelve other projects, including a day hospital and community hospital
* Further capital allocations worth eight million pounds to improve housing stock

Nick Edwards, my predecessor as Welsh Secretary, had given the go-ahead for a range of improvements on the A55 in North Wales to make it dual carriageway from one end to the other. I gave approval for a couple of extensions to the road. We were approaching the position when there was going to be a motorway equivalent for the whole of North Wales. It created, in my view, great opportunities, so I asked Wyn Roberts, my minister and himself a North Wales member, to ask all the local authorities in North Wales what was needed to take full advantage of this motorway. I wanted to know what they could do in planning, what was required in housing and new factory sites and feeder roads. After completing a thorough exercise, beautifully done by Wyn, who knew every inch of North Wales and spoke fluent Welsh, we drew up a programme. It included derelict land improvement, new roads, WDA investment in new factory sites. We called it *The Road to Opportunity*.

When I arrived at the Welsh Office, I spent about four weeks assimilating all the basic information about Wales. I got the department to analyse where the unemployment was and to look at the public expenditure patterns. My wish was to identify all those places in which performance was below the national average and where, over five or six years, I intended them to be brought up to scratch.

Unemployment was one area, housing was another, large tracts of derelict land a third. It was not so much that there was a shortage of housing, but that many houses needed improvement. On top of this, I tried to see there was a diversity of education opportunities and retraining programmes. Wales needed a great deal of retraining as workers moved from the old to the new industries. I drove down each valley myself, identifying some of the things which needed to be done. I remember going into one shop to buy a newspaper and being told, 'You look just like Peter Walker.' I said I was relieved.

The analysis showed up what I needed in action and resources. I found that the totality of the problem was not that big. Although the unemployment percentages, for example, were high, the actual numbers involved, given Wales's population, were quite small. We calculated that by creating new businesses, helping existing companies grow and attracting inward investment from Britain and overseas, we could bring down unemployment to the lowest figure in England.

I quickly realized that my best instrument for achieving all this was the Welsh Development Agency. It was flexible, could help with the property side, offer grants in line with the EEC rules. I gave it more money to expand the job.

In South Wales we had the motorway. The M4 did suffer hold-ups and needed improvement, but the biggest obstacle in the way of the future of South Wales was the Severn Bridge. It was already crowded and a second Severn Bridge was obviously going to be needed quickly.

To my horror, I discovered that the Ministry of Transport had plans to build this second bridge, but were saying that it would not be needed until the middle or late part of the 1990s. I had some difficulty in getting the papers, but insisted and did so eventually. The Ministry of Transport stuffily claimed that the papers were theirs and not ours. I discovered from the papers that the policy rested on a survey made in 1986. Here I was in 1988. I asked what up-to-date survey work showed. It showed that their earlier estimates had been exceeded and there was already more traffic on the bridge than had been forecast for 1992.

I sent a memorandum to the Transport Secretary, the Prime Minister and the Cabinet, saying the original estimates were clearly wrong and a go-ahead on the second Severn Bridge must be given as quickly as possible. The Ministry of Transport admitted that their earlier figures were outdated. They gave the absurd explanation that the bridge was being repaired for three years, so that the volume of traffic using it would be sharply reduced. I asked officials how on earth they thought the traffic was going to be reduced. What were drivers to do? They said drivers might use the other route. I asked them if they had ever done so. As the other route was sixty miles longer, it was ridiculous to think they would not wait to cross the bridge.

The expansion of the Welsh economy, with new buildings and new factories, simply underlined the need for a new bridge. I am glad to say we then had the co-operation of the Ministry of Transport and quickly decided where the second bridge would go. It is now to be erected as swiftly as possible. Even so, it will not be built before 1995 and I am afraid that a year or so before then the existing bridge will be badly overcrowded. Afterwards, Wales will have excellent communications.

When it came to enticing overseas investment, I looked closely at Japan. Japan had already established some factories in the Principality and Wales did have a good reputation. Japan would remain a prime target, but we wanted, too, to pull in firms from the United States and parts of Europe where it was in their interests to have manufacturing in Britain. I conducted a study of the international possibilities and set up a small group to manage the strategy, attracting high-calibre people like Sir John Harvey-Jones, the immediate past chairman of ICI, and Desmond Watkins, one of Shell's top men.

They worked, without any reward, to try to bring much needed investment to their native country. Gwyn Jones at the WDA was quite outstanding. I personally went on visits to Japan, Korea, Germany and the United States, contacting the chief executives of top industrial companies, pointing out all the advantages of coming to Wales and the facilities they could expect. We had an office in Japan, Japanese speakers working for us in Tokyo. When they heard a company was contemplating coming to Europe, they would alert us and I would top and tail a letter to the chief executive. If I discovered the top man could speak English I phoned him at his offices in Japan, saying, 'I am the Secretary of State for Wales. Wales is part of the United Kingdom . . .' As a result, we did get leads and positive responses.

By the time I left Wales unemployment had been more than halved, from thirteen to six per cent, and was only one and a half per cent higher than in south-east England. It was the biggest drop in the United Kingdom.

As we had in the pipeline the large-scale investment of Bosch, the Toyota plant, a range of medium-sized investments, we were clearly in sight of the target I had set three years before.

There were always some closures and set-backs, but nothing to interfere seriously with the steady flow of heavy inward investment. The important thing about the Bosch, Toyota and Ford investments was not just the projects themselves, providing hundreds of jobs, but the potential for component suppliers. Component suppliers came to Wales to service the big factories. The demand for components for Ford, Toyota and Bosch, when they are fully working, will give another immense opportunity to Wales.

What we achieved in Wales as a result of close government co-operation with industry, councils and trade unions does underscore the weakness of our post-war performance in the rest of the country. We have simply failed to create the right relationship between government and industry. France has an interface through the civil service: the French civil service operates to benefit the French industrialists against foreign competition. The United States, with heavy expenditure by the Pentagon and individual states, ensures that there is a strong bias in favour of American industry. The build-up of American technology and electronics has been due to American government intervention. You have the same story in Japan. The government has a complete interface with its industry and the department responsible for industry is probably the most powerful in the country. All departments work in close liaison with Japanese industry, seeing that industry is protected from imports and exports have every possible advantage.

Britain, with its free-trade attitude belonging to another century, adopted under Margaret an arms-length relationship between government and industry. In addition, we have had the destructive battle between Socialism and free enterprise in which Tories say they are in favour of free enterprise and Labour favour nationalization.

What we really need is the co-operation with industry achieved by other governments in different ways. The classic example is the Bundesbank in West Germany which was set up post war as a so-called independent institution to stop inflation ever happening again. But the Bundesbank has a tight relationship with the three German banks, the Deutsche, the Dresner and the Commerce Bank. If the German government wants something achieved, it operates through the banking system.

When it wanted to reorganize Volkswagen, the Bundesbank spoke to the main German bankers and they got rid of the bad management in the car firm. The German banks financed the restructuring on hugely favourable terms, including equity injections and the funding of new production lines. The VW disasters ended, the company flourished again. The equivalent in Britain was the nationalization of British Leyland. That, quite obviously, did not have the same dynamism.

I was concerned by our attempts to contain inflation and our dependence on interest rates to the exclusion of other weapons. I did write to Nigel Lawson to say that we should look at the way the Bundesbank operated to see that inflation did not go through the roof because institutions were providing too much credit.

This was at a time when the banks were pouring out money to anyone who would take it. Our letter boxes were stuffed with invitations to take out personal loans, holiday companies were offering credit and so were the shops. Inflation was created by a credit boom. I argued that interest rates were not the only weapon and the Germans were demonstrating this.

When the Germans faced any threat, the government told their main clearing banks they had to meet liquidity ratios and hold more cash so they had less to lend out. That type of policy has worked in restraining inflation. The Chancellor replied that the Germans had stopped doing this, but he was wrong. They are still doing it.

The other feeble reason for inaction put forward by the Treasury is that foreign banks and overseas financial interests in Britain can evade the controls. That is absurd. Exactly the same applies in Germany. There are a great many foreign banks there and anyone can finance projects in Germany from outside.

The reality is that if you put such restraint on your main credit providers, the banks and building societies, you have an impact on about ninety-five per cent of the economy. If five per cent avoid it, so what? You are interested only in the overall deflationary effect.

Selwyn Lloyd did have a system which compelled the banks to put money on deposit. It was an effective instrument then and it could be used today.

The housing market was an illustration of what was wrong. It has always been thought prudent not to lend anyone more than two and a half times their income when they are buying a house. Suddenly High Street banks were competing with the building societies and the societies fought back. House buyers were getting mortgages of three, four or five times their annual salary. Doubtless many of these people are now in default and repayments put a tremendous strain on many families.

If, instead, the Bank of England had been saying to the clearers that they must increase their cash ratios so they did not have all the money to hand out, the boom would have been controlled. Instead we were forced to watch a serious house price and inflation boom which was credit-led. I did argue in Cabinet that it was important to introduce curbs rather than relying entirely on high interest rates.

At the Welsh Office, I came forward with a modification of my earlier, rejected scheme to make it easier for tenants to buy their own council homes. It started when I told one particularly bright official in the housing section of the Welsh Office, Adam Peat, about my earlier wish to enable many more tenants to buy their council homes. He went away and came back with his idea of converting rents into mortgage repayments and for tenants to become the immediate owners of their homes. I cross-examined him and we developed a scheme which produced a saving in public expenditure. A tenant who had lived in a house for a long time would be entitled to perhaps a fifty per cent discount and have the house immediately in his or her name. If he had capital, he raised his stake still more. If not, he converted his rent into a mortgage, the money to be held by the Housing Corporation. If he died, the half he owned went to his family and the other half to the Housing Corporation for refinancing arrangements. The formula gives the state a continuing equity in the house until the mortgage is paid off. The tenant is not asked to pay more than his current rent.

I asked to see the Prime Minister and told her I had something to discuss which I thought was of fundamental importance.

She invited in Professor Brian Griffiths, head of the Cabinet's policy unit and right-wing guru. I gave the scheme, sheet by sheet, as I took them through it.

Margaret asked some seemingly hostile questions, but they were easily answered. Then she turned to Brian Griffiths and asked: 'What do you think of it?' He said it was the most remarkable proposal he had ever seen, it was fantastic and the government should do it.

She said the Cabinet would have to look at it for any problems. I did not want it to go round Whitehall because it would leak and not be fully explained, so she proposed, instead, to call a meeting of all concerned, including John Major, the Treasury Chief Secretary, Malcolm Rifkind, at Scotland, Norman Fowler, the Social Services Secretary, and the Environment Secretary, Nicholas Ridley. We were all invited for dinner at No. 10 to discuss it. It became clear that there was only one opponent. His attitude was that tenants could not be expected to take these decisions. They should be looked after. It was very much the approach of the landed gentry to their tenants. He said also that people with mortgages would complain they were losing their advantage.

There was always some resentment being felt by major departments when a small one took an initiative. I was conscious that the high ranking the Prime Minister gave me in the Cabinet pecking order, above the Secretaries of State for the Environment, Trade and Industry and Defence, meant that the officials from major departments had to come to my small department to discuss proposals. That is Whitehall protocol. I suspect the officials who worked for me in a series of small departments positively enjoyed this reversal of the normal roles and senior civil servants having to come to them.

John Major was in favour, but did not say too much. He wanted it looked into in greater depth. Norman Fowler was in favour. Local administration on housing benefit would disappear. The Prime Minister asked for more work to be done on it, but no objections could be found. I had made sure it was foolproof.

Mrs Thatcher was in a dilemma. A close ally was strongly opposed, I was strongly in favour. She made it clear to me that she thought it was a good idea and wanted it in the next General Election manifesto, but the immediate compromise was that we had two experiments, one in Wales and the other in Scotland. Since then two experiments in England have been agreed. Wider application of the idea will, I am sure, be in John Major's election manifesto.

We did not have, in Wales, the same problems over hospital opt-outs. I did not see many advantages of opting out in Wales and expressed the view I did not think many would do so. If they did not, nothing would happen. If they did apply, then their application would be looked at objectively. While in England there was a push to persuade every hospital to opt out, in Wales there was no such campaign.

This did not stop Labour and some misguided doctors making the most of the issue in the Vale of Glamorgan by-election. All the doctors decided to launch a well-organized campaign. They even had their own candidate, but they did the real damage by writing to their patients opposing the changes, putting up notices in waiting rooms and urging their patients not to vote Conservative. They said that a bad result in the by-election would demonstrate the wish of the people of Wales to have nothing to do with the new proposals.

The by-election result was actually quite good. It showed a smaller swing against the government than in any mid-term by-election for a decade. Opinion polls showed my personal popularity in Wales was greater than that of Neil Kinnock or Margaret Thatcher. *The Times* did a survey which showed that my popularity was a big plus to the Conservative candidate, but the health service issue did considerable damage and brought about our defeat. Not even an announcement during the by-election campaign that Bosch was to come to Wales made much difference.

We persuaded Bosch to come by first phoning Dr Marcus Beirich, the chairman of the firm, and then going to Germany to see him. When I phoned him, I explained that I was a Cabinet Minister and in charge and knew he was looking for a site. I thought that I could prove to him we had the best facilities and decision-making process available anywhere in Europe.

I think he was impressed that a Cabinet Minister was taking such a personal interest. Bosch picked a good site, we told them of the grant available and alerted the local council to consider the planning application quickly. The company said it had developed plants throughout Europe, but had never before dealt with such an efficient organization. That was what we wanted to hear. The WDA, the Welsh Office, the local authorities all worked as one team. Phase one of the Bosch project could well be followed by later phases. The Bosch factory in Wales is likely to become one of the biggest engineering plants anywhere in Western Europe.

We adopted the same tactics with Toyota. We had a terrific relationship with the heads of the firm and there was no doubt that we were to get the plant. Inexplicably, the main plant then went to Derby. I discovered later from Toyota that the switch had been made because the Prime Minister had called in the Toyota boss and said she personally wanted the factories to go to Derby.

The Toyota boss said that he appreciated my understanding, but he did have difficulty when approached by the Prime Minister. She

had told him that the government would provide financial arrangements as good as those being offered in Wales, but after all we
had done he was still anxious to locate a factory in Wales. He said he
would be putting the engine plant in Wales and subsequently did so.

I think the Derby scheme was pushed because there was criticism
by the Department of Trade and Industry that Peter Walker was
taking all the inward investment for Wales and that England was
doing badly. The Prime Minister was almost certainly also concerned
that the important East Midlands area, with its high number of marginal constituencies, was complaining about its small share of investment, despite high unemployment. That is the only explanation I
can think of for Trade and Industry Secretary David Young and the
Prime Minister putting pressure on Toyota to go to Derby.

In the middle of all this, I made a speech which proved to be
controversial, though I was only repeating the views I had made
plain over a number of years. Newspapers suggested that this must
be the moment to get rid of Peter Walker, but I then read to my
astonishment that leaders of the Welsh CBI, TUC and National
Farmers Union were all publicly calling for me to be kept. They had
taken the newspaper speculation seriously and sent messages to the
Prime Minister saying that it was vital I stayed in Wales. I doubt if,
even for a moment, she considered sacking me.

We continued to have a good working relationship. I was doing
in Wales the job I said I would do and which she wanted. What was
more I was doing it successfully.

I did tell her that there was talk that she had not been to Wales
since I was Secretary of State and this was unfortunate. She and her
government should take the credit for what was happening and she
should pay an official visit. I said I thought there were Welsh seats
we could gain in the General Election by showing Wales had
improved faster under her administration than under any post-war
government. The people of Wales were already beginning to appreciate this.

Margaret agreed and No. 10 prepared a programme, but I did not
think the officials had it right. I said I would prepare the programme
and that she should start off by going to the valleys. She asked if the
controversy which surrounded her would not cause demonstrations.
I said, 'No.' As always, in the valleys of Wales, there would be
a warm welcome to a visitor and she should see the remarkable
transformation taking place.

We flew down by helicopter and were met by the Labour mayor, the Labour leaders of the council and the county council, all dressed in their best suits and coats. As she climbed down from the helicopter she was given a warm greeting. Indeed, I think she was pleased when the Lady Mayor of the Rhondda, a good Socialist, welcomed her as 'Mam'. We looked at the clearance of derelict sites, the new housing, the factory building; she was impressed. Later she sent me an inscribed picture of the two of us standing in the Rhondda with the words 'To Peter. Thank you for a marvellous day in the Rhondda.'

At the first stop in the Rhondda we were met by an army of newspapermen and television crews. She answered the questions fully, but as she walked away I thought she failed to catch a question about Peter Walker doing a good job. I just caught it. Margaret did not. I knew the journalist and had a nasty suspicion that he could come out with the headline saying: 'Thatcher Refuses to Back Walker'. I told her what had happened and understood that she had not heard it, but the reporter would be at the next stop and it was important he should not be able to write the story I thought he might want to do.

She said this was incredible, but at the next stop began with a long eulogy of me, what I had done for Wales and how popular I was. I think it was nevertheless quite a surprise when later she addressed three or four hundred party workers over coffee. Quite early on she remarked what an outstanding job I had done for Wales and there were then several minutes of loud applause. This was going too far!

16

BOWING OUT

Three years into the job as Welsh Secretary, I realized I needed to take decisions about my future. I had thoroughly enjoyed every moment in Wales. It was going well and I liked it, but I had laid down the Valleys and the A55 'Road of Opportunity' initiatives and negotiated the public spending over the next three years. If I stayed as Welsh Secretary, there would be few big decisions left to be taken.

At that time, I presumed that Margaret would fight the next General Election. If she won, I thought she would ask me to stay on as Secretary of State for Wales and I would have another five years of rather repetitive work. I felt I had done the innovation and by the time of the following election I would be sixty-five.

If she was defeated, there would then be a contest for the leadership, either because she decided to hand over to someone younger, which I thought was probable, or because there was a challenge.

In theory, I could still be a contender in that contest, offering myself as a Cabinet Minister of long experience on the more liberal wing of the party. But if we lost the next election and I did win the leadership, I would be fighting my first General Election at the age of sixty-five. It was not an attractive proposition for my party.

I had another reason for stepping down. I thought there were emerging at least two likely politicians of the younger generation who would be contenders for the leadership, were of the right age and of whom I fully approved, John Major and Chris Patten. I did touch on these possibilities when I went to see Margaret about a disagreement shortly after she had appointed John to be Foreign Secretary and Chris to the Environment job.

At the end of our conversation, I complimented her on her

219

decision to appoint John and Chris. I said that of all the Cabinet changes she had made, these were probably the most important. Rather defensively, she demanded, 'What do you mean?' I said she and I were the only two politicians to have served in Cabinets and Shadow Cabinets since 1967 and we had seen many come and go. Of all the people who had come and gone, I thought John Major was quite outstanding. He was not a friend of mine, but he had immense ability, charm and was also a thinker of considerable quality. Even in politics few knew him well outside the Treasury circle where he had been Chief Secretary. The public did not know him at all, but I was sure he would be a superb Foreign Secretary and become a national and international figure. I thought Chris Patten was also excellent and should have been in the Cabinet a long time ago.

I told her she had brought two people of the next generation into key positions and started to prepare for the succession and I thought this was right for the party. She said, 'Oh, Peter! I am so pleased you said that. I think John Major is very high quality and he will do well, but everyone has been so beastly to me over how nasty I have been to poor Geoffrey. You are the first person to recognize what I really wanted to do. As for Chris Patten, you know he has helped me to write every one of my election manifestos and I have always thought highly of him and I am delighted he is in the Cabinet.'

Neither of us thought that twelve months later John Major would be Prime Minister.

The emergence of these two in top positions helped me make up my own mind. I felt that if there was going to be a leadership struggle after a General Election, I should not take part. There would be no need. Michael Heseltine would certainly be there. John Major and Chris Patten were likely to be significant contenders and it was right for the Tory Party to move to a younger age group.

If we lost the General Election, it would be wrong for whoever won the leadership to include in his Shadow Cabinet someone who would be sixty-five at the time of the next General Election. If I declined to join a Shadow Cabinet then, would I be satisfied to sit on the back benches for another five years? I have always found former ministers on the back benches, with some notable exceptions, rather boring people, pontificating on how much better things were in their days. I never wanted to become one of those long, lingering, retiring politicians.

The alternative was much more attractive. If I left Cabinet, I would be only fifty-eight and could have ten years of activity in other spheres, undertaking some challenging and interesting assignments.

My family was another important consideration. I have always been lucky in being close to my family in spite of the pressures of Cabinet. Having a house almost next door to the House of Commons, and deliberately having my children live at home, instead of going to boarding schools, has helped.

But close as we have been, there have been inevitable drawbacks. If you are a Cabinet Minister you cannot get away at half-term. There are always Cabinet committees to attend. You can never plan ahead with any certainty to go to the theatre, the ballet or the opera. You are never sure what is going to come up. My two eldest children, Jonathan and Shara, are at Oxford and at an interesting stage in their lives, starting on their careers. The younger ones, Timothy, Robin and Marianna, are active at school. I was left reflecting that from the family point of view, after all those years of division bells, it would be enjoyable to go out to dinner and not come back to red boxes and to be able to go to the opera and the ballet and to plan overseas trips with the family.

All the considerations combined to make it an easy choice. Giving myself ten years of other activities, bowing out at a time when the future succession of leadership looked to be in good hands and the prospect of seeing more of my family, were compelling reasons. I discussed the options with Tessa and we agreed to do it that way.

I went to see Margaret and said I wanted to go. She said she was sorry and asked me to continue at Wales until the General Election. I said I could not. I would have to let my constituents in Worcester know that I was going, so that they could adopt a new candidate. I had been at Worcester for thirty years and the new candidate would need time to travel around and become known. And once I announced I was going, I should not have the same weight in Cabinet and would not want to go on.

This conversation with the Prime Minister took place in September 1989 and we agreed I would stay on without telling anyone until the Easter of 1990. She asked whom she should make Secretary of State for Wales. I suggested there were three candidates. William Waldegrave, who was MP for Bristol, close to Wales, would be good and personable; Michael Howard, who was Welsh and already in the Cabinet, might also be suitable; but by far the best choice was likely to be David Hunt, who had been a junior minister with me. His constituency bordered on Wales. Even better he had been born in Wales and possessed all the qualities to be an excellent Secretary of State. Margaret said, 'You are quite right, Peter, David would do it superbly, so we shall fix on David.'

It was agreed we should keep the arrangement to ourselves until Easter, when I would announce it. The story did not leak and I did not tell anyone with the exception of my family, but one Saturday afternoon in March I was phoned by Julia Langdon, the political editor of the *Sunday Telegraph*, who said she had heard I was resigning.

I said something like, 'Dear Julia, these ridiculous rumours you are always spreading. I am long past denying rumours. There are rumours like this about me every other week.'

I hoped I had killed the story, but she had decided that as I had not specifically denied it, it must be true. I discovered afterwards that Kenneth Rose, the paper's diarist, first included the story in his section of the paper. Julia had picked it up and the editor had put it on the front page, much to the annoyance of Kenneth. They led with it in their first editions and I phoned Margaret at Chequers to tell her what had happened and that every other newspaper was about to phone me up. I could not tell a pack of lies all evening and I thought we must announce it. She agreed that was all we could do. We quickly consulted on what we would both say and organized an exchange of letters for release on the Monday. The letter I wrote reflected my genuine feelings at going and my admiration for Margaret.

Dear Margaret,
    Like you I have been fortunate throughout most of my life to be involved in the Conservative Party in Parliament and in the government of our country.
    It is thirty-five years ago that I became the candidate for Dartford and we first met.
    For much of the last quarter of the century I have had the privilege of serving in Shadow Cabinets and Cabinets, a quarter of a century in which we have witnessed such rapid change both nationally and internationally.
    You were very understanding when last September I explained to you my decision not to contest the next General Election and my belief that when that was announced I should be replaced in the Cabinet by somebody who would continue in the Cabinet after

the election and who would make an important contribution to the production of our manifesto for the following five years.

You know that I am delighted that you have chosen David Hunt to take my place. He will be a Secretary of State that the people of Wales will both admire and work with.

When we come to the next election your government will be able to claim that during this decade of Conservative administration, Wales has become one of the most lively and fastest expanding economies in Western Europe: a diverse free enterprise economy in which the young and lively Welsh no longer have the choice of going down the pit or leaving Wales but have new horizons of opportunity and choice.

It is under a Conservative government that we have cleared the dereliction of the past, built the new factories and offices and attracted investment from throughout the world. Socialism would have achieved none of that.

I am grateful to have had the opportunity to have made a contribution, and be assured that I will help in every way to see that we do not return to the outdated doctrines of Socialism and that our party remains in government to fulfil the aspirations of the British people.

Yours ever,
Peter

Dear Peter,
Sadly the day has come when – as we arranged previously – you are leaving government to return to private life. There is so much to thank you for and I would like to place on record the very special contribution you have made to political life over more than three decades.

After joining the front bench in Opposition in 1964, you have served in Cabinet for fifteen years, as Secretary of State for the Environment, for Trade and Industry, for Energy and for Wales and as Minister for Agriculture, Fisheries and Food. That is a record which few can match this century. To all these posts you have brought exceptional drive and vision. And in our discussions in Cabinet you have been a most valued and perceptive colleague, whose political judgement has been widely respected.

In Wales you have been particularly successful in transforming the environment and in revitalizing the economy. The prominent role you have taken personally has been invaluable in capturing a number of major inward investment projects. You can take pride in these achievements.

I know I can count on you to give your support not only to your successor, David Hunt, but also to the government and the Conservative Party.

May I say a warm thank you to Tessa. I know she has given you wonderful support throughout your political career. Denis and I send our best wishes to you both for the future.

Yours ever,
Margaret

All the newspapers and television crews rushed down to my house in the country at Abbots Morton. It produced a family joke. One of the television crew asked my five-year-old daughter, Marianna, 'Do you know what this is all about?' She replied, 'Yes, Daddy is getting a new car.'

Tessa and my two eldest children were the only people who knew of my decision to step down. If we had been able to announce it, as I intended, during the Easter recess I would have been able to phone some close friends and family the day before and warn them it was about to happen. The *Sunday Telegraph* dashed those plans.

I stayed in office for two months because I had agreed with Margaret that I would hand on to my successor in May. The person we both wanted to do it, David Hunt, was, in any case, involved in the poll tax.

Resignation must have been in the air.

Nigel Lawson chose a much noisier exit in October 1989, complaining that comments made by Sir Alan Walters, the Prime Minister's economic adviser, about the EMS were only 'the tip of a singularly ill-concealed iceberg'.

Nigel has one of the finest brains of any politician with whom I have been associated. I can imagine his fury at having someone like Alan Walters, close to the Prime Minister, expressing opinions directly opposed to his own. But disagreement with an outside adviser should not, in itself, be justification for resignation. What has never been clear is whether there were other proposals to counteract inflation – apart from the use of the interest and exchange rates – that the Treasury were stopped from pursuing.

The credit boom was on a far greater scale than we had witnessed since the war and I personally believed we should have given the problem more attention and much earlier. When Nigel's chancellorship is examined, the sharpest judgement will doubtless be on the rise he allowed in inflation.

There will, however, also be judgements of his radical and reforming budgets. Some of the innovation helped to create a wider property-owning democracy, but I believe he made a fundamental mistake in linking capital gains tax with high levels of taxation. No free enterprise country in the Western world of any importance operates on the basis of a forty per cent capital gains tax. Capital gains tax at this level discourages investment and decisions necessary for a healthy economy. People hold on to old investments to avoid paying the capital gains tax instead of switching to new and exciting investments which would bring economic growth.

Nigel surprised me when, soon after John Major's election as leader, he intervened in the Budget debate to criticize the degree of consultation being offered by the government and the new council tax. It was, after all, during Nigel's period as Chancellor that the original poll tax was born. Any Chancellor determined to defeat it should have rallied his Cabinet colleagues at that point.

I hope John Major will continue to consult widely and sensibly. This is important in building up a sense of national unity. To listen as well as to pronounce is important for any Prime Minister.

When I announced my resignation, I said it would give me more time with the family and I would return to business. 'Giving more time to the family' is not a phrase easily understood in hard-bitten political circles when many are driven by powerful ambition. But after nearly twenty years at the top, in Cabinet or out, it was heartfelt. If you are running a major business you can, more or less, plan your life, to have weekends off and to go on holiday. I looked forward to that.

What was pleasant about the reaction was that colleagues like Michael Heseltine made complimentary comments and I had many letters from fellow MPs. Particularly rewarding were the letters I received from Wales, from Labour MPs, trade union leaders, leaders of Labour councils and miners.

I had no choice jobs lined up before I took my decision, but I did begin to think about what the fresh fields might offer. Obviously, I had acquired skills in business and in insurance, which I knew and liked, particularly the international aspects. I believed there was scope for improving the management and marketing of many British businesses. The knowledge I had acquired of, say, the energy and the food industries, gave me a wider insight than many others. As a former Trade and Industry Secretary, attracting inward investment, knowing the European scene, I was able to think internationally.

I felt if I let it be known that I was interested in returning to business, former colleagues in insurance or industry might want me back. Whatever I did I would be non-executive. I did not want to have to deal with the detail which is part of the job of a chief executive. My strength should be in looking at the strategy in a particular business.

I was surprised and flattered by the number of approaches I did receive. Smith New Court asked me to become a non-executive director. I liked the idea because they were a major market-maker with important operations in New York, Sydney and Tokyo as well as Britain. I wanted to make a contribution to Britain's success as an international player in the business world. Smith New Court has given me the base I was seeking, providing a steady flow of information about what is happening throughout the world.

Rothschilds, the merchant bankers, asked me to be an outside director of Rothschilds in Wales. Since I had actually persuaded them to go to Wales in the first place this was a happy accident. The press did not appreciate fully what was happening. There was a suggestion that given my background as Welsh Secretary I should not be making money out of Rothschilds in Wales. The reality, of course, is that a non-executive directorship of a small part of Rothschilds in Wales is not particularly rewarding financially. Non-executive directors get £5,000 a year which, less forty per cent tax, means £3,000 a year. This is not the way to make a fortune, but I wanted to do it because of my connections, and because it was a fascinating task where I could continue to benefit the Welsh economy.

There were two areas in which I had experience and knew Britain had the potential to be a world player, energy and food.

In energy Britain is unique in being the possessor of coal, gas, oil and high technology in electricity. As the world grows so will the demand for energy and energy conservation. Joining British Gas has given me the chance of being part of the biggest gas utility in the world, a company restricted for decades while it was in the public sector, but now with the might and freedom to become another world player.

I did hesitate initially. To my surprise, a number of oil companies asked me to join their boards and I was attracted. They knew I possessed a great deal of knowledge about the industry worldwide and thought I could make a contribution, but I was then approached by the chairman of British Gas, Robert Evans, who asked to come and see me at the Welsh Office.

I assumed at first he was coming to talk about gas in Wales, but he announced that at its board meeting the previous week British Gas directors had decided unanimously to ask me to join the board as a non-executive director. My immediate reaction was that this was a mistake. I had been involved in the privatization, and political opponents would be critical. I said I would love to join the board, with its enormous international potential, but I thought it was in their interests that I did not do so.

The chairman asked, 'Are you telling us that the only energy company in the world whose board you will refuse to join is British Gas?' I insisted that I was not thinking of my interests, but of the board's. There would be political criticism from the Labour Party and others and it would be plain silly. But I was in an embarrassing position. I knew, as I spoke, that I had been approached by three major oil companies, competitors to British Gas, to join their boards.

He said he would like me to think about the proposition and speak to him again. British Gas needed someone with my knowledge of the oil industry internationally. It was to diversify worldwide and my experience would be of immense value.

I discovered that the fees of a non-executive director of British Gas were a long way below those of the oil companies. Here was a dilemma. If I accepted the British Gas job, I would be shot at. If I said 'No' and a few weeks later joined oil company X, one of its competitors, for appreciably more money, I would be shot at again. The British Gas board would believe that I had gone elsewhere for more money. I decided that, on balance, I should do what I wanted to do and go to British Gas. I knew, if no one else did, that I was not going to make a lot of money out of it and British Gas should benefit from the wider international connections I had.

On the food side, I was lucky enough to be invited to join the boards of Tate and Lyle and Dalgety, two of Britain's finest companies and both enjoying international reputations. The chairman of Dalgety was my former Permanent Secretary Sir Peter Carey. He could not have thought too badly of me as a minister.

I have ended up with a number of attractive business positions of an international nature. Another is the chairmanship of Thorntons, one of the most successful investment managers in Far Eastern equities. It is owned largely by one of the strongest German banks and to be part of a company in which German and Japanese expertise combine is providing another insight into world economic developments.

The break from government has also enabled me to give encouragement to young businessmen and to become involved in two small companies – as I see them, the saplings of British commerce, one day to become mighty oaks. One is Radio Business, run by a young man called Brendan Harris, who is building up a specialist company making advertisements for sound radio. The big advertising agents have concentrated on television. Brendan has identified a gap. The second is the Kalshas Group. They were management trainees who joined a big management consultancy and then decided to start on their own. They spotted the need for strategic advice and are now acting for some of the biggest firms in the world.

It is refreshing being in a different atmosphere, not having to attend Cabinet committees, not having to argue with the Treasury. If I have an idea my colleagues think is good, the investment is made. You are not making decisions of the importance you make in politics and you do not have the excitement of political infighting, but there is satisfaction in working for a firm which is efficient and enthusiastic.

Politics remains my real love. I decided that I wanted to devote my life to politics and went into business to achieve the independence to do that. I have enjoyed thirty years in Parliament, in Cabinets and Shadow Cabinets. If I was asked by my children whether they should go into politics or devote their lives to business, I would recommend politics as the more fulfilling. There is, however, a time for change.

As it happens, a bit of philosophizing on my part has landed me, totally unexpectedly, another job. Smith New Court were brokers to Maxwell Communications at the time of the flotation of the *Daily Mirror*. I went to a number of meetings, as part of the Smith New Court team, to discuss tactics and how to arrange the finance. Robert Maxwell, whom I had known as an MP, and his son Kevin, as well as other Maxwell executives, were there. We got on well. I think the advice I was giving was appreciated and I was impressed by Kevin, who is extremely able. On a later occasion I said to Robert Maxwell that I found a similarity between his relationship with his son and the relationship of an entrepreneur of the past and his son, Isaac and Leonard Wolfson.

BOWING OUT

When I was younger, Isaac was a great entrepreneur, buying and selling businesses, making profits out of property. He worked up a substantial business, but his son, who was also very talented, was a different personality from a different background.

Isaac had come from the Glasgow slums, but his son had been to a public school and enjoyed a good education. It was interesting that at the end of the day Isaac handed over the business to his son, who stopped buying and selling other concerns, disposed of many of the companies and concentrated on being a mail order house, Great Universal Stores, one of the most successful businesses in Britain today. It was a switch from the entrepreneur to the able son.

I told Robert I thought he was lucky to have such a capable son and it might be in his interests to pass over the business to him while he was young. We laughed and discussed it. I dropped him a line, saying that he should have a look at the history of GUS and see how the father played a major part in creating it all, but the son was important in changing the nature of it. I said it struck me that his publishing group had such high quality, international businesses, like Macmillan in New York and Berlitz Languages, that there was a lesson to be learned. I admired what Leonard has done for GUS and thought that Kevin had similar ability and talent. Having made my point, I thought no more of it.

Then Kevin and his wife came to our home for dinner one evening. It was purely social: nothing to do with business. They have four children. Tessa had not met them and I wanted her to do so. Over coffee, Kevin turned to me and said, 'Peter, I want you to consider taking over the chairmanship of Maxwell Communications from my father.' With the flotation coming off, Robert wanted to concentrate on the *Daily Mirror* and his new newspaper in New York. I was astounded.

Kevin said that he had discussed the question with his father and he wanted to take over the running of the business and become chief executive. They both wanted me to be chairman.

I pointed out my ignorance of publishing, but Kevin insisted that the combination of my knowledge of commerce and the world at large would be a great benefit to him. I did discuss it with Robert Maxwell and whether Kevin and I would genuinely run the business. He said that from the moment he retired as chairman in July 1991, after presenting his report, the two of us would be in total command and able to pursue the policies we thought were right.

STAYING POWER

My inquiries showed that the company was one of the leading publishers in America, far advanced in emerging electronic publishing techniques; one of the biggest companies in business information; and the proprietor of the biggest language tuition school in the world. Given the right team approach and application, it could become a great international company in the next decade. I decided to go into partnership with Kevin.

In preparation for taking over the chairmanship I visited the main American companies. They were staggering companies: Macmillan, one of the finest American publishers; the Berlitz Language School, the world's largest language tuition centre; Macmillan McGraw-Hill, one of America's biggest educational publishers; OAG, the world's dominant information service on airlines and tourism. Other companies include the largest publishing company in the world of books on computers.

Ninety per cent of the profits of the company came from the American subsidiaries. On my return to London I said to Kevin Maxwell that I thought it was absurd for such companies to be run from the head office in Holborn and that he should look carefully at de-merging the American assets to create one strong American publisher, with the best of American management in charge and with the greatest American financial institutions as shareholders. This idea was looked at by both the family and the board and they concluded that it was a correct idea which would benefit all concerned with the company.

I therefore persuaded them that instead of me being the chairman there should be a top American commanding most of the company. I am sure this was the correct approach and decision and, although I much enjoyed America, there is no way I would wish to live in the United States or spend a great deal of my time there as opposed to England. But I have no doubt the new American company will be a major force in world publishing.

While I was sorting out my future, the futures of others were being determined on the centre of the political stage. I was shaken at the speed with which Margaret fell. I had always believed she would go on until the next General Election. If she won, I thought, because of age, she would hand over in perhaps two years and probably to John Major. She had made him Foreign Secretary and then Chancellor. It was clear how her mind was working.

If she lost, I thought there would be a challenge with John Major, Chris Patten and Michael Heseltine contending. I would have been happy with any one of the three as leader. At that time I thought it would be wrong for anyone to challenge her before the General Election, because it would split the party.

What did emerge after I had left the Cabinet in May 1990 were the wide differences between the Prime Minister and others on European issues and the question of German reunification.

With hindsight, Nicholas Ridley's offensive comments in July, accusing the Germans of a rushed take-over of Europe and forcing his resignation, may have been a sign of heightening tension over Europe and an omen of what was to come. Nicholas was right to go. His words were inexcusable. It is all too easy to play on the emotions and residual hostility towards a former enemy. The reality is that for more than forty years Germany has shown herself not only to be a genuine democracy, but also to be highly successful. We should be trying to have consistently friendly relations with our German partners in the European Community. Both in Europe and internationally, we share many common objectives.

The anti-European tone of Margaret's remarks and the seeming hostility to German unity was not shared by the Tory Party or, in particular, her Foreign Secretary or Chancellor. Sir Geoffrey was no longer a main player, or so it seemed. When Willie Whitelaw was Deputy Prime Minister the job did matter. She conferred with him and depended on his advice to avoid mistakes. She did not have the same relationship with Geoffrey. She had sacked him as Foreign Secretary and this must have soured their relationship. If you simply have the tag of Deputy Prime Minister, it is a non-job. I am not trying to belittle Geoffrey, but it was the people with the big jobs who counted at that moment.

Chatting to PPSs and MPs, I quickly discovered that the Foreign Secretary and the Chancellor were deeply unhappy about her negative attitude to Europe. That unhappiness grew and grew. After the Rome summit, she clearly agreed with John Major and Douglas Hurd the statement she would make to the Commons. But the moment she finished the statement and started answering questions, she became more hostile to the Community.

Tension was heightened because the Prime Minister and the party were lagging in the polls. That, in itself, did not matter too much. Margaret had lost and recovered ground umpteen times before. The danger to her was the combination of her low standing in the polls plus the differences over Europe with her Chancellor and Foreign Secretary and a large part of the Parliamentary party.

The situation exploded when Sir Geoffrey resigned. No one had predicted it. I believe he felt strongly on the European issue and that she was not listening to him, the Chancellor or the Foreign Secretary. It was said that if Geoffrey disagreed so strongly with policy he should have resigned sooner.

We were all, at different times, antagonized by the way Margaret rode roughshod over Cabinet, but outsiders do not appreciate fully the patronage power of a Prime Minister who won a General Election in 1983 and then again in 1987. The only way you get into Cabinet is if the Prime Minister decrees it. The only way you can move up from being Minister of Agriculture to Foreign Secretary is if the Prime Minister ordains it.

The politician who keeps in favour is not being unprincipled. He or she has to recognize that the Prime Minister will decide. You say to yourself, 'If, with the views I hold, I become Foreign Secretary, that would be terrific. I must keep a good relationship with her so that she recognizes all my talents.' That is perfectly honourable.

To resign causes a stir. You become a fascinating and interesting figure, for a few days. If you resign on an issue which is popular with the public you go out as a hero. If I had resigned over the poll tax people would have said how courageous Walker was. When it is proved to be a bad tax, people say, 'Look, he was right.'

But the much more courageous and difficult action is to stay, to stick to your guns and try to influence policy. You do not reject resignation because you want to keep your job or stay as a popular politician, but because you realize that if you go it will destroy the unity of the party. Unity has been a strong characteristic of the Tory Party over the years and lack of it has debilitated Labour in the past. Inside the Cabinet I and others were able to influence policy to some extent. When Peter Carrington was Foreign Secretary, he had differences with the Prime Minister and usually won her over. His advocacy led to the setting up of an independent Zimbabwe.

The shock to Geoffrey was considerable. I never took up Margaret's brief and she accepted I had a different brief. The arrangement worked in practice and it was better to have me in than out. Had she dropped me in 1983 or 1987, I would have gone without ill-feeling. There was none when she sacked me in the 1970s. Geoffrey's position was different. He had taken up her brief. Both he and Elspeth were clearly very upset when she moved him.

Whatever the reasons, his resignation speech made it devastatingly clear he thought she was taking a line he considered disastrous for the country. The Chancellor and the Foreign Secretary could not rush to her aid with any great conviction. Everyone knew they were in disagreement with her. That changed the whole scene.

On the day of the State Opening of Parliament, which followed the resignation of Sir Geoffrey Howe, Michael Mates, who conducted Michael Heseltine's campaign, stopped me in a corridor of the Commons and asked, 'Don't you think Michael Heseltine should stand now? It is either now or never.' I was non-committal, but did say he should be careful. If he got the timing wrong, it would be never. Michael Mates asked if it would make a difference if Sir Geoffrey proposed Michael. I said, 'Is he going to?' He said, 'Yes.' I said that did create a different atmosphere which required thinking about carefully.

Then, a few days later, Geoffrey made his sensational resignation speech.

As I listened to Sir Geoffrey, it was clear to me that there would be a leadership contest and Michael Heseltine should stand. Michael phoned me that night and I told him I thought he should stand and he would have my support. In the light of that Howe speech, it was perfectly reasonable for Michael to challenge for the leadership.

I also checked on the intentions of people who were close to me, but the campaign was run by Michael Mates, Neil Macfarlane, Keith Hampson and William Powell. I knew Michael was going to get a substantial vote on first ballot.

We exchanged calls each day. On nomination day I was surprised that Geoffrey did not propose Michael and neither his proposer nor his seconder were political heavyweights. The soundings for the first ballot looked promising, however, and suggested Michael would get well above a hundred votes. We discussed the part I might play in his campaign and he agreed that it might be against his interests if I had too high a profile in the early stages. He would take all the votes from the 'wets' and my public support would not be particularly helpful in delivering some votes from the right, essential if he was to win a second round.

I did warn him, from my experience of Ted Heath's campaign in

1975, that it was important to double-check every pledge. A good tactic was to go up to those already pledged, say 'It looks as if Margaret will win' and then wait for the reaction.

I told him I thought the crucial paper was the *Sunday Times* and believed that Andrew Neil would support him, though there could be pressure from the proprietor to go the other way. As it turned out, the proprietor did disagree, but left his editor to take his own decision.

We discussed how Michael should counter the charge that abolition of the community charge would mean an increase in taxation. He was to point out that everyone already knew that the poll tax was taxation. It was simply necessary to arrange it in a fairer and more acceptable way.

I suggested that Alick Buchanan-Smith might help, since he was so highly regarded by other Conservative MPs. We agreed Michael must stress the need for party unity and his willingness to have a Cabinet made up of ministers from all sections of the party.

The outcome of the first ballot was close to what Michael's team predicted and, in my judgement, it was impossible for Margaret to stay. No Prime Minister could continue with more than one third of her MPs expressing the wish she should go. She must have known that her vote included others who did not want Michael, but still wanted her to step down.

It was a terrible mistake for her to declare immediately that she would battle on and that provided she won the second ballot she would remain Prime Minister. It was plain that this stand was unsustainable and that many MPs recognized this and were deserting her. If she had fought on, I have no doubt that Michael Heseltine would have won the second ballot and she would have been humiliated.

There was an amusing moment close to the crucial vote when I was writing a letter in one of the voting lobbies. Michael Heseltine walked through and encountered, at the other end, a cluster of seven or eight Cabinet Ministers, obviously deeply concerned and discussing what they should do. On seeing Michael, Cecil Parkinson said, 'We are discussing the weather, Michael.' Michael replied, 'Whether to stand or not?'

By the following morning that had become a crucial question for John Major and Douglas Hurd. I knew that if the party took to either they had a good chance of winning.

When Margaret changed her mind and announced she was not

standing, John Major came into the reckoning and I was faced with another dilemma. I did have a high regard for him. He had several times asked me to go to the Treasury for private chats about the economy. I liked him, admired him and thought he would make a good leader of the party.

Richard Ryder, who played a key part in John's campaign, asked for my support. I said that I would, quite sincerely, be extremely happy to have him as leader and if there was another ballot and the choice was between John and Douglas, I would vote for John. But Michael Heseltine had been my junior minister twice, he was a close friend, I was trustee to his children's trust and I would vote for him.

Richard said that was fair and when I saw John later that day he said he fully understood my position and thanked me for explaining it. I did think Michael was unlikely to win the second ballot. The probability was that his vote would fall away and most of the Thatcher vote would go elsewhere. This is what happened. It became obvious that more were going for John than Douglas. The majority of the right looked upon John Major as the right-wing candidate and many in the middle thought he had a balanced view of politics, was a good performer and an approachable man.

What I did find impressive over the next few days was that you had three men arguing cogently they should be leader with no personal animosity. The Tory Party must be one of the few parties in the world where you can have a contest to become not only leader, but also Prime Minister without rancour and then have all three working together as a team.

I saw David Hunt, who had been in Tokyo and not at the Cabinet when Margaret had resigned. He had therefore not been present when she said she was standing down and others must be free to stand, but must be united in opposing Michael Heseltine. None of the Cabinet had supported Michael. David sought my advice and flatteringly said he had followed it throughout his political career. I said I was voting for Michael and gave my reasons. David said that was his choice. I warned him that it would not be easy to stand alone as the only Cabinet Minister to back Michael Heseltine, but it would appeal to Wales. The other two members of the Welsh Office team, Wyn Roberts and Ian Grist, had said they would go the same way as David.

I phoned Michael at the crack of dawn next morning to say he should call David immediately, as pressure was bound to be exerted upon him. David said he would declare after consulting his Wirral constituency party executive. My warning of pressure was not misplaced. Notwithstanding the pressure, David had the courage to make his declaration on Sunday morning – for Michael.

I heard the result of the leadership election on television. Michael immediately came out and declared his support for John Major in an effective manner. Perhaps even more effective was John Major's response. He phoned Michael within two minutes to say 'thank you' and to ask him to be part of the Cabinet team.

There was never a sinister plot by the Major camp to engineer Margaret's fall, as has been suggested. John certainly went into action quickly, but this should be easily understood. When I ran Ted Heath's leadership campaign there was no preparation. I had no idea that I was going to do the campaign until Ted asked me on the Thursday when the election was on the following Tuesday. Most people would say that the Walker campaign was well done, but the explanation was that there was not much to organize. You have 320 MPs. You determine who are your friends and how you will contact them to make sure of their support. You quickly go down the list, find out your supporters and ask them whom they should contact. When you find a doubter you get those of his friends who are on your side to talk to him.

It is a simple exercise. The moment John stood he had Peter Lilley, Norman Lamont, Richard Ryder, David Mellor, all able organizers, who quickly formed a group to do the task.

However strongly I was supporting Michael it was impossible not to feel sadness and sympathy for Margaret in being forced to relinquish her post. Margaret is, and this is something I admire, deeply patriotic, she has considerable ability and limitless energy and application.

But, given the history of the Conservative Party, I believe she was wrong to think any single economic doctrine could solve all economic problems. For too long, she was hooked on dogma which is not in the Tory tradition and this made us look as though we were opposed to public expenditure on health, education and pensions. The message of her early years was *laissez-faire* capitalism and I disagreed.

We fought the Liberals in the nineteenth century because we disagreed with *laissez-faire*. We believed in intervention. We favoured protection. The One Nation theme of Disraeli was that you used the wealth created by capitalism to tackle the social problems of the day. That, in my view, was the Tory tradition.

Much as I disagreed with Margaret, I never doubted that she held her beliefs sincerely and thought they were for the good of the country. The reality was that, in the end, her record on public spending was good, but the over-emphasis on doctrine did give the wrong impression.

She got it wrong on Europe. This was partly because of her patriotic feelings and her reluctance to give up sovereignty. Yet sovereignty is no longer that relevant. The world is so interlinked. We give up sovereignty on defence to belong to NATO and on trade to be part of the European Community. It is to our advantage.

The prospect of European monetary union and a single currency has upset some Tory MPs. It should not do so. My children will see a united Europe and a European currency. It is only the timing which is in doubt. What has been done will lead inevitably to greater conformity in Europe's economic performance, on inflation, wage levels, investment. Once that is achieved a single currency and union will be easier to agree.

Two factors will determine the speed at which it all happens. The first is external pressure and the second the personalities of the leading politicians. Economic threat from the current giants like America or Japan or from emerging countries like China, India and even South America could speed up the process. It is conceivable that raw material producers coming together, as oil producers did when they formed OPEC, could endanger European prosperity.

I know personalities are important. I witnessed how Heath, Pompidou and Brandt were at one in their European objectives. If they had only been in power together for five years there would have been a sharp acceleration in European unity. Perhaps in the 1990s Major, Kohl and the new French president will have a similar impact.

Margaret ran into a snare on Europe. She was rightly conscious, as I found, that you gain nothing in the Community by saying how European you are. The French have won all they have out of the market by tough, ruthless negotiation, as have the Germans, the Italians and everyone else. Margaret transformed the community budget deficit by hard, rough negotiation, as I did on agriculture and fisheries. It meant her going through a series of confrontational negotiations which gave her the image of being anti-European. I think she felt, too, a personal animosity towards Europeans whom she thought knew what a nonsense the budget was and how unfair it was to Britain.

All this was understandable. What did her so much harm was her failure to come out with anything positive about Europe, to say: 'Why don't we do this together?' That was a mistake.

As a human being, she is kind and generous and warm. I know of people who have been in real distress and she has moved quietly behind the scenes to help them. But the truth is that she actually enjoyed the reputation of being the Iron Lady. This was fine during a Falklands War, but it rebounded later on. The country would have found her more attractive if they had known what a kind and compassionate person she really was and is.

I met her in the voting lobbies after she had made her last speech and it was difficult to find words. Colleagues were going up to her to say what a good speech she had made, but I was too conscious that here was someone who had devoted her life to politics, reached the top and become one of the major figures in the world, working eighteen or nineteen hours a day to achieve it. She had done the job with great vigour and sincerity and then over the space of a few days found the power stripped away, leaving her again on the back benches. For so long she had been Prime Minister or party leader, surrounded by large staffs, arranging for her to move round the world. Then no staff and no organization. She was not being removed because she had done anything wrong, but because her colleagues decided they disagreed with her and it would be better to have a change of leadership. Words seemed inadequate.

Politics is tough at the top. I thought of Disraeli's greasy pole and how easy it was to slip.

It will be difficult for her to find a new role, other than as a dignified, not very active, elder stateswoman. Few succeed in finding a new role in their political lifetime. Winston Churchill remained as a backbencher. He refused to go to the Lords because he looked upon himself as the great Commons man and never wanted to go anywhere else. He wanted to stay in Parliament as long as he could because he loved the atmosphere, but he never spoke.

Anthony Eden resigned, went to the Lords and made some visionary speeches on foreign policy, but nothing which was party contentious. Sir Alec Douglas-Home was an exception. He went because he felt people wanted him to do so and came back as Foreign Secretary, but that was because of his personality and because he was more than happy to work with Ted Heath. He did it with great skill, but clearly had no desire to come back as leader of the party.

I do not believe there is any possibility of Margaret Thatcher becoming Foreign Secretary. I cannot think of any likely Prime Minister who would want someone with such strong views of her own. It would be a Thatcher foreign policy and not one of a Prime Minister or a Cabinet. Nor do I think that having been a world player, negotiating with Gorbachev, Reagan, Mittérand and Kohl, Margaret would want to start going to councils of foreign ministers.

The only real role for her is to write an important work of ideas as part of her autobiography and deliver thoughtful lectures on international issues or less controversial domestic ones. Perhaps she should encourage some of the younger politicians.

She is right to leave the Commons. If she stayed, she would find groups constantly trying to attract her to their cause and repeated accusations of disloyalty to the leader. Every word she says from now on will be examined to see if it marks a difference with the new Prime Minister. Every speech Ted Heath has ever made since he was deposed has been interpreted as being hostile to her, sometimes quite unfairly.

I found the same when I was in the wilderness from 1974-79. Journalists looked at my speeches only to see if they could be interpreted as an attack on Margaret Thatcher. Political journalists will find it irresistible to look for phrases which can be construed as an attack on John Major. I do not believe that she would want that.

POSTSCRIPT

In February 1978 I made a speech to the Parliamentary Press Gallery in the House of Commons on the important themes of Harold Macmillan. A few days later I received a letter from Harold in which he wrote: 'There came into my hands the other day the press release of a speech you made to the Press Gallery. May I say with what pleasure I read this. You seem to me to understand exactly what had been the dominating purposes of my political efforts during all these years. Many people foolishly thought that the work and writing in my pre-war years were merely the extravagance of youth. On the contrary, I have tried to pursue the same theme throughout. It is a great pleasure to me to feel you understand this and are carrying on the work.'

I have endeavoured to pursue the 'Middle Way' of Harold Macmillan and as I leave the stage, I have been reflecting upon the words he used in one of his first speeches to the Commons, when he was new and representing Stockton, a seat suffering from terrible unemployment and social problems. He said: 'The ordinary man of today wants freedom, responsibility and status. He rejects the old individualism which, beginning with the Reformation and going on with the Industrial Revolution, did not quite destroy but fatally injured the old organic conception of society. He wants to see it rebuilt. He does not want Socialism or individualism. He wants neither the Jekyll nor the Hyde. He wants an organized system of society in which he has a place, in which neither the rights of the community nor the rights of the individual are over-emphasized and in which he can feel himself to be something different from what he has been in the past.'

That, to me, is a perfect description of the approach the Conservative Party should always take.

There are many problems to be tackled. We have again the spectre of unemployment, the problems of homelessness and the inner cities, aggravated by increasing crime.

Only an approach based on a series of pragmatic and compassionate decisions can give everyone a fulfilling life. I am optimistic that the Tory Party is well equipped to take on these challenges. I see in John Major and his colleagues men who recognize that if everyone is going to have greater equality of opportunity, there has to be a better educational system and better training. I believe they are dedicated to continuing a health service available to all our people, but also one of higher quality, and more efficiently run.

I think giving people the ability to participate will be an important theme of the new government as it brings forward radical policies to see that every family has a home of their own and every worker can share in the profits of a free enterprise system. Ministers will look at the regions where unemployment is still a deep-seated problem. These can be tackled with the types of policies I was allowed to follow in Wales.

On the international scene, we have leadership which recognizes we need to play a prominent part and, if we do so, we can have greater influence than at any time in our history. We have a party determined to see that the message of One Nation Toryism, expounded by Disraeli more than a century ago and followed by Conservative politicians during most of my political lifetime, will be repeated. It is the only message which will unite our nation and the only one on which we can continue to be the party of government.

INDEX

INDEX

INDEX

Thorneycroft, Peter 44, 136
Thorntons 227
Thorpe, Jeremy 125
Times 115, 137, 216
Todd, Alec 46–7
Tory Reform Group (TRG) 136–7, 183
Toynbee Hall 40
Toyota 211–12, 216–17
Trade & Industry
    Department of 76, 92–4, 96–7, 99, 105–6,
        108, 114, 127, 142–3, 165, 217
    Secretary of State 88, 92, 116–17, 121, 142,
        226
Trades Union Congress (TUC) 122, 173,
    177–9, 217
trade unions 121–2, 124, 136, 173, 177, 204–5
training policy 209, 241
Transport
    Ministry of 77, 165, 210–11
    Shadow Minister of 46–7
Transport & General Workers' Union 124, 173
Transport Bill (Labour) 47–8, 82
transport policy 77, 82
Trust the People 195

underwriting 57
unemployment 1, 4, 9, 121, 135, 159, 184, 203,
    208–11, 241
Unicorn Trust 61–2
United States 102, 211–12, 237
unit trusts 60–2

Vale of Glamorgan 216
Valleys Initiative 207–9, 219
van Straubenzee, William 19
Vantreuse Caterers 60
Varney, John 57
Venezuela 107
Vicky 34
Videla, President 162–3
Viola, President 163
Volkswagen 212–13

wage restraint 97, 124
Waldegrave, William 221
Walden, Brian 27
Wales 112, 183, 187, 200, 202–12, 215–19,
    222–3, 225–6, 235
    Secretary of State for *see* Welsh Secretary
Walker, Jonathan 29, 74, 109, 221
Walker, Marianna 221, 224
Walker, Robin 221
Walker, Rose 3, 7–8, 17, 22, 24
Walker, Shara 29, 221
Walker, Sydney jnr 5, 7, 50

Walker, Sydney snr 3, 8, 16–17, 22
Walker, Tessa 29, 41, 50, 70, 74, 82, 90–1, 95,
    108–9, 130, 221, 224, 229
Walker, Timothy 206, 221
Walker Anti-Labour League 9
Walker Moate & Company 59
Walker's dining club 67
Walker-Smith, Sir Derek 34
Walker Young 63, 69–71, 127
Waller, Frank 66
Walters, Sir Alan 224
Ward, Geordie 25–6
Ward, Dame Irene 84
water industry 88
Watkins, Desmond 211
Weatherill, Jack 48
Webster, David 48
Welldon Park primary school 4, 8–9
Wellington Barracks 90
Welsh Development Agency 113, 203–4,
    208–11, 216
Welsh Language Board 204
Welsh Language Society 205
Welsh Office 146, 206, 208–9, 214–16, 235
Welsh Secretary 187, 199, 202–5, 219, 221–3
West Indians 139
Westland crisis 187–8
West Midlands 27
'wets' 41, 159, 172, 233
Whitelaw, Willie 84, 115–17, 122, 125, 137,
    143, 159, 186, 231
Wigg, George 40
Wigham Poland 71
Wildman, Miss 5
Willis, Norman 177–9
Willis Faber 59
Wilson, Harold 18, 38, 76, 104, 143
Wolfson, Isaac 100, 228–9
Wolfson, Leonard 100, 228–9
Worcester Conservative Association 24
Worcester constituency 24–7, 126, 143, 221
Worcestershire 78
Worcestershire County Cricket Club 17, 24
World War II 5–7, 9

Young, David 217
Young, Jimmy 62
Young & Rubican 193
Young Conservatives 10, 19–20, 23
    Brentford & Chiswick 18
    Gloucester 16, 55
    Home Counties North 18
Younger, George 186

Zitzavitz, Herr von 58